Power Tools for REASON 2.5

Master the World's Most Popular Virtual Studio Software

BY KURT KURASAKI

Backbeat Books

San Francisco

Published by Backbeat Books
600 Harrison Street, San Francisco, CA 94107
www.backbeatbooks.com
email: books@musicplayer.com

An imprint of the Music Player Network
Publishers of *Guitar Player*, *Bass Player*, *Keyboard*, and other magazines
United Entertainment Media, Inc.
A CMP Information company

CMP
United Business Media

Distributed to the book trade in the US and Canada by
Publishers Group West, 1700 Fourth Street, Berkeley, CA 94710

Distributed to the music trade in the US and Canada by
Hal Leonard Publishing, P.O. Box 13819, Milwaukee, WI 53213

Text and cover design by Doug Gordon
Illustrations by Andrew Hamilton

Library of Congress Cataloging-in-Publication Data

Kurasaki, Kurt, 1969–
  Power tools for Reason 2.5 : master the world's most popular virtual studio software /
    by Kurt Kurasaki.
      p. cm.
  Includes index.
  ISBN 0-87930-774-9 (alk. paper)
  1. Reason (Computer file) 2. Sequencer (Music software) 3. Music—Computer
    programs. I. Title.

ML74.4.R43K87 2003
786.7'6—dc22

                                    2003063619

Printed in the United States of America

04 05 06 07 08   5 4 3 2 1

Contents

Foreword

It is a pleasure to have been asked to write the foreword for Kurt's book. Reason has played a large part in the process of making music for Neil Davidge (Producer of Massive Attack's *Mezzanine* and *100th Window*) and myself since it first became available, and will continue to do so in the future. Reason has taken the whole premise of the virtual studio into a new domain. With each version upgrade, Reason has become an increasingly powerful tool for creating and arranging music in a way that is spontaneous and seemingly limitless.

The graphic interface, as users will already know, makes the process of creating and using the virtual studio very simple, yet gives the user the potential for endless permutations as the piece of music he or she is creating develops. The flow of the music need never be broken while auditioning new sounds or introducing new components, as all these functions can be performed without having to stop the sequencer. Both Neil and I have found this feature invaluable when an idea needs to take shape quickly, without losing the vibe of the moment. The other key thing for me as a programmer is that the sequencing engine is as tight as anything I have used. There is little point building up layers of grooves if they are going to sound loose. Reason holds it all down, effortlessly.

One of the things that I loved about Reason's predecessor, ReBirth, when I first began using it to create drum loops in the early stages of *100th Window*, was the wealth of resources available on the web to enhance it. Makers of electronic music from all corners of the globe have given up their time to create "mods" (in essence, *their* version of ReBirth, which featured their favorite samples and sound effects), and posted them to the Propellerhead website. These were available for free download, and were often of a very high standard. This gave rise to a real sense of interaction with the online musical community.

This spirit of generosity and sharing has been carried on by Kurt at his website, www.peff.com. Visitors to this site will find a wide range of useful supplements to Reason. In keeping with his own musical diversity, you will find everything from lovingly multisampled 303 patches and vintage rhythm boxes to faithful representations of Rhodes pianos, Stradivarius violins, and shakuhachi. In addition to such downloadable goodies, Kurt is happy to share a wealth of tips and tricks for the creators of music in the virtual domain. It is a hugely rewarding site to visit, even if you are just starting out in the field of virtual studio technology.

Kurt's wealth of knowledge now comes to the wider stage in the shape of *Power Tools for Reason*. As I was writing this foreword, the document was only available as an unfinished draft, but even so I was amazed by the breadth of ideas and examples Kurt had put together. Each aspect of Reason's versatility as a music production tool has been revealed in great detail, with care being taken to explain why particular techniques or configurations have been used.

I would recommend that even the most avid fan of Reason pay close attention to the first two chapters, which provide invaluable guidance on the first principles of using the software. The section that deals with shortcuts is rightly described as essential, as the key commands listed will save a lot of repetitive mouse movement, leaving the user with vital headspace to concentrate on the music. Kurt's sensible advice on file management, including the use of customized songs as a starting point for each new project, is well worth understanding and implementing. Take care also to read up on copy and paste techniques with the various devices, as these again will save precious time which you can spend being creative.

Once these basics are under your belt, feel free to progress to more intricate maneuvers. Pattern-controlled vocoding and side chain compression are not just useful pieces of jargon to impress your buddies with; they can help you in your music making! By following the examples found in this book, you will learn to use the software in new and inventive ways. Not only that, but you will also have taken in a lot of very useful knowledge of music production in general, because the author has taken a lot of care to explain what is actually happening to the audio once you begin to manipulate it. In other words, you're not just getting great sounds out of your software synth, you're learning *how* you're doing it. I had a lot of fun trying out some of these ideas, and found myself falling in love with Reason all over again.

Therefore, I wholeheartedly recommend this book to newcomers and experts alike.

—*Alex Swift*

Alex Swift's programming credits include Massive Attack's 100th Window *and Peter Gabriel's* Up.

A Note from the Editor

This is not a book to read. It's a book to *use*. While preparing the manuscript of *Power Tools for Reason* for publication, I went through all of the examples step by step. In the process, not only did I learn a tremendous amount about Reason, I also came up with a number of song files that expanded on the ideas Kurt Kurasaki presents. I spent a lot more time on the editing job than I would normally have done, because I kept stopping to try out new musical and patching ideas that occurred to me.

This book is not a substitute for the Reason owner's manual. But if you've already learned the basics of Reason from the manual, going through the examples in the book step by step will not only inspire you but turn you into a Reason power user.

—*Jim Aikin*

Chapter 1
All You Need Is Reason

Propellerhead Software Reason is a powerful virtual studio application, with all of the tools necessary to produce music of almost any style. Reason runs solidly on even a basic computer setup, which has made it one of the most popular music programs used by enthusiasts, and the convenience of having so many creative tools on a computer has made it popular with professionals as well. It's common to find Reason used in the home or project studio, but a growing trend is to use Reason as a portable synthesizer rig running on a laptop. With the ease and convenience of instantly recalling songs stored on a hard drive, live bands use Reason as a portable sampler or as a drum machine. There are even artists who put on complete live performances using Reason alone. It's really quite remarkable how Reason has helped musicians realize their creative visions.

The main part of Reason is a virtual equipment rack with a visually stunning graphic user interface that balances aesthetics with an intuitive control layout. The rack devices can be used in any configuration necessary to complete a song project. The rack devices include a 28-input mixer, two types of synthesizers, a sample-based drum machine, samplers compatible with the Akai S1000/3000 series, a high-quality reverb, a vocoder, and distortion and other effects processors, all with audio quality that meets current professional specifications. Reason also features patchable modulation controls like those found in modular synthesizer systems, as well as an analog-style pattern sequencer. Like their hardware counterparts, Reason devices must be cabled together — using, in this case, virtual cables. The entire rack of equipment can be controlled by Reason's sequencer, which records MIDI note events and parameter changes.

Having a seemingly endless number of devices at your disposal makes Reason very flexible. A rack of devices can be saved and recalled at a moment's notice. A Reason song file can be modified by altering the sequence or reconfiguring rack devices to quickly create variations and remixes of the original song. The fact that Reason is completely software-based also makes access to audio sample archives very convenient, and the software comes with a versatile sample set for electronic music as well as a large set of orchestral and percussion samples.

Anyone with the desire to create music can quickly learn how to use Reason. The motivation to create far outweighs the importance of understanding the concepts behind producing music, and using Reason is a great way to learn about music production. To fully understand every aspect of Reason, however, one must possess some knowledge of music theory, composition and arrangement, MIDI and sequencing, synthesizer programming, modular synthesizer patching, sampler programming, acoustics, and audio engineering. Knowing some math and the physics of sound wouldn't hurt, either. It's not necessary to possess this knowledge to compose great music using Reason, and novice users starting with little or no understanding of these subjects should not be discouraged, because Reason provides an ideal learning environment. Keep in mind the old adage, "Practice makes perfect." As with any musical instrument, it takes practice and experience to gain proficiency with Reason.

Most of this book discusses signal processing and the principles behind routing cables to different Reason devices. The emphasis on the technical language and history of audio engineering should help you understand the processes occurring in the devices. In each section, several examples demonstrate how to implement the principles in Reason, and schematic diagrams illustrate the connections between the devices. These examples can be used to spark new life into tracks already created with Reason, but the intent is to inspire you to experiment and discover your own unique wiring configurations.

Although Reason is software and all of the functions are based on over 700,000 lines of code, the results you'll get are much like what you'd achieve using hardware. The principles are easier to understand when you regard cables in Reason as carrying real signals instead of as software processes, and the content of this book relies on the hardware metaphor to describe the functions. This is especially important in the sections on control voltages and audio signals.

Prerequisites for Using This Guide

In order to get the most out of the resources in this book, you should be familiar with the basics of using Reason, such as creating and cabling devices, loading patches, adjusting parameters, recording MIDI sequences, and programming patterns on the Matrix and Redrum. These are necessary in order to work your way through the examples. The directions for the examples are comprehensive, so new users can follow the directions and hear the results of the examples, but this book will not cover the basics. For that, you'll need to read the manual.

Most of the examples in this book require nothing more than a fast computer with a soundcard and the latest version of Reason. While the minimum system requirements claim that Reason will run on older processors and older operating systems, a newer system with plenty of RAM (at least 256 megabytes) running the latest operating system from Apple or Microsoft is recommended.

Some of the examples can be used with Reason Adapted, but most of the examples require the full version of Reason. Some examples require a MIDI keyboard or a MIDI controller with knobs or faders. The events generated by a MIDI control device can be substituted, however, by programming events in the sequencer.

The most important requirement for getting the most out of this book is an open mind about music technology and a respect for music of all styles. Creative use of technology has become a form of art, and different styles of music have developed different methods of using technology. One may not be keen about a certain style of music, but much can be learned from the production methods that may be part of that style. The examples in this book are inspired by many different genres of electronic music, ranging from *musique-concrète* to hip-hop, and the production techniques from one style can be used to add a new dimension to music you're creating in a different style.

The *Power Tools for Reason* CD

Learning by example is the most efficient way to grasp the versatility of Reason. Included on the CD-ROM accompanying this book are several tracks produced by different artists. Listen to these productions and study the cabling methods and patch settings used to achieve the sound of each track. Also included with the book are a number of ReFill sample libraries, audio samples, and Reason song files that provide examples to illustrate the concepts described in the book.

Chapter 2
Essential Shortcuts

With only one mouse for manipulating all of Reason's controls, access to the mouse cursor is a precious commodity, especially when you're performing tasks in real time. In complicated Reason song configurations with dozens of rack devices, hundreds of control parameters are available. When accessing a menu item in real time, you have to find the cursor destination, move and click the mouse, then move the cursor back to the device in the rack. During this brief moment, the creative process is suspended while your focus of concentration shifts from the rack to the menu bar. Contextual menus and Reason key commands help eliminate the task of moving the mouse up to the menu bar, and allow you stay focused on the user interface.

Contextual menus are remote menus that appear at the location of the mouse cursor, which eliminates the need to move the cursor up to the menu bar. Typically, the contextual menu lists the items found in the Edit and the Create menus. The Edit menu items change from one type of device to another, and the contextual menu will reflect the change depending on the device selected. When the contextual menu is accessed on an empty area of the rack, only the Create menu is shown, and new devices can be quickly added. When the Create menu items are accessed while another device is selected, effects will be automatically inserted in the signal path on the output of that device.

Reason key commands are keystrokes or combinations of keystrokes with mouse clicks. One of the basic key commands (one that every Reason user should know) is the Tab key, which flips the rack from the front to the rear view. This key alone saves a few seconds of time compared to accessing the Option menu "Toggle Rack Front/Rear" command. Other important key commands handle the tasks of copying, pasting, undo, redo, saving your song file, and creating a new Reason song file.

Depending on where the cursor is, the set of key commands will change. The same keys may perform different functions on different devices. For example, holding down the Shift key and clicking on items selects multiple items in the rack, but this same combination will behave differently when you click on the pattern edit interface of a Matrix pattern sequencer. It's important to understand that the behavior of a given key command is not necessarily consistent. With practice, using the key commands will become second nature. The entire list of shortcuts and key modifiers is described in the "Reason Key Commands.PDF" document.

Being organized is probably the most important time-saving process. Being able to access samples for editing and finding song project files quickly will save you a lot of time as your projects become more complex. The end of this chapter describes a few strategies for organizing song files and audio samples for Reason projects.

Menus

Reason employs contextual and pop-up menus that display at the location of the cursor. This eliminates the need to move the cursor to the menu bar then back down to work on items in the sequencer or rack. The items in the menu vary depending on the cursor location and selection focus, but the primary menu palettes include the Create menu items, Edit menu items, and patch and sample listings.

Contextual Menus

Contextual menus are accessed by using the right mouse button (right-click) on computers using Microsoft Windows. Macintosh users can access the contextual menus by holding the Control key while clicking. Two-button mice are available for the Macintosh, and the software drivers can be configured so that the right button sends a Control-click.

The Edit menu changes depending on the device focus in the Reason rack. The edit features are very different for an NN-XT Advanced Sampler, by comparison to a Matrix Pattern Sequencer. The right-click contextual menu simplifies the confusion by listing the appropriate menu items for the device selected. When you right-click on various areas of the sequencer window, contextual menus also appear with a selection of items for modifying the sequence or duplicating tracks.

Pop-Up Menus

Several Reason devices can load and save parameter settings as patches. Once a patch is loaded into a device, other patches can be loaded by using the browser buttons. The entire list of patches will appear on a pop-up menu list when you click on the patch name. In order to switch to a different directory, the patch browser window must be used to navigate to a different directory or ReFill location, but to jump to various patches within a given directory, the pop-up menu is the best way to audition sounds.

The devices with patch pop-up menus include the Subtractor and Malström synthesizers, both the NN19 and NN-XT samplers, the RV7000 Reverb, and the Scream 4 Distortion Unit. The Redrum Drum Computer has pop-up menus for patch browsing and also on each of the drum channels for sample browsing.

Although the Dr.REX Loop Player does not save parameter settings as patches, ReCycle loops can be browsed using the pop-up menu by clicking on the file name. When browsing through REX loops, click on the Preview button, which plays the loop at the current song tempo. When the new loop is selected from the pop-up menu and loaded, the REX loop will play. This can also be done while a sequence is playing, but make sure to either delete or mute any previous REX slice data that triggers the Dr.REX.

The Malström synthesizer has pop-up menus for selecting patches and pop-up menus that list the oscillator graintables. The graintable menus allow you to quickly select a desired graintable from the list.

Copy & Pasting

Music has a certain degree of repetition, and using Reason's copy and paste to duplicate phrases will help you develop a complete track more quickly. Reason's context-sensitive copy and paste features work much like those in other computer programs: There are copy and paste items in the edit menu, but the Command/Ctrl-C (copy) and Command/Ctrl-V (paste) key command shortcuts are more convenient. There is also a drag-and-drop duplicate key command, by far the most convenient way to duplicate items in Reason.

Drag & Drop Duplicate

The fastest way to copy various items in Reason is to use drag-and-drop duplicate. The drag-duplicate feature is enabled by holding down the Option (MacOS) or Ctrl (Windows) key, clicking and holding the left mouse button, and then dragging an item.

The Reason rack devices have "hot spots" where dragging is enabled. The hot spot is on the rack ear at either end of the user interface. This location is where you click to drag and move a device to a different location in the rack. Clicking on other parts of the device interface will not enable the drag-move or drag-duplicate feature. With several devices selected in the Reason rack, the drag-duplicate feature will copy all selected devices and the cables between them.

The drag-and-drop duplicate feature also works on sequencer tracks and groups. Using the Option/Ctrl key while clicking and dragging on a sequencer track or group of sequencer tracks will create copies of the selected track or tracks. (When doing this, click and hold first, then press Option/Ctrl.) When duplicating groups (chunks of data that you've defined using the Group command in the Edit menu) in the sequencer arrange view, it's recommended to have the snap-to-grid feature enabled with the grid resolution set to bar or 1/2 bar. The duplicate groups will advance in steps according to the resolution, but the relative positions of all data within the group will remain the same. With several groups from different tracks selected, entire regions of songs can be quickly duplicated.

Duplicating events on a smaller scale works well in the sequencer's edit mode. With the snap-to-grid feature enabled, set the resolution to 1/8 or 1/16 (eighth-note or sixteenth-note) steps. Groups of note events or parameter automation events can be selected and drag-duplicated.

Copy & Paste Between Files

Data from one Reason song file can be copied and pasted into another. This includes devices in the Reason rack, as well as groups of devices, sequencer tracks, Redrum patterns, and Matrix Pattern Sequencer data. The effect configurations described in this book can be tedious to recreate each time one uses them in a production. Once you create the configuration and save it to a Reason song file, you can open this file alongside the song you're working on, select the devices you need, copy the devices (their connections will also be copied), and paste them into a different Reason song.

Entire sequencer tracks can also be duplicated to other Reason song files. For instance, you can copy crucial timing information such as a Dr.REX slice track that is used as a quantization template. Also, parameter automation and pattern selection data can be copied, so any control change information can be applied to a different song. Sequencer tracks pasted into a new song are not automatically routed to a device. Before the track sends out any data, the track must be assigned to a device in the rack.

Redrum and Matrix patterns can be copied regardless of the song file, but it's usually easier to copy the whole device instead of the pattern. When a Redrum or Matrix is selected and duplicated, all of the patterns in it are duplicated. When a Redrum is duplicated, the sample assignments and parameter settings are duplicated as well.

Cable Routing

When new devices are created in the Reason rack, the modules automatically connect to sensible destination sockets. This is the "auto-routing" feature in Reason. The auto-routing feature is quite powerful, as it saves time in connecting devices in the rack. It's not a perfect process, however, and there are certain rules that should be followed when using it.

Automatic Routing Rules

Automatic routing occurs when a new device is created in the Reason rack. The outputs from the new device are typically connected to the first available inputs above it. Creating a mixer as the first device in the rack ensures that all subsequent sound modules will be automatically be connected to mixer inputs. New effects devices, such as reverb modules, are automatically routed to the mixer effect send and return sockets.

Automatic routing will recognize when you insert an effect. If you need to insert a distortion module between a Subtractor and the mixer input, it is not necessary to manually reconnect the audio cables. First, click on the Subtractor to select it in the rack, then select the D-11 Distortion from the Create menu. The audio output from the Subtractor is automatically connected to the D-11 audio input, and the D-11 audio output is routed to a mixer channel input.

When a song becomes complex, with many modules and effects, there may be times when you've deleted sound modules while their insert devices remain in the rack. If a new sound module is created below the open insert devices, it will be automatically cabled to the open inputs, not to the mixer. To prevent this, navigate to the top of the rack and click on the mixer before creating a new sound module. The new device will be automatically cabled to the next available mixer inputs.

When a device is copied and pasted, its audio outputs are not automatically cabled. Hold down the Shift key when pasting or drag-duplicating to automatically route the duplicate device. This also applies to duplicating groups of devices, such as a sound module with several insert effects. The last output of the signal chain will be automatically cabled to the next available mixer input.

CV cables are only automatically cabled with the Matrix Pattern Sequencer and the Spider CV Merger & Splitter. The Matrix Pattern Sequencer gate CV and note CV sockets will automatically connect to a sound module's sequencer control inputs. With some effects devices, the Matrix curve CV socket will be automatically connected to a modulation input. The Matrix gate CV and note CV are also auto-routed to Spider inputs, and the Spider will be auto-routed as an insert between a Matrix and a sound module's sequencer control inputs.

Bypass Auto-Routing

When automatic routing doesn't give you the connections you need, manual routing of cables is needed. There is a key command that will bypass automatic routing: Hold down the Shift key when clicking on a device item from the Create menu or contextual menu.

When a second mixer is created below the primary mixer, automatic routing connects the Aux send and master outputs of the second Mixer to the primary Mixer's chaining aux and chaining master inputs. This is not desirable if the second mixer is used as a submixer for drum sounds, so use the bypass auto-routing feature when creating the submixer. Once the connections to the second mixer have been set, drag the second mixer above the primary mixer, so new devices created at the bottom of the rack will be automatically routed to the primary mixer.

There is a second use for this feature. When connecting a cable from a device with stereo audio outputs to a device with stereo inputs, both the left and right channels will automatically be cabled. If this connection is made with auto-routing disabled, only one connection is made.

Auto-routing also works when disconnecting cables. If the left cable is disconnected from a stereo connection, both the left and right cables are automatically disconnected. When auto-routing is disabled, only one cable is disconnected.

Pattern Controls

The Redrum and Matrix are pattern-based devices with mini-sequencers built into them. Reason has several key commands that make pattern programming very efficient.

Redrum Dynamics

The key to programming effective drum patterns on the Redrum Drum Computer is to use dynamic changes. Programming hard, medium, and soft events that vary through the pattern will give you a more interesting feel than static patterns that use all medium step events. When you're programming Redrum patterns, you'll need to change the dynamics switch before programming a step with a louder or softer event. Once the event is programmed, the dynamics switch has to be changed back to the previous setting for a different step event, and this becomes very tedious.

There is a useful set of key commands that saves time in programming Redrum patterns. Set the dynamics switch to the default, medium. Hold the Shift key and click on a pattern button to program a step with hard dynamics. Hold the Option/Alt key and click on a pattern button to program a step with soft dynamics.

Pattern Shifting

Redrum and Matrix are based on pattern sequences. The edit and contextual menus for Redrum and Matrix have items that allow you to offset a pattern. Using the edit menu or contextual menu to shift a pattern several times is time-consuming, and using the keyboard commands simplifies this task.

Shifting the Redrum and Matrix pattern left or right is achieved by holding down the Command (MacOS) or Ctrl (Windows) key and pressing "J" or "K." To shift the pattern to the right eight times, one would hold down the Command/Ctrl key and press "K" eight times.

The Matrix Pattern Sequencer has another set of keyboard commands to transpose the note events. Transposing the Matrix pattern up or down in semitones is done by holding down the Command (MacOS) or Ctrl (Windows) key and pressing "U" or "D."

Matrix Modifiers

The Shift key commands associated with the Matrix Pattern Sequencer provide several time-saving features. The Shift key performs three different editing functions in the Matrix. These functions differ depending where the cursor is located on the Matrix interface.

Holding the Shift key and clicking on gate events will create tied gate events. When the shift key is released, normal gate events will be created.

In the key view mode, holding the Shift key and clicking on note events will enable the line tool, which is a quick way to program scale patterns. This can be used to quickly transpose note events using the mouse. While holding the shift key, click on a note event on any step, drag the mouse cursor to another step, and then drag the mouse up and down the key lanes until a horizontal line appears across the key view.

The line tool also applies to the Matrix curve edit mode, and works in a similar manner. Hold the Shift key and click on the curve editor on one step, set the start value of the ramp, then drag the mouse to another step and drag up or down to select the destination value of the ramp.

File Management

Like any computer application, Reason creates and uses a variety of computer files. The following tips offer a few ideas on keeping these files organized on your system, as well as methods for localizing files so that song projects can be moved to other systems. There are also a few file handling shortcuts that will help when creating tracks in Reason.

Custom New Song File

When the New Song item is selected in the File menu, the default song is opened. When you get tired of listening to the factory song, you can go to the Edit menu, select Preferences/General, and choose an empty rack for your default song. But there's a better way. Usually, the first few items you'll create in the empty rack are a mixer, a few effects processors, and perhaps a few sound modules. This base configuration for a song can be saved and used as the default new song file. This song file should be saved in the Reason application folder so it can be easily located.

Select Preferences/General and click on the radio button for Custom Default Song. Click on the file browser button, locate the custom song file, and click on Open. When a new song is created, your customized file will be used.

You may also want to modify the song information on the custom default song.

This will save you the time of typing the copyright, website, and email information for each Reason song you create.

Project Folders

A Reason song can easily become quite intricate with the use of samples and ReCycle loop files, so it's wise to organize song projects in unique folders. When starting a new song project, create a project folder on your hard drive, and save the Reason song file into this directory. All files associated with the song, like patches and samples, should also be saved in this folder.

Saving Duplicate Song Files

You should save copies of each Reason song file you're working on as the project progresses. This will create a working history of the song development. If you make drastic changes and later decide they were a mistake, you can easily revert to an older version of the track. Establish a numbering system to keep the history organized. For example, save the first file as "My Reason Track 000.rns", and increase the digits as the song progresses. The files should be named in sequential order — "My Reason Track 001.rns", "My Reason Track 002.rns", etc. Make sure to save these files into the folder you've created to hold the project. Don't save song files to the desktop and later move them into the project folder. Reason is sensitive to file paths, and moving files around can cause problems.

Patches & Samples

Patch settings are easily lost, especially when you're making several parameter changes. Since Reason is limited in the number of undo levels it supports, it's wise to save synth, sampler, and effect patches. These should have appropriate subdirectories in the project folder, and a numbering system can be used with patch names so you'll remember when they were created.

A directory for samples should be created inside the project folder. Having the samples localized with the Reason song file makes them easier to access if they need editing. Reason is sensitive to file paths, so the samples should be moved into the project folder before loading them into a sampler. In the worst-case scenario, Reason will prompt you to find and replace samples that have been moved. To avoid this problem, you can move a copy of the sample into the save directory level along with the song file. When Reason opens a song, it will look in the same directory for the samples.

There is an option to save a Reason song file as a self-contained file, but once the files are compiled with the Reason song, it's not easy to access them. If you're collaborating with another Reason user or moving the track to another computer, the self-contained option works well. The song project folder can also be moved. As long as the relative file paths between the original song file and the samples do not change, Reason will have no problem finding the samples. Reason song files with self-contained samples can be very large, and if duplicates are saved, each of the duplicates will be as large as the original. This can consume a lot of disk space.

Loading Multiple Samples

Typically, the browser windows in Reason only open one file at a time. For example, only one patch can be selected from the Malström patch browser. The sample browsers on the NN19 and NN-XT are different. All samples listed in the browser can be selected and loaded in a single operation. Once the samples are loaded, they can be quickly mapped using auto-mapping features.

When the sample browser lists the audio files in a directory, use the key command Command/Ctrl-A to select all, and then click on the Open button. Specific audio files can be selected by using the Shift-click command, and the chosen samples will be loaded when the Open button is clicked.

Organizing ReFills

Many free and commercial ReFill Sample Libraries are available, and with the introduction of Reload, users can create their own ReFills from Akai S1000/S3000 CD-ROMs. The number and size of ReFills can grow incredibly fast, and you may find the need to move these to another hard drive location.

Create a folder called "ReFills," and move your ReFill files into this directory. The ReFill folder can be on any drive mounted on your system, including external FireWire devices and network drives. Reason looks within the application directory for the Factory Sound Bank and Orkester ReFills. These two files should remain in the application folder. Open the Preferences, select Sound Location from the pull-down menu, and click on the browser button. Using the browser, navigate to your ReFills folder and click on the Choose button.

On the *Power Tools for Reason* CD-ROM are a number of ReFill sample libraries. These should be copied from the CD-ROM into your ReFill folder.

Back Up Song Files

Back up your files — this should be the mantra of any computer user. With the time and energy you put into creating songs, taking a little time to back up the Reason song files after each work session is the only way to prevent the loss of critical data. File backup should be performed in addition to the process of saving multiple files as a project develops. Saving multiple files will safeguard your project if one file becomes corrupt, but backing up the entire project folder to a separate physical device will protect your work in the horrible event of a fatal hard drive problem or a stolen computer. While this isn't a shortcut, it can be considered the mother of all shortcuts. It will save a lot of time and headaches, should disaster strike.

Chapter 3
Control Voltages

Electrical currents called control voltages govern the processes of analog synthesizer systems. Vintage modular synthesizers manufactured by companies like Moog Music and Buchla & Associates have multitudes of connector jacks on the front panels of the modules. Some of these jacks are for sending audio signals from one module to another. The rest of the jacks are used for connecting control voltages (CVs). Using patch cords, CV signals can be sent from a control voltage source to trigger events or modulate parameters of other modules. Using patch cables, complex sounds can be generated by routing CV and audio signals between modules. This is the origin of the term "synthesizer patch." Patching CV and audio signals between devices is an incredibly powerful way to create unique sounds.

While Reason doesn't use true control voltages (it's a digital device), it's designed to operate very much as if it did. So understanding the theory behind control voltages is essential to getting the most out of Reason.

In any CV cable routing, there is a source, a destination, and an amount (also known as scale or sensitivity) control. Control voltages do not directly modify audio signals. Instead, a module like a filter alters the audio signal, and the CV affects the behavior of the filter. When a control voltage causes a parameter change, it's called *modulation*. A typical modulation routing is an LFO triangle wave output patched to the pitch control of a voltage-controlled oscillator (VCO). As the voltage level from the LFO rises and falls, the oscillator pitch increases and decreases, creating vibrato. The LFO CV is not combined with the audio signal. Instead, the CV signal from the LFO is added to another CV that controls the basic oscillator pitch.

Another common modulation is an envelope generator patched to a voltage-controlled amplifier (VCA). When a key is pressed on the keyboard, a gate CV (basically, a voltage that works like an on/off switch) is sent to trigger the envelope generator. The envelope generator's CV output signal rises and falls, and this signal changes the VCA loudness level. The audio signal passing through the VCA increases and decreases in level according to

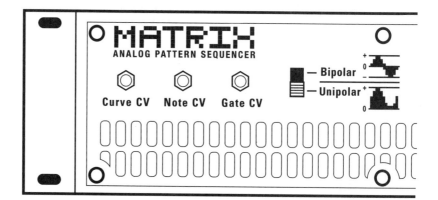

Figure 3-1.
The Matrix Pattern
Sequencer's CV outputs.

the level of the envelope CV. On most analog modular systems, multiple patch cords can be connected from the same source, so an envelope CV can be routed to the VCA, a voltage-controlled filter (VCF), and the VCO simultaneously.

In contemporary synthesizers, modulation routings tend to be less flexible. Patch cords are no longer an option, and CV signals from an LFO or envelope source are often limited to a single destination. A modulation routing within a synthesizer works much the same way as a CV signal on a modular synthesizer. For instance, on the SubTractor synthesizer front panel, the LFO 1 signal can be routed to modulate only one parameter at a time. Envelopes are also limited in their modulation routings, but this only applies to the front panel. There are some benefits to the compromise: Patches in a modern synth can be easily stored and instantly recalled without the trouble of remembering how the modules were patched.

On the rear view of the Reason virtual rack, most of the devices have sockets, graphically depicted as minijacks, for patching modulation routing inputs and outputs. Reason incorporates CV features similar to those on modular analog synthesizers. Modulation signals generated within the sound modules can be routed with virtual patch cords to different destinations on different devices in the Reason rack. These CV signals can also be split from a single source, just as they can in modular analog synthesizers. In essence, Reason is a modular synthesizer with an endless number of modules and patch cords.

Reason CV Sources

Many CV patching options are available in Reason, but there are only a few specific types of sources: the note, gate, and curve outputs from the Matrix, plus LFOs, envelopes, Malström modulators, the Scream 4 envelope follower, the BV512 Vocoder band levels, and the Spider CV.

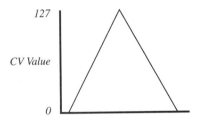

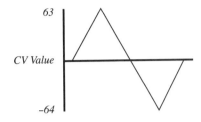

Figure 3-2.
Unipolar and bipolar CV curves both have a total range of 128 steps.

Modulation routings within Reason devices and the Reason CV signals available on the modulation output jacks are the same type of data. The LFO 1 signal operating within a SubTractor is the same signal available from the LFO 1 modulation output. The values of CV and modulation routings have a range of 128 steps. This range falls in either the unipolar domain of 0 to 127 or the bipolar domain, which is offset downward to between –64 and 63. In either case, only 128 values are possible in the signal, and the offset is determined by the source of the signal. Incoming CV values are added to the existing parameter settings, but the sum can't exceed the 128-step range.

While all of Reason's CV signals are basically interchangeable, it's often useful to think of them as falling in three different categories: curve, gate, and note CVs. Curve signals are general-purpose modulation signals, and can have any value between 0 and 127 (or between –64 and 63). Gate CVs are used to trigger events, but like other CVs, they can have any value between 0 and 127. When they're used simply to trigger other events, any value greater than 0 will produce a trigger, but in some situations the value of the gate CV will be interpreted as velocity, in which case the full range of values between 1 and 127 is meaningful. Note CV signals correspond to the MIDI note numbers in the chromatic scale (where Middle C has a value of 60).

Note CV
Note CV signals are used to send note values to the different sound modules, and are generated by the Matrix Pattern Sequencer. The CV value is determined by the note programmed in the key edit view of the Matrix. The lowest value is at C1, which has the numeric equivalent of 36, and the highest value is C6, which has the numeric value of 96. The Matrix Note CV does not take advantage of the full 128-step range, but for most musical applications, notes outside of this range are irrelevant.

Gate CV
Gate CV signals are pulses and are normally at zero. When an event occurs, the

gate CV value jumps to a value between 1 and 127, then returns back to zero. The Redrum, Dr.REX, and Matrix have gate CV outputs, which are usually connected to other gate CV inputs. Each of the Redrum channels has a gate CV output, and when the channel is triggered, a gate impulse appears at this socket. The Dr.REX has only one gate CV output; each time a slice is triggered, a gate impulse appears on this socket. The Matrix gate CV signals follow the values of the gate events programmed in the pattern.

With Matrix patterns, gate CV impulses are typically paired with note CV signals. The gate CV triggers a note event on the sound module to which the Matrix is patched, and the note CV specifies the pitch of the event. Velocity values are determined by the gate CV value, and these can be used to modulate the dynamics of the note events.

The duration of a gate CV is limited. Normal Matrix gate events are half the duration of the step resolution. These gate events can be tied for longer durations. Redrum gate CV impulses vary depending on the module's decay/gate and length settings. If the Redrum channel is set to decay mode, the gate CV duration is very short, but if the Redrum channel is set to gate mode, the gate CV duration is determined by the length setting. Dr.REX gate signals are very short and are very similar to those coming from the Redrum when it's set to decay mode.

Matrix Curve CV

The curve CV coming from Matrix can be used to modulate any parameter in Reason for which there is a rear-panel CV input jack. A common use of the curve CV is to modulate the cutoff frequency of an ECF-42 Filter module. Different values for each step of the pattern will generate a CV signal that modulates the filter in a unique way, repeating each time the pattern cycles. The same signal can be easily applied to any CV input on any device in the rack.

Matrix curve CV signals come in two varieties, called unipolar and bipolar. You can choose either mode using the switch on the rear of the Matrix. The curve edit view of the pattern differs depending on the mode. Unipolar curves have a value range from 0 to 127. Bipolar curve mode has a range from −64 to 63. When the Matrix is set to bipolar mode, the curve edit view changes to show a zero-crossing line across the middle. Events above the line are positive signals, and events below the line are negative signals. With higher pattern resolutions, the Matrix curve can be used to emulate an LFO signal.

Low-Frequency Oscillator CV

LFO CV signals are one of the most common types of modulation signal found on any synthesizer. While many devices and some effects have LFO features, only the SubTractor, NN19, and Dr.REX have LFO CV outputs. The LFO CV functions are the same for all three devices. LFO CV signals are bipolar with a range of values between –64 and 63. The CV value is determined by the shape of the waveform, and the period of the cycle is set by the LFO's rate knob.

A SubTractor LFO set to a triangle wave generates a CV signal that behaves as follows: The signal starts at zero, rises to 63, falls back to zero, dips to –64, and then rises back up to zero. The ramp waveforms will generate CV curves that rise from –64 to 63 or fall from 63 to –64. The square wave is an impulse signal that starts at 63, drops to –64, then jumps back up to 63. The last two waveforms are random signal generators. The first random waveform is stepped, and a random CV is held for a moment before jumping to a new random value. The other is a smooth random waveform where the CV signal randomly sweeps between values.

The LFOs usually run freely and are not synchronized to a note event, but they can be synchronized to the tempo of the Reason song. The sync button on the SubTractor or Malström panel enables the tempo synchronization. When the LFO is synchronized with the tempo, the values available from the rate knob change to note value durations, and the phase of the waveform is locked to the start of the sequence so that the sweep will produce a reliable rhythmic effect.

Envelope CV

Envelopes are common to every synthesizer for controlling dynamics. Envelopes can be used to modulate other parameters, which is why devices like SubTractor have three envelope generators. Every sound module in Reason has some form of envelope generator, but envelope CV sources are found only on the SubTractor, Dr.REX, NN19, and Malström.

Envelope modulation output CV signals are unipolar and start at zero, then rise up to 127, then fall back to zero. Until the envelope is triggered, the CV signal from the envelope generator is zero. The rate of the change is determined by two factors — the envelope's attack, decay, sustain, and release parameters, and the duration of the gate event triggering the envelope.

The attack, decay, and release values control the length (time) of the envelope. The sustain value controls a CV level value. When a trigger is received by either a gate CV event or a MIDI note-on event, the envelope CV value increases from 0 to 127 at the rate determined by the attack setting. Once the envelope peaks at 127, the CV value decreases at the rate set the by the decay setting. The destination CV value of the envelope decay is set by the sustain parameter. The envelope CV value will stay at the sustain setting until the gate CV or MIDI note-on event switches off. When the gate is switched off, the envelope CV will fall from the sustain level back to zero. The time it takes the CV signal to fall back to zero is determined by the release setting.

The release time is the only parameter that works independently of the gate duration. If the gate stops at a point in the middle of the attack phase, the CV output

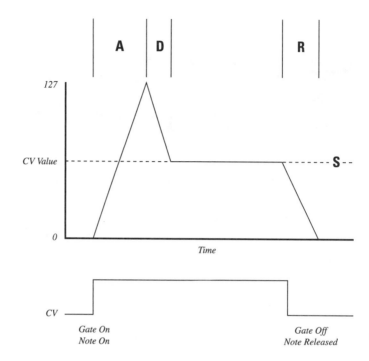

Figure 3-3.
An ADSR envelope CV
signal rises to a level of
127, and falls back to 0
when the gate ends.

will stop increasing and start decreasing back toward zero at the rate of the release setting. This also applies if the trigger stops in the middle of the decay phase of the envelope.

If the attack and decay rates are set to zero, the envelope CV signal will instantly rise from zero to the sustain level when the envelope is triggered. When the gate ends, the CV signal will return to zero at the release rate (see Figure 3-4).

The envelope CV is crucial for modulating the volume of synthesizer or sampler note events, but this time-controlled CV can be used in a variety of applications like changing pitch or filter cutoff frequency.

Malström Modulator CV
Each Malström Graintable Synthesizer has two modulation sources labeled "Mod A" and "Mod B." Both have the same basic functions, but they have different modulation routings within the synthesizer. On the rear of the Malström, a CV modulation output socket is provided for each modulator.

The modulators have the same basic features as LFOs, but there are 32 different waveforms to choose from, and the output CV range varies depending on the waveform. Some waveforms are unipolar, while others are bipolar. The waveform

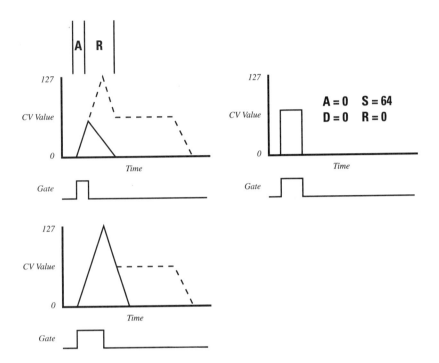

Figure 3-4.
The gate duration changes the ADSR's output curve.

icons will indicate the mode of the signal. Icons that only use the upper half of the waveform display are unipolar with a range from 0 to 127. Icons that use the entire display are bipolar with a value range from −64 to 63.

The modulation source resets each time a note event starts. Until another note event is received, the output behaves like a free-running or tempo-synchronized LFO source. Within the Malström, there is a modulation generator for each voice of polyphony, so the phase of the waveform is locked to the trigger event of each voice. The CV signal sent to the modulation output socket will be from the last note triggered. If the modulation source is used to generate CV signals, it's best to disable the oscillator and filter sections and not use the Malström's synthesizer features.

The one-shot feature of the modulation generator changes the behavior so that it's more like an envelope generator rather than an LFO. With the one-shot button enabled, the Modulator waits for a gate event. Once a gate event is received, the modulator cycles through the waveform. The CV values change according to the waveform and rate settings, then stop, returning the CV value back to zero. In one-shot mode, the rate knob controls the duration of the modulator cycle.

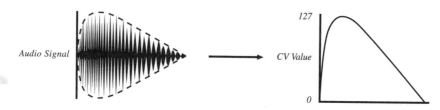

Figure 3-5.
The Scream 4 Envelope
Follower's CV output.

Scream 4 Envelope Follower CV

The Scream 4 Sound Destruction Unit has a unique CV output labeled "Auto CV Output." The Scream 4 has an internal envelope follower. An envelope follower creates a CV signal based on the loudness of the audio signal being received by the Scream 4.

The auto CV output values are unipolar with a range between 0 and 127. When the input audio signal is silent, the CV value is zero. When the input audio signal peaks to maximum, the CV value is 127. Unless processing is desired on the input signal, the damage, cut, and body features can be disabled and the audio signal will pass through the Scream 4 unaffected. The audio signal will still be attenuated by the Scream's master level knob unless it's set to 100 (unity gain). This setup allows you to insert the Scream into any audio signal path and use the envelope follower without affecting the signal.

The envelope follower feature opens up a wide variety of modulation possibilities, because it links audio signals with CV signals. The Scream's auto CV output can be connected to the pitch modulation of a SubTractor, for instance, while a Dr.REX loop feeds a signal into the Scream 4. The pitch of the SubTractor is then determined by the loudness of the drum hits: Louder hits will drive the pitch higher than softer hits.

Vocoder Band Level CV

The BV512 Vocoder device has another unique CV source similar that of to the Scream 4 envelope follower. Each of the 16 band level CV outputs acts as a frequency-dependent envelope follower. Each band level output is derived from one of the frequency spectrum bands in the BV512's audio input. When the vocoder is set to four-, eight-, or 16-band mode, the band level outputs correspond to the band levels on the analyzer. In 32-band or FFT mode, the CV outputs reflect the levels of adjacent pairs of bands.

The Band Level CV signals are unipolar with a range from 0 to 127. When the

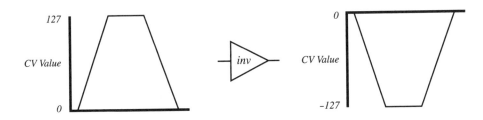

Figure 3-6.
A CV inverted by the
Spider CV Splitter.

analyzer detects frequencies in the range associated with a vocoder band, a CV signal is generated depending on the intensity of the frequencies in that range.

The attack and decay parameters on the BV512 contour the way the envelope followers change levels. When the attack and decay settings are at zero, the band levels and the corresponding CV values change as rapidly as possible. The attack parameter controls the maximum rate that a band level can increase, while the decay parameter controls how fast it can decrease. Higher decay settings can be used to generate a lag effect, because the peak level will be held for a short duration before the band level CV decays to zero.

Spider CV

The Spider CV Merger and Splitter module does not generate CV signals, but it contains a signal inverter, which can be used to modify CV signals. The inverted signal can then be used as source to modulate other devices.

A CV signal connected to splitter input is inverted on the fourth splitter out socket. This means that a CV signal with a value of 32 going into the splitter will have a value of –32 on the inv jack. An LFO signal connected to the splitter can be routed to the pitch modulation inputs of two devices. One device is connected to the normal splitter output (Out 1, Out 2, or Out 3), and the other device is connected to the inverted Out 4. The pitch modulation will be opposite for the two devices.

CV Trim Knobs

The trim knobs located next to the modulation input sockets on various Reason devices attenuate incoming CV signals. These controls function like the LFO amount, mod amount, and envelope amount knobs located on the front of the device, and scale the modulation. With the exception of the signals generated on the Matrix Pattern Sequencer, all CV signals have a range of 128 steps in either

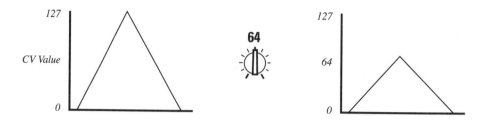

Figure 3-7.
The trim knob scales
CV values.

bipolar or unipolar mode. The full modulation range is not always desired, and the CV trim knobs can be used to limit the range.

When the trim is set to zero, no modulation is applied from incoming CV. Turning the trim knob to 127 will allow the full modulation range of 128 steps. The default setting is 64, which scales the value range from 0 to 63. As mentioned in the beginning of this section, incoming CV values are added to existing parameter settings. If a filter cutoff frequency is currently set to 64, the value from an envelope generator CV will be added to 64. Once the sum reaches 127, it will be held at 127 until the sum of the CV values is less than the maximum amount. Using the trim knob to scale the envelope generator value range will prevent this type of control signal clipping.

CV Signals Are Universal

CV outputs must be connected to CV inputs, and any of the three types of CV signals can be used as a source (output). Typically, the Matrix gate CV and note CV outputs are connected to the corresponding gate and CV inputs on the sound modules, but you can switch these, or use the curve CV output as the source of gate signals, or use gate signals to modulate note CV inputs. The result of mismatching CV source types and destination types is not always predictable, and the process of finding a patch that produces something interesting is usually trial-and-error. The next few examples will demonstrate that these signals are interchangeable.

LFO Triggering Gate Events

A square/pulse waveform from an LFO can be used to generate gate CV signals that trigger events on the sound modules or the ECF-42 Envelope Controlled Filter. Since the SubTractor LFO is free-running, note events will occur as soon as the LFO connection is made to the gate input socket. Enabling the Sync feature on the LFO will trigger these events in time with the master tempo of the track.

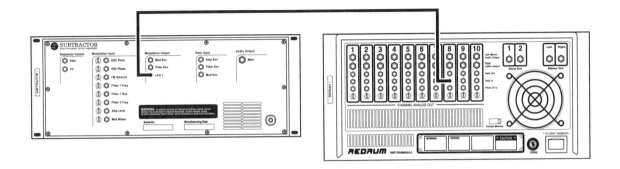

Figure 3-8.
SubTractor LFO connected
to Redrum gate CV input.

- In an empty rack, create a mixer.
- Create a Redrum Drum Computer and load the patch "Abstract Kit 01.drp" from the Reason Factory Soundbank\Redrum Drum Kits\Abstract HipHop Kits directory.
- Create a SubTractor Synthesizer Module.
- Connect the SubTractor Modulation Output LFO 1 output to the Redrum channel 8 gate input.
- Set LFO 1 to a square wave. (Some of the other waves will offset the LFO wave in relation to the beat.)
- Adjust the LFO 1 rate knob lower for regular hi-hat hits, adjust the rate higher for some unique rapid hi-hat sample smearing, or adjust it to 16/4 so the hi-hat channel triggers only once every four measures.

Matrix Curve as a Gate CV Source

The Matrix curve CV can be used as a gate CV source. Since the duration of a curve CV event is a full pattern step, it behaves like a tied gate event. In fact, there is one

Figure 3-9.
Matrix curve CV
connected to Malström
gate CV input.

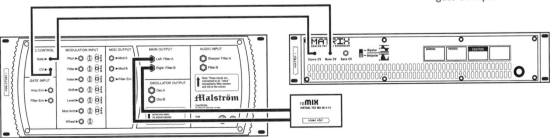

application of this configuration that works better than gate events. The maximum value of a Matrix gate event is 126. If the Matrix is used to trigger an NN-XT sample zone mapped to a velocity of 127, the Matrix gate will not trigger the zone.

- In an empty rack, create a mixer.
- Create a Malström Graintable Synthesizer.
- On the Malström, set the LVL:A velocity setting to 41.
- Bypass auto-routing by holding down the Shift key, and create a Matrix Pattern Sequencer.
- Connect the Matrix curve CV output to the Malström seq control gate input.
- Connect the Matrix note CV socket to the Malström seq control CV input.
- Program the following pattern on the Matrix. The curve values shown are approximate:

Matrix 1 (Steps 1–16)

Step	1	2	3	4	5	6	7	8	9	10	11	12	13	14	15	16
Curve	64	0	32	0	96	0	10	0	80	0	64	0	96	0	24	0
Note	C4	C4	C4	C3	C3	C3	C4	C4	C4	C3	C3	C3	C4	C4	C4	C3
Gate																

- Press Run on the Matrix to hear the curve events gate the Malström.

Using a Gate to Control a Note CV Input

The Matrix in the preceding example isn't doing anything you couldn't do with its gate CV output. The point of the experiment is simply to show that the curve CV can be used as a gate. This example demonstrates that note and gate CV data are interchangeable. The only specific difference is the behavior of the source signals. Gate CV signals last for half of the time value of a Matrix step, and then fall back to zero. Note CV outputs from the Matrix are fixed for the duration of the step, as are curve CV outputs. The resolution of curve CV values is not as precise as that of the note CV values, because the note values will correspond to the MIDI note number, but the note CV will always be between 36 and 96, while the curve value can be as high as 127 or as low as –64, depending on whether you choose unipolar or bipolar mode.

- In an empty rack, create a mixer.
- Create a SubTractor Synthesizer Module.
- Connect the SubTractor modulation output from LFO 1 back to the sequencer control gate input of the SubTractor. The SubTractor will start to beep.

- Bypass auto-routing and create a Matrix Pattern Sequencer.
- Connect the Matrix gate CV to the SubTractor sequencer control CV input. The beeping will drop to a low pitch.
- Program gate events from step 1 through 16 on the Matrix.
- Press Run on the Matrix.

Envelope CV Gate Source

Envelope curves with short durations will behave like gate CV impulses. The SubTractor envelope modulation output can trigger a Redrum channel, for instance. A chain of gate CV events can be created to trigger several different sources simultaneously.

- Start with an empty rack and create a mixer.
- Create a SubTractor Synthesizer.
- Set the mod envelope attack and decay to 0, sustain to 127, and release to 0.
- Create a Matrix Pattern Sequencer.
- Program the following Matrix pattern (note: the letter 'H' in the Gate row indicates that you're to put a normal gate event on that step):

PROGRAMMING TABLE ABBREVIATIONS. Throughout this book, the letters H, M, and L are used in programming tables for Matrix and Redrum patterns. H refers to a high-velocity event, M to a medium-velocity event, and L to a low-velocity event. In the Matrix, the values will be approximate. The letter T is used in Matrix tables to refer to a tied gate event.

Matrix 1 (Steps 1–16)

Step	1	2	3	4	5	6	7	8	9	10	11	12	13	14	15	16
Curve																
Note	C3	C3	C3	C3	C3	C3	C3	C3	C3	C3	C3	C3	C3	C3	C3	C3
Gate	H				H				H		H		H			

- Create a Redrum Drum Computer.
- Load the Redrum patch "Electronic Kit 1.drp" from the Reason Factory Sound Bank\Redrum Drum Kits\Electronic Kits directory.
- Connect the SubTractor mod envelope modulation output to the Redrum channel 3 gate in socket.
- Run the Matrix pattern.

The Matrix sequence triggers note events on the SubTractor Synthesizer. As each note event occurs, the modulation envelope is triggered, sending a gate-like CV signal to the Redrum.

Modulator as a Note CV Source

This example should eliminate any question about the nature of control voltage

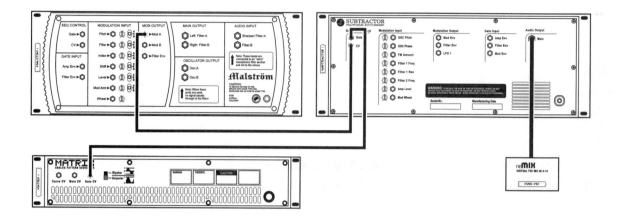

Figure 3-10.
Malström modulator CV
sending note CV events.

signals. Instead of using a Matrix note CV to control the pitch of a SubTractor synthesizer, a ramp signal from a Malström modulation source will send note CV data
to the SubTractor.

• Start with an empty rack and create a mixer.
• Create a SubTractor Synthesizer.
• Set the SubTractor Polyphony to 1, and Filter 1 Freq to 127.
• Create a Matrix Pattern Sequencer.
• Set the Matrix pattern to one step and program a tied gate event on Step 1.
• Disconnect the cable connected to the Matrix sequencer control CV output.
• Bypass auto-routing and create a Malström Graintable Synthesizer.
• Connect the Malström mod A output to the SubTractor sequencer control CV
  input.
• Set the Malström mod A rate to 1 and modulator curve to 12 (ramp).
• Run the Matrix.

As the ramp signal from the Malström increases, the SubTractor note pitch also
increases. Each value of the control voltage signal is equal to a half-step.

Merging & Splitting CV Signals

The Spider CV Merger & Splitter performs the simple functions of merging CV
signals the way an audio mixer does, and splitting CV signals so you can distribute

one output to several inputs. The CV signal inverter was discussed earlier, but this section will illustrate a few common uses of merging, splitting, and inverting CV signals.

Matrix CV/Gate Splitting

This is a method for creating polyphonic tracks from a single Matrix pattern. Although the intervals are fixed to the oscillator tuning, splitting the Matrix CV/gate signals can be used to layer or stack oscillators for thicker sounds.

- Start with an empty rack, and create a mixer.
- Create three SubTractor Synthesizers.
- Bypass auto-routing and create a Matrix Pattern Sequencer.
- Bypass auto-routing and create a Spider CV.
- Connect the Matrix note CV output to the Spider CV split A input.
- Connect the Matrix gate CV output to the Spider CV split B input.
- Connect the split A outputs to each of the SubTractors' sequencer control CV inputs.
- Connect the split B outputs to each of the SubTractors' sequencer control gate inputs.

Figure 3-11.
Splitting the Matrix note CV and gate CV to three SubTractors.

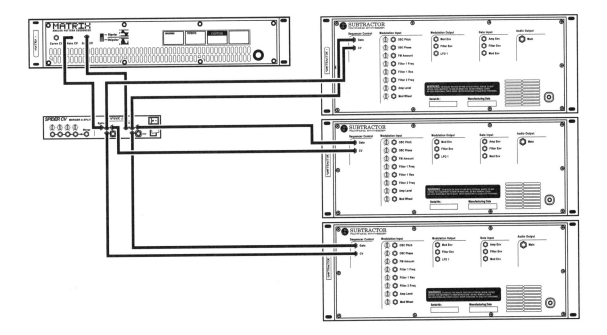

• Program the following Matrix pattern:

Matrix 1 (Steps 1–16)															
Step	1	2	3	4	5	6	7	8	9	10	11	12	13	14	15	16
Curve																
Note	C3	C2	C3	C3	C2	C3	C3	C2	C3	C2	C3	C3	C2	C3	C3	C2
Gate	H	H	H	H	H	H	H	H	H	H	H	H	H	H	H	H

• On all three SubTractors, load the patch "Acid Saw 2" from the Reason Factory
  Sound Bank\SubTractor Patches\MonoSynth directory.
• On SubTractor 1, adjust osc 1 and osc 2 semitone settings to 7.
• On SubTractor 2, adjust osc 1 cent setting to 0 and osc 2 cent setting to –8.
• On SubTractor 3, adjust osc 1 and osc 2 octave settings to 4.
• Pan mixer channel 1 to –63.
• Pan mixer channel 2 to 64.
• Run the Matrix.
• Adjust the values of the Matrix gate events to produce an accent pattern.

Merged Modulator CV Signals

Complex modulation patterns can be created by merging several CV sources together. This examples uses modulators A and B from a Malström, merges them, and
modulates the pitch of the oscillator.

• In an empty rack, create a mixer.
• Create a Malström Graintable Synthesizer.
• Enable sync on mod A and mod B.

Figure 3-12.
Merging two Malström
modulator CV signals.

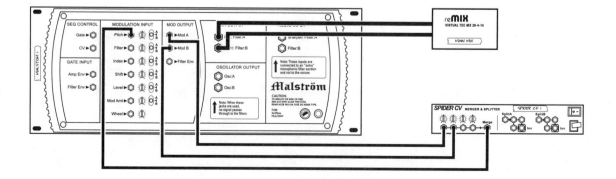

• Set the mod A rate to 1/8.
• Set the mod B rate to 4/4.
• Set the mod B waveform to curve 9.
• Create a Spider CV while disabling auto-routing.
• Connect the Malström mod A and mod B outputs to the Spider CV merger input
    1 and input 2.
• Connect the Spider CV merge output to the Malström pitch modulation input.
• Play a note from a MIDI controller directed to the Malström to hear the effect
    of the combined modulation signals on the pitch of the note.

Matrix-Controlled Cross-Pan
The mixer pan parameter is bipolar with a range of −64 to 63. This example
demonstrates using the Spider CV inverter to modulate panning. Using the Spider
CV signal inverter and splitter, the Matrix curve CV modulates panning on two mixer
channels. The modulations are reversed causing the mixer channels to cross-pan.

• In an empty rack, create a mixer.
• Create two Dr.REX Loop Players.
• On Dr.REX 1, load the Recycle file "125_Moogerized2_mLp_eLAB.rx2" from the
    Factory Sound Bank from the Music Loops\Variable Tempo (rex2)\Uptempo Loops
    directory.
• Copy the REX data to the Dr.REX 1 sequencer track.
• From the Same directory, load the file "130_Circle_mLp_eLAB.rx2" into
    Dr.REX 2.
• Copy the REX data to the Dr.REX 2 sequencer track.
• Create a Spider CV Merger & Splitter.

Figure 3-13.
Spider CV split and
inverted signals
modulating mixer
panning.

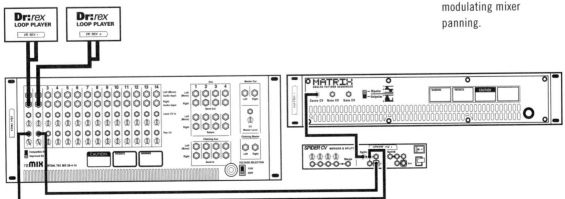

- Bypass auto-routing and create a Matrix Pattern Sequencer.
- On the rear panel, set the Matrix to bipolar mode.
- Connect the Matrix curve CV output to the Spider CV split A input socket.
- Connect a Spider CV split A output to the pan CV in socket on channel 1 of the mixer.
- Connect the Spider CV split A inv output socket to the mixer's channel 2 pan CV input.
- Set the mixer's rear-panel pan CV trim to 127 on input channels 1 and 2.
- Set the Matrix pattern to 32 steps.
- On the Matrix, draw a curve ramp from –63 to 64 starting at step 1 and ending at step 32.
- Click the play button in the sequencer control panel.

As the sequence runs, the Matrix curve CV modulates the panning on channels 1 and 2. The inverted curve CV signal causes channel 1 to pan left while channel 2 pans right, and vice-versa.

Matrix CV Examples

The Matrix Pattern Sequencer is the most versatile source for control voltages in Reason. Its primary function is to generate monophonic music patterns that trigger note events in the sound modules, but it has many applications beyond note sequencing. The following examples demonstrate a variety of uses, and others are described throughout this book.

Matrix Curve LFO

This technique creates an LFO modulation curve that is synchronized to the tempo. This might be considered obsolete since the LFO sources in all Reason devices have tempo sync, but you can't control the phase (waveform starting point) of these

Figure 3-14.
Patching two Matrix
Sequencers with offset
patterns.

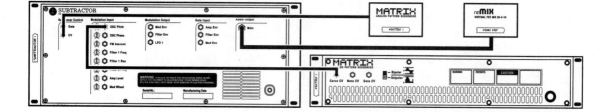

LFO sources. The Matrix curve can be offset by shifting the pattern using the edit menu or keyboard commands, thus altering the phase of the modulation shape.

- In an empty rack, create a mixer.
- Create a SubTractor Synthesizer.
- Create a Matrix Pattern Sequencer.
- In the Matrix, program tied gate events from step 1 through step 16.
- Bypass auto-routing and create another Matrix. ✓
- On pattern A1 of Matrix 2, set the pattern length to 32 steps and the resolution to 1/128.
- Hit the Tab key to flip the rack to the rear view and switch Matrix 2 to bipolar mode.
- Cable the Matrix 2 curve CV output to the SubTractor osc pitch modulation input socket.
- Set the SubTractor osc pitch mod trim to 12.
- Switch Matrix 2 into curve edit mode.
- Enable the line tool and draw a triangle wave starting at the zero crossing on step 1 with a peak on step 9 and a trough at step 25.
- Select the two Matrixes and the SubTractor. Hold down the Alt/Option key and drag the duplicate group of devices to the bottom of the rack.
- Connect the SubTractor 1 Copy to mixer input channel 2.
- Select Matrix 2 Copy.
- From the Edit menu, select the item Shift Pattern Right, or type Ctrl-K. Repeat this 15 more times until the triangle wave trough is in the first half of the pattern and the peak in the second half.
- Pan mixer channel 1 hard left and mixer channel 2 hard right.
- Start the sequence by pressing the Play button.

Matrix Arpeggiator Effect

An arpeggio is a musical chord where the notes are played in a sequence rather than simultaneously. Some electronic instruments have built-in arpeggiators that perform this musical task. Typically, when a chord is played on the synthesizer keyboard, the arpeggiator plays a sequence starting with the lowest key and moving up to the highest key, then back down to the lowest key. Reason does not have an arpeggiator, but this effect can be simulated in several ways. The configuration below is a polyphonic arpeggiator and requires note events from a MIDI keyboard or from the sequencer.

- In an empty rack, create a mixer.
- Create a SubTractor.
- Load the SubTractor patch "Sweeping Strings" from the SubTractor Patches\Pads directory in the Reason Factory Sound bank.

• Edit the SubTractor patch by changing the osc 1 and osc 2 octave setting to 2.
• Bypass auto-routing and create a Matrix.
• Cable the Matrix note CV output to the SubTractor osc pitch modulation input.
• Set the SubTractor osc pitch modulation trim to 127.
• Switch the Matrix Keys view to Octave 1.
• Set the Matrix pattern length to 6 steps.
• Edit the pattern to create a C minor arpeggio:

Matrix C Minor Arpeggio (Steps 1–6)						
Step	1	2	3	4	5	6
Curve						
Note	C1	E♭1	G1	C2	G1	E♭1
Gate	H	H	H	H	H	H

• Press Run on the Matrix.
• Enable MIDI on the SubTractor sequencer track and play octaves or open fifths on the keyboard.

This effect is handy for creating arpeggio chord effects since the Matrix is used to transpose rather than send note values. Because the Matrix output value of the note CV starts at 32, the oscillators must be transposed down to compensate for the increase in pitch value. With the osc pitch CV input trim set to 127, the note CV value will modulate the pitch in chromatic steps.

Dual Matrix Arpeggiator

This example demonstrates how two Matrix note control voltages can be merged in a Spider CV merger to create an arpeggio pattern sequence. One Matrix pattern controls the root note of the chord, while the second Matrix pattern generates the cascading chord notes in C minor. The second Matrix can easily be programmed to other chord variations such as major or dominant seventh, but the root note must be C1. The actual root value is set by the first Matrix. The pitch value is the sum of these two control voltages merged in a Spider CV Merger.

• Start with an empty rack, and create a mixer.
• Create a SubTractor Synthesizer.
• Set the polyphony to 1 and osc 1 octave transposition to 0.
• Bypass auto-routing and create a Spider CV Merger & Splitter and two Matrix Pattern Sequencers.

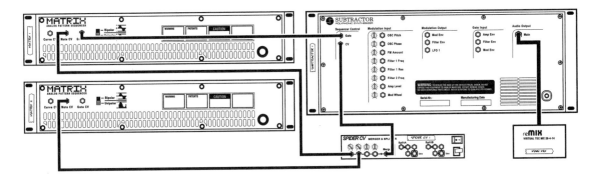

Figure 3-15.
Matrix note CV signals
merged to create a
summed note CV for the
SubTractor.

- Matrix 1 will control the gate events and the root note of the arpeggio, so connect the Matrix 1 gate CV output to the SubTractor gate sequencer control input.
- Connect the Matrix 1 note CV output to the Spider CV merge input 1.
- Set the Spider CV Merge input 1 trim to 127.
- Set Matrix 1 pattern length to 32 steps, and program the following on Matrix 1 pattern A1:

Matrix 1 Root Note and Gate Events (Steps 1–16)

Step	1	2	3	4	5	6	7	8	9	10	11	12	13	14	15	16
Curve																
Note	C3	C3	C3	C3	C3	C3	C3	C3	G3	G3	G3	G3	G3	G3	G3	G3
Gate	H	H	H	H	H	H	H	H	H	H	H	H	H	H	H	H

Matrix 1 Root Note and Gate Events (Steps 17–32)

Step	17	18	19	20	21	22	23	24	25	26	27	28	29	30	31	32
Curve																
Note	B♭3	B♭3	B♭3	B♭3	F3	F3	F3	F3	E♭3	E♭3	E♭3	E♭3	C#3	C#3	C#3	C#3
Gate	H	H	H	H	H	H	H	H	H	H	H	H	H	H	H	H

Matrix 2 generates the chord sequence of the arpeggio. Only the note CV values are used, and the chord structure will be based on C minor.

- Connect the Matrix 2 note CV output to the Spider CV merge input 2.
- Set the Spider CV merge input 2 trim to 127.
- Set Matrix 2 pattern length to 8 steps.
- Program the following on Matrix 2 pattern A1:

Matrix 2 Arpeggio Chord								
Step	1	2	3	4	5	6	7	8
Curve								
Note	C1	E♭1	G1	C2	E♭2	C2	G1	E♭1
Gate								

• Connect the Spider CV merger output to the SubTractor CV sequencer control input.
• Press Play in the sequencer.

The numeric value of C1 is 36 and the value of C3 is 60. The resulting sum is 96, which is the equivalent of C6. In order to compensate for the high pitch, the SubTractor's oscillator has to be transposed down to octave 0. Because the maximum CV value is 127, the root note is limited in range between octave 1 and octave 3 on Matrix 1. Anything higher than octave 3 will create note values that pin at 127. Another method of compensating for the sum of the note values is to start the root note pattern on octave 1 or octave 2, then increase the SubTractor octave transposition to 1 or 2.

CV Examples

CV routing is one of the features that make Reason so versatile. The following examples illustrate a few other ways CVs can be used. "Real-Time CV Control" is a particularly important example, since this configuration is used several times in other examples in this book.

Envelope-Controlled Panning

The SubTractor has two envelope generator outputs, making it the most useful source of a general-purpose envelope CV. Since the SubTractor won't be used to generate a sound in this type of patch, the polyphony should be set to 1, low bandwidth (BW) should be enabled, and the audio output should be disconnected. These steps economize CPU resources.

• Start with an empty rack, and create a mixer.
• Create a SubTractor, and set its polyphony to 1.
• Set the filter 1 frequency to 62 and resonance to 63.
• Set the mod envelope attack to 65, decay to 0, sustain to 127, and release to 72.

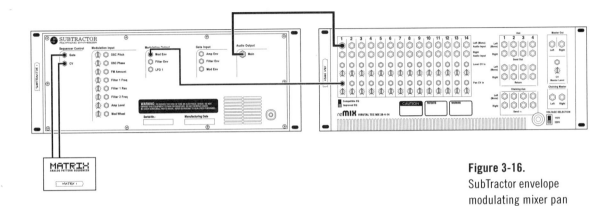

Figure 3-16.
SubTractor envelope
modulating mixer pan
CV input.

- Set the filter envelope attack to 0, decay to 57, sustain to 87, release to 75, and amount to 63.
- Set the amp envelope attack to 0, decay to 0, sustain to 120, and release to 72.
- Set the velocity filter envelope modulation level to 0.
- Connect the SubTractor mod envelope modulation output to the mixer channel 1 pan CV in.
- Set the mixer channel 1 pan CV trim to 127.
- Set the mixer channel 1 front-panel pan to about −28.
- Create a Matrix Pattern Sequencer.
- Program the following in Matrix pattern A1:

Matrix 1 (Steps 1–16)

Step	1	2	3	4	5	6	7	8	9	10	11	12	13	14	15	16
Curve																
Note	C3	C3	C3	C3	C3	C3	C3	C3	C3	C3	C3	C3	C3	C3	C3	C3
Gate	TH	TH	TH	TH	TH											

- Press Run on the Matrix. You should hear each note start in the left speaker, pan across to the right speaker, and then pan back to the left.

Envelope generator CV outputs are always unipolar. The inverter option next to the ADSR settings only applies to modulation routings within SubTractor. The CV output is always in the positive range of 0 to 127. The Spider CV inverter can be used to invert the modulation signal, however. By using the Spider CV to split and invert the envelope CV, this configuration can be modified to cross-pan two signals.

Real-Time CV Control

The Spider CV module, introduced in version 2.5, has opened up the possibility of creating endless numbers of modulation routings in Reason. In most cases, control of the CV signals is limited to envelopes and LFOs. This example illustrates a method of sending a CV signal from a slider, which opens up the possibility of changing CV signals in real time. This effect uses the modulation and filter envelopes on the SubTractor. When the sustain level of the envelope is altered, the CV modulation output signal changes accordingly.

The Matrix Pattern Sequencer is used to send a constant note-on message to the SubTractor. A one-step pattern with a tied gate event on step 1 ensures that whenever the song is running, the SubTractor will constantly play a single note. When the Matrix is stopped, the CV modulation will also cease.

- Bypass auto-routing and create a SubTractor.
- Enable the Low BW (bandwidth) button.
- Set the SubTractor's polyphony to 1.
- Set the Mod Envelope ADSR settings all to 0.
- Set the Filter Envelope ADSR settings all to 0.
- Create a Matrix.
- Program the following Matrix pattern:

Matrix 1 — Pattern Length = 1 Step

Step	1
Curve	
Note	C3
Gate	TH

This pattern will play and hold a note while the Matrix or Sequencer is running. This is like a single note that plays for the entire length of a song.

- Bypass auto-routing and create a Spider CV Merger & Splitter.
- Connect the SubTractor mod env output to the Spider CV split A input.
- Connect the SubTractor filter env output to the Spider CV split B input.

The sustain sliders on the mod envelope and filter envelope now control the CV signal sent out the modulation outputs. These signals are split by the Spider CV, and they can be routed to any CV destination for real-time control. Automation of these controls can be recorded on a sequencer track, and can be assigned to an external knob or slider controller. (When sending MIDI controller data from external hardware, you can either use the controller assignments listed in Reason's MIDI Implementation Chart, or choose Options/Enable MIDI Remote Mapping and then select the controllers of your choice in each slider's pop-up mapping window.)

Chapter 4
Audio Signal Routing & Busses

This chapter introduces the terminology and concepts of the audio electronics applied in Reason. The key issues discussed are routing audio devices in series, splitting signals in parallel connections, audio busses, merging and mixing signals, attenuation, and feedback. Having a grasp of the terms and concepts will make it much easier to understand some of the more complex configurations described later in the book.

Audio signals can be connected among devices in Reason in a nearly infinite number of ways, and cabling modules together without some kind of plan can easily become confusing. By simplifying the process and looking at some basic circuit configurations, we can outline a framework in a way that's easy to grasp. Not only does this framework help in making the proper connections among devices, it allows one to understand how to make variations in existing connections.

Devices in Series

A *series* connection is where the outputs from a given device are wired into the inputs of the next device. If there are more than two devices, the inputs of each device in the chain are connected to the outputs of the previous device. In traditional mixers, effects that are connected to a channel in series are said to be *insert* effects. Adding an effect is commonly described as "inserting an effect" into the signal path. For instance, let's say the output of an ECF-42 Envelope Controlled Filter module has too much bass. Inserting a PEQ-2 Parametric Equalizer to contour the low frequencies is required. The resulting signal could have very drastic changes in loudness, so a Comp-01 Compressor would be inserted after the PEQ-2 to control the dynamic changes. Almost limitless numbers of devices can be connected in series, especially in Reason, where adding a device to the signal chain is as easy as a mouse click.

Many modern keyboards have effects parameters built into each sound patch.

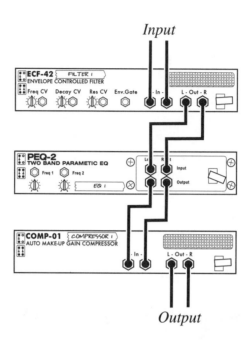

Figure 4-1.
Three effects devices
connected in series.

Connecting several effects in series is a technique used to create sonically rich sounds from merely pressing a single key on these keyboards. If you remove the effects from the patch, the sound is reduced to a simple tone. With the variety of effects available in Reason, and the ability to connect these effects in any order, it's quite easy to create an amazing sound from the output signals of a single synthesizer module.

There is a limit beyond which adding more effects yields no significant benefit, especially when economizing CPU usage becomes an issue. Every computer has a specific limit in terms of the number of modules, processors, and effects devices you can add. The CPU usage meter on the Reason Transport Bar will indicate when the amount of information being processed is taxing the processor's resources. In the example described above, a bass shelf equalizer could be used instead of adding a PEQ-2 to roll off the bass frequencies, thus saving a few CPU cycles.

Parallel Circuits

In a *parallel* circuit, a signal is split into branches, each carrying the original source signal. At a later point in the signal path (often the main mixer or output), the parallel signals will be joined back together. When it's necessary to route the same audio signal to different devices, a signal is split and a parallel circuit is created.

A useful example of a parallel circuit is where you want the mono output of a SubTractor to go into stereo inputs on a mixer. In the hardware realm, you would

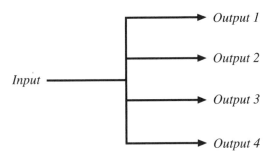

Figure 4-2.
A four-way splitter splits
the incoming signal into
four parallel paths.

use a Y-cable. The SubTractor audio output can be split into two parallel signals that connect into the left and right inputs of a mixer channel. There are several methods of splitting audio signals in Reason, but the Spider Audio Splitter is specifically designed to handle this task.

Spider Audio Splitter

Each Spider Audio Splitter can distribute a mono input signal to seven outputs at once. To do this, patch the input to splitter A, and then patch one of the A outputs into the B input. When stereo connections are made with input connections on both inputs A and B, the stereo signal can be split four ways.

A pair of outputs from one splitter can be chained to the splitter inputs of a second Spider Audio module, creating a series of stereo "taps." Because these signals are running in parallel, each effect patched to the Spider outputs receives the original signal. For instance, six split signals can be directed to six DDL-1 Digital Delay Lines, each with a different delay time, to create a multi-tap delay. This chain of splitters can continue to create as many taps as necessary.

Other Methods of Splitting Audio Signals

Prior to Reason 2.5, audio signals could be split using the mixer. The pre-2.5 mixer has two master outputs and four effects sends. A mono signal can be routed through an input channel. When the fader and aux send levels are set to 100, the input sig-

Figure 4-3.
Two Spider Audio
splitters chained.

nal is distributed to each of these outputs, providing a six-way splitter. In version 2.5, the mixer is modified so that each aux send bus is stereo, thus expanding the aux bus with four more outputs. A mono input signal can be split to as many as ten outputs through the mixer.

For a simple Y-cable, or two-way splitter, a mono signal can be routed through a CF-101 Chorus/Flanger effect with the device set on bypass. The mono input signal is split to the CF-101's left and right outputs. These techniques can still be applied in newer versions of Reason, but the Spider Audio module is designed specifically for this purpose.

Audio Signal Busses

Once the signals of a parallel circuit are routed to different effects, the outputs of these devices need to be combined together back into a mono or stereo signal. A Mixer 14:2 or a Spider Audio Merger will combine signals from various sources. The Merger is the more limited of the two. In either case, signals are combined, the difference being that the mixer has features to control signal levels.

The Spider Audio Merger has two busses, and each combines four incoming signals. The mixer has ten signal busses. There is a stereo bus for the left and right master mix output. Each of the mixer channels is connected to this mix bus, where the signals are combined. The mixer chaining master inputs are also connected to the mix bus. The mix bus goes through the master fader, and the combined signal output is available at the master output.

The four aux sends are individual busses that combine signals from the channel aux sends. Like the master mix bus, the aux send busses are stereo and create the common connection from the individual channel input aux sends. The aux send busses also have direct inputs through the mixer chaining aux send in sockets. The combined signals on the aux send busses appear on the aux send out sockets.

Spider Audio Merger

The Merger combines the signals from four input signals to one output signal. There are two sets of mergers, which provide either a stereo bus with four inputs or two mono busses with four inputs each. The two mergers can be connected in series for a seven-input monophonic bus on one Spider Audio Merger. Likewise, several mergers can be connected in series to combine as many stereo signals as necessary.

The Spider Audio Merger can be used to group signals being sent to a mixer channel. Connect signals from different sound modules into a Spider Audio Merger, then route the Merger outputs into the mixer channel. This creates a bus for the mixer input channel, with the sum of the signals controlled by one fader.

Individual levels are then controlled from the output levels of the various sound modules. Effects devices don't have output level controls, so a mixer is usually more suited for combining effects signals.

Bussed Redrum Sends

The Spider Audio Merger can also be used to expand the inputs on a mixer's chaining aux busses. A Redrum module has two effects send outputs, which are automatically routed to the mixer chaining aux input 1 and input 2. If more than one Redrum module is used, the second Redrum effect send can't be routed to the mixer send bus. Using a Spider Audio Merger, effects sends from several Redrum modules can be merged, then routed into the chaining aux connections on the mixer module. The chaining aux inputs are inputs to the mixer's aux busses, so any signal received at these inputs will be passed on to the corresponding aux send sockets.

• Start with an empty rack, and create a mixer.
• Create a Spider Audio Merger & Splitter.
• Connect the Spider merger output A to splitter input A.

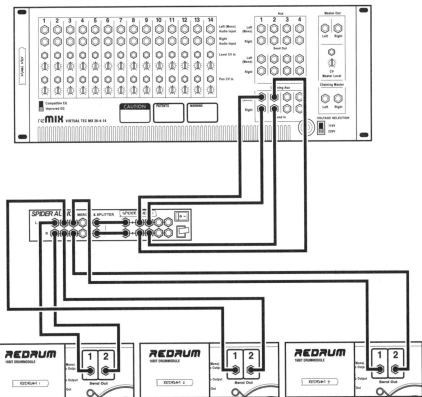

Figure 4-4.
Redrum sends merged in a Spider Audio Merger. The merged signals are connected to the mixer's chaining aux inputs.

- Connect the Spider merger output B to splitter input B.
- Connect the Spider splitter A out 1 and out 2 to the mixer chaining aux 1 inputs L and R.
- Connect the Spider splitter B out 1 and out 2 to the mixer chaining aux 2 inputs L and R.
- Create three Redrum Drum Computers.
- Connect the send out 1 from each Redrum to the Spider merger inputs L/mono 1, 2, and 3.
- Connect the send out 2 from each Redrum to the Spider merger inputs R 1, 2, and 3.

With this patch, all of the Redrum channel sends can share effects with the main mixer's aux 1 and aux 2 sends. The Redrum send 1 outputs are combined on the merger A strip and the Redrum send 2 outputs are combined on the merger B strip. The output of each merger is then split to connect to both the left and right inputs of the mixer chaining aux inputs, which feed directly to the mixer's aux sends. The pseudo-stereo connection is necessary, especially if you are using the RV-7000 Reverb module on the mixer's effect send bus. If the aux send uses a mono signal, then splitting the merger outputs is not necessary.

Rack configurations in Reason can become very intricate. Sometimes several mixer devices must be chained together. In such circumstances, the merged sends from the Redrums should be disconnected before adding the second mixer to the rack. Once the second mixer is chained into the first mixer, the merged Redrum sends can be connected to the chaining aux send inputs on the second (or last) mixer with free inputs available.

A signal on an effects send is equivalent at any point in the path, so an alternative method of bussing send signals would be to merge the mixer aux send outputs with the Redrum effect sends, and bus the result to the effect.

Attenuation

The main difference between a mixer and a Spider merger is that a mixer will attenuate signals. To attenuate means to decrease the signal level. This is the primary function of a mixer input channel. Combined signals sometimes need to be balanced so that they don't overload or overshadow the other signals. The mixer bus combines incoming signals, and the mixer input channels attenuate the signal before they reach the bus.

The fader on a mixer channel controls the input signal attenuation to the stereo mix bus. A fader setting of 0 is the same as $-\infty$ dB, or silence. Unity gain refers to 0dB of attenuation where the input signal is passed through without any increase or decrease of level. A fader setting of 100 is unity gain on the mixer 14:2. Settings above 100 will add gain to the incoming signals, making them louder. A fader setting of 127 adds about 7dB of gain to the incoming signal. These parameter settings also apply to the aux send controls, since they attenuate the signal levels going to the aux send busses.

Panning

Panning is another form of attenuation. It affects simultaneously the levels of two output signals coming from the stereo mix bus. When an input signal is panned center, an equal amount of attenuation is applied to the left and right input signals. When the input signal is panned all the way to the left, the left channel signal increases while the right signal is attenuated to silence ($-\infty$ dB). When the input is panned all the way to the right, the left signal is attenuated to silence while the right signal is brought up to unity gain. The shift in levels is perceived as a change in the location in the stereo field.

Dual Mono vs. Stereo Mixer Channels

Stereo input signals on the left and right input sockets of a single mixer channel sound different from connecting the stereo inputs to two mono mixer channels panned hard left and hard right. The cause of this is uncertain, but the levels are slightly louder when two mixer channels are used. This indicates that center pan of stereo inputs attenuates each signal slightly. Connecting stereo signals to two mixer channels offers more panning flexibility, as the separation can be decreased to fit in a narrow space in the stereo field instead of occupying the full range between left and right.

Several signals from effect outputs can be panned to different locations between the left and right speakers to create rich stereophonic effects. From the example mentioned earlier, in which four delay units are running in parallel, the outputs of the four delays can be combined in a mixer with different pan positions and levels. One possible result would be a multi-tap delay with echoes starting from one speaker and moving toward the other speaker, gradually becoming louder as the echo is heard from each delay unit.

Aux Send Busses

Digital signal processing effects such as reverb units are typically connected to the aux send and return sockets of a mixer. Four different effects can be connected to a single mixer in this way. These effects are shared by the sends on all of the input channels. Signals routed to the aux send bus are tapped after the channel fader, so both the channel fader and aux send knob attenuate the signal. This is called a post-fader send, because the relative loudness of the send and the channel signal itself remains constant.

Effects connected in aux send/return loops typically return a 100% wet signal, so the aux send knob works like a dry/wet balance control. When the aux send is set at unity gain, the incoming signal is split equally between both the mix bus and the aux send bus. The aux return from the effect processor is then combined with the dry signal on the mix bus. A parallel circuit is created after the fader: One branch is processed through the effect, then combined with the dry signal. When the aux send and aux returns are set to unity gain, the result is a 50% dry/wet balance. With post-fader effect sends, the dry/wet balance cannot exceed 50% by more than a small margin. (If the send is raised past unity gain, more wet than dry signal will be heard.) The range of 60% to 99% wet signals can be achieved either by using the effect as an insert or by using the pre-fader option on aux send bus 4.

Pre-Fader Effects

Mixer aux send bus 4 has a pre-fader option. When the pre-fade button is enabled on a channel's aux send bus, the signal bypasses the fader and is attenuated only by the aux send 4 knob. Sometimes a signal may need to have more effect processing without an increase of the dry signal to the mix. In this situation, the dry signal from the fader can be mixed low and the effect level, controlled independently with the aux send 4 knob, can be set higher.

Figure 4-5.
Pre-fader effects
are routed through
the mixer's aux 4 send
and return.

Mute FX on Solo

When the Solo button is enabled, signals are still routed to the aux send busses, and the effects signals are still heard in the mix. Instead of using the aux return inputs,

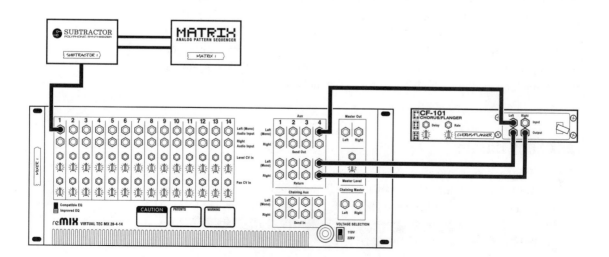

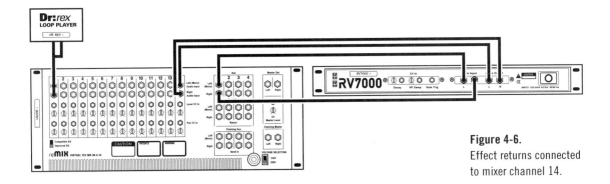

Figure 4-6.
Effect returns connected
to mixer channel 14.

effect returns can be connected to mixer input channels. If you do this, when the Solo button is enabled for a channel, the channel's effects will be muted. Make sure not to create feedback loops in the effect devices by keeping the aux send amount to 0 on mixer channel 14! It's best to avoid feedback loops, so return signals from the aux 1 effect should not be added back to the aux 1 send bus. There are special cases where audio feedback can be used constructively, but it usually causes problems.

- Start with an empty rack.
- Create a mixer, a RV-7000 Reverb, and a Dr.REX Loop Player.
- Load the ReCycle loop "Elc16_Sequential_110_eLAB.rx2" from Reason Factory Sound Bank\Dr Rex Drum Loops\Electronic directory.
- Copy the REX slice data to the Dr.REX 1 sequencer track.
- Set the mixer channel 1 aux send 1 level to 79.
- Run the sequence and click on the channel 1 Solo button to verify that the Dr.REX loop is soloed with the reverb aux send/return.
- Disconnect the RV7000 outputs from the aux return 1 inputs, and reconnect them to the mixer channel 14 inputs.
- While running the sequence, click on the channel 1 Solo button to solo the signal and hear the signal without the aux return from the reverb module.

Panning Effects

There are some other benefits to routing effects returns into mixer channels. The effect returns can be quickly muted. They can be processed with some equalization. For some extra processing, effect returns can be mixed to other aux send busses. Instead of routing pairs of effects into one mixer channel, effect returns can be routed to the mono inputs of two mixer channels. The individual returns can then be panned to different locations in the mix. For example, the RV7000 returns could be panned just a little off center to create a hollow cave reverb effect.

Another example is panning PH-90 Phaser inputs to −18 and 19. The stereo separation is not as wide as panning the effect hard left and hard right. Too many effects connected to aux returns can fill the stereo field, cluttering the mix. Routing and panning effects to different locations in the mix is an effective means of controlling the balance of the mix.

Submixers

Any number of mixer modules can be created in the Reason rack. Multiple mixers can be bussed together using the chaining aux and chaining master inputs. This is useful when more input channels are required to accommodate more than 14 sound modules. When extra mixers are created, auto-routing is set to make the proper connections to chain the series of mixers.

Secondary mixers can also be used as submixers for grouping inputs. A common type of submix would have input signals from Redrum channels and ReCycle drum loops. The relative levels between the drum sounds can be balanced in the submixer, and the submixer can then be connected to the input channel of the primary mixer. When creating a submixer, bypass auto-routing to avoid chaining the secondary mixer to the primary.

Submixer Shortcut

A submixer that groups drum signals is usually an afterthought, and is needed after a considerable amount of the song is done. In the process of creating the track, fader, EQ, and effect send settings have been set, and duplicating them on a submixer can be tedious. Instead of creating a new submixer, simply duplicate the primary mixer. The cables from the primary mixer can then be manually moved to the submixer, and the parameters will not need adjustment. The submixer outputs can be chained to the primary mixer, or grouped to a primary mixer input channel.

If this is a specific drum group mixer, you might want to copy effects like reverb along with the mixer. Select the mixer and the effects, and then duplicate them below the main mixer. The drag-and-drop duplicate shortcut works really well in this situation. Select the mixer and appropriate effects and drag-duplicate them. Connect the duplicate mixer master outputs to a free input channel on the primary mixer. A CF-101 Compressor can be inserted on the master output of the submixer to control the dynamics of the entire drum submix.

Once the input channels have been connected to the submixer, collapse it to conserve user interface space. The submixer should be moved to a position above the primary mixer. This will prevent auto-routing from cabling new devices into the submixer.

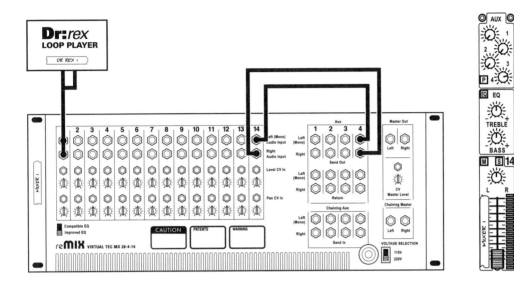

Figure 4-7.
Aux 4 send outputs
connected to mixer
channel 14 inputs.

Aux Send 4 Submix Bus

The aux send 4 bus can also be used to group input signals when the pre-fader button is enabled. The aux send 4 outputs are then connected to mixer channel 14 audio inputs, so all signals routed to the aux 4 bus will be routed into mixer channel 14. Channels routed to the aux 4 submix bus should have faders set to 0.

• In an empty rack, create a mixer.
• Create a Dr.REX Loop Player.
• Load the ReCycle loop "Rnb14_Original_100_eLAB.rx2" from the Dr.Rex Drum Loops\RnB HipHop directory in the Reason Factory Sound Bank.
• Copy the REX slice data to the Dr.REX 1 sequencer track.
• On the mixer, connect the aux send 4 left and right sockets to the channel 14 input sockets.
• Set the mixer channel 1 fader level to 0.
• Enable the pre-fader option on mixer channel 1 and set the aux 4 knob to 100.
• Run the sequence.

The signal from mixer channel 1 is routed through the aux send 4 bus, which leads back into mixer channel 14. This creates a submix group controlled on mixer channel 14. (At the moment the submix group contains only one mixer channel, but you can add more channels to it as needed.) The individual levels are attenuated using the aux 4 knobs, and the mixer channels must be set to zero; otherwise

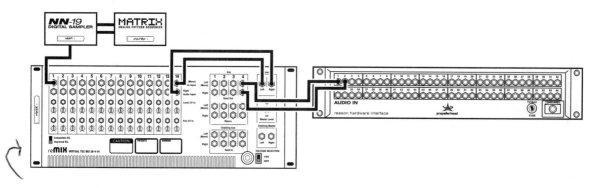

Figure 4-8.
Master outputs
connected to mixer
channel 14 inputs.
Aux 4 send outputs
connected to Reason
Hardware Interface
inputs 1 & 2.

the signal will be routed through both the aux bus and the master mix bus. The aux 4 knob on mixer channel 14 should be set to zero; otherwise a feedback loop will occur.

Devices like a Comp-01 Compressor/Limiter or PEQ-2 Equalizer can be inserted between the aux 4 send outputs and the mixer channel 14 inputs. This must be manually cabled. Since the input channels from the grouped signal will not direct signals to aux sends 1, 2, or 3, aux effects can be applied on mixer channel 14 for the entire submix. An RV7000 Advanced Reverb can be inserted, for instance, to add reverb to the submix signal.

Master Outs with Mixer EQ

The "Improved EQ" settings of the mixer in the latest version of Reason can work wonders with the final mix. To apply this EQ to the mix, the mixer's master outputs can be routed back into mixer channel 14, then through the aux 4 send bus. Before connecting the master outputs into the channel 14 inputs, set the channel 14 fader to 0, as otherwise a feedback loop will occur. Aux send 4 for channel 14 should have the pre-fade option enabled, and the send should be set to 100 (unity gain). The master output signal will then be available from the aux 4 send outputs, which can be connected to the Reason Hardware Interface inputs.

CV Control of the Mixer

On each of the mixer channels, there are CV inputs to modulate the level and pan parameters. Using different CV sources, a variety of panning and dynamics control effects can be created. The level CV is unipolar and matches the fader level range from 0 to 127. Pan is bipolar and has a range of –64 (hard left) through 0 (center) to 63 (hard right). The incoming CV signals are added to the current fader and pan settings, and the sum of the two will not exceed the value range. An envelope CV

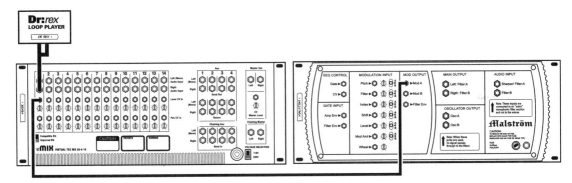

Figure 4-9.
Malström modulator
connected to mixer level
CV input.

signal will go from 0 to 127, so if the fader is set to 100, the modulation will only have an effect when the envelope CV value is between 1 and 27.

This section contains several examples of modulating the mixer parameters. More examples of modulating level CV are described in the chapter on dynamics processing.

Modulated Mixer Level

In this example, the Malström Modulator CV is used to control the level of a mixer channel. The Malström Graintable Synthesizer Modulator is Reason's only source of a sine wave CV LFO. There is a slight difference between a sine and a triangle wave, but in this example the sine wave sounds better because the duration of the peak is longer than with a triangle wave.

- In an empty rack, create a mixer.
- Create a Dr.REX Loop Player.
- On Dr.REX, load the ReCycle file "100_PhaseRhodes_mLp_eLAB.rx2" from the Factory Sound Bank from the Music Loops\Variable Tempo (rex2)\Downtempo Loops directory.
- Copy the REX data to the Dr.REX 1 sequencer track.
- Bypass auto-routing and create a Malström Graintable Synthesizer.
- Set the Malström polyphony to 1 and disable OSC A, filter A, filter B, and Mod B.
- On the Malström Mod A, enable sync and set the rate to 1/16.
- Connect the Malström output mod A socket to the mixer channel 1 level CV in socket.
- Set the mixer channel 1 level CV trim to 120.
- Set the mixer channel 1 fader level to 0.
- Run the sequence.

The sine wave modulation creates the effect of a smooth fader increase and decrease synchronized to the tempo of the track. This configuration is sometimes more appropriate than gating effects because the transitions are smoothed by the curve of the sine wave.

Matrix-Controlled Crossfader

A crossfader is a type of attenuator commonly used on DJ mixers to mix between the input signals from two turntables. When the crossfader is centered, the two sources are mixed equally. When the crossfader is set to the extreme left or right, only one of the two sources is heard. The following two examples show methods of simulating the crossfader effect by using split and inverted CV signals modulating mixer levels.

- In an empty rack, create a mixer.
- Create two Dr.REX Loop Players.
- Create a Spider CV Merger & Splitter.
- Bypass auto-routing and create a Matrix Pattern Sequencer.
- Connect the Matrix curve CV socket to the Spider CV split A input.
- Connect a Spider split A output to the mixer channel 1 level CV input.
- Connect the Spider split A inverted output to the mixer channel 2 level CV input.
- Set the mixer channel 1 and 2 level CV trim to 127.
- Set mixer channel 1 fader level to 0.
- Set mixer channel 2 fader level to 127.
- On Dr.REX 1, load the Recycle File "125_DaftChord_mLp_eLAB.rx2" from the Factory Sound Bank from the Music Loops\Variable Tempo (rex2)\Uptempo Loops directory.
- Copy the REX data to the Dr.REX 1 sequencer track.

Figure 4-10.
Spider CV Splitter and Inverter routed to two mixer level CV inputs.

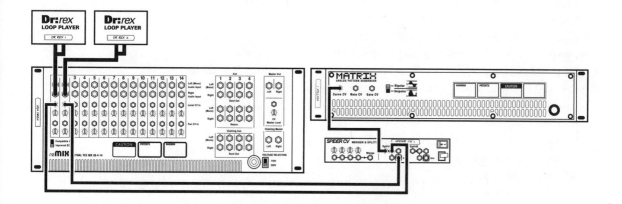

• From the same directory, load the file "130_Looped_mLp_eLAB.rx2" into Dr.REX 2.
• Copy the REX data to the Dr.REX 2 sequencer track.
• On the Matrix, select curve edit mode.
• Set the Matrix pattern length to 32 steps.
• Draw a ramp curve on the Matrix from step 1 to 32 from 0 to 127. (Hold down the Shift key to enable the line tool.)
• Run the sequence to hear the Matrix curve crossfade between mixer channels 1 and 2.

Try experimenting with different Matrix curve patterns to create some unique beat mixing.

MIDI Crossfader

This example uses the Real-Time CV Control example to modulate the crossfader CV configuration. The SubTractor envelope sustain sliders are assigned to MIDI faders or knobs, which will control the CV outputs that modulate the crossfaders. This example shows the benefit of an external MIDI controller, since you can send multiple controls at the same time.

• In an empty rack, create a mixer.
• Set the tempo to 130.

Figure 4-11.
MIDI crossfader block diagram.

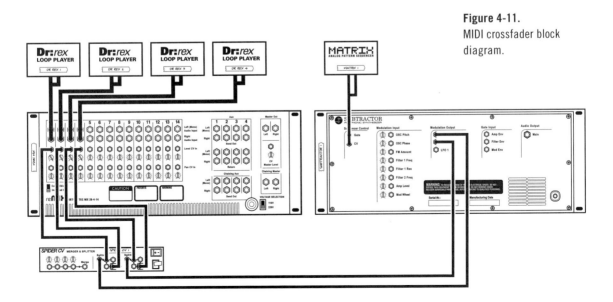

- Set mixer channel 1 and channel 3 fader levels to 0.
- Set mixer channel 2 and channel 4 fader levels to 127.

Crossfade CV Section
- Create a Spider CV Merger & Splitter.
- Connect the Spider CV split A out 1 to the mixer channel 1 level CV input.
- Connect the Spider CV split A out 4/inv to the mixer channel 2 level CV input.
- Connect the Spider CV split B out 1 to the mixer channel 3 level CV input.
- Connect the Spider CV split B out 4/inv to the mixer channel 4 level CV input.
- Set the level CV trim to 127 on mixer channels 1 through 4.

Real-Time Control Section
- Bypass auto-routing and create a SubTractor Synthesizer.
- Enable the Low BW button and set the SubTractor polyphony to 1.
- Set the mod envelope ADSR settings all to 0.
- Set the filter envelope ADSR settings all to 0.
- Patch the SubTractor mod env output to the Spider split A input, and the SubTractor filter env output to the Spider split B input.
- After making sure the SubTractor is still selected, create a Matrix Pattern Sequencer.
- Set the Matrix pattern length to 1 step.
- On the Matrix, program a tied gate event on step 1.

MIDI Control Section
- Select "Enable MIDI Remote Mapping" from the Options menu. When enabled, this item has a check mark.
- Assign the SubTractor's mod envelope and filter envelope sustain sliders to MIDI knobs or sliders.
- In Edit/Preferences/Advanced MIDI, make certain Reason is set up to receive MIDI control data from your control device.

Audio Example Section
- At the bottom of the rack, create four Dr.REX Loop Players. These will be used as loop sources to mix using the crossfaders. Verify their auto-routing to the inputs on mixer channels 1 through 4.
- On Dr.REX 1, load the ReCycle file "135_Techniq_mLp_eLAB.rx2" from the Reason Factory Sound Bank\Music Loops\Variable Tempo (rex2)\Uptempo Loops directory.
- Copy the REX data to the Dr.REX 1 sequencer track.
- On Dr.REX 2, load the ReCycle file "130_Circle_mLp_eLAB.rx2" from the Reason Factory Sound\Music Loops\Variable Tempo (rex2)\Uptempo Loops directory.

- Copy the REX data to the Dr.REX 2 sequencer track.
- On Dr.REX 3, load the ReCycle loop "Chm07_Skint_130_eLAB.rx2" from the Reason Factory Sound Bank\Dr Rex Drum Loops\Chemical Beats directory.
- Copy the REX slice data to the Dr.REX 3 sequencer track.
- On Dr.REX 4, load the ReCycle loop "Chm18_Dustbin_125_eLAB.rx2" from the Reason Factory Sound Bank\Dr Rex Drum Loops\Chemical Beats directory.
- Copy the REX slice data to the Dr.REX 4 sequencer track.

- Run the sequence and start moving the sliders assigned to the SubTractor envelope sustain levels.

Feedback Loops

One normally associates the term "feedback" with the howling noise heard when a P.A. microphone picks up a signal from the loudspeaker. The audio signal between the microphone and the loudspeaker starts looping, causing an unpleasant oscillation. In other cases, feedback is used in a musical way, such as when an electric guitar pickup is placed near the speaker cabinet of the amplifier. Both of these types of feedback can be applied in Reason, but only the latter is likely to be useful. When applied carefully, audio feedback loops can create interesting results.

In Figure 4-12, the feedback loop schematic, the audio input signal is merged with the output signal, creating a direct feedback loop. This circuit is unpleasant to listen to, but it shows the basic method with which feedback loops are established. This effect becomes much more practical when used in conjunction with an effect like a digital delay, which is why there is a feedback control on the DDL-1 Digital Delay Line. The feedback control attenuates the processed delay signal being combined with the input signal. With the DDL-1 feedback setting at zero, there is no feedback within the device, so any amount of external feedback

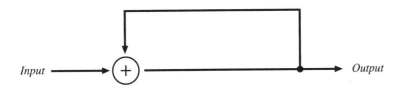

Figure 4-12.
Feedback loop schematic.
(Don't try this without turning down your speakers!)

Figure 4-13.
Delay feedback loop
schematic.

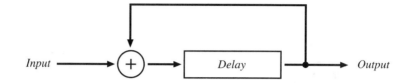

signal, when combined with the incoming signal, will result in an echo effect with the delayed signals repeating at the rate set on the DDL-1.

Instead of using the built-in feedback control of a DDL-1, a feedback loop can be created in Reason using a mixer. The input signal is combined with the feedback audio signal in the mixer, and the channel fader will attenuate the feedback signal going into the digital delay module. The advantage of using a wired feedback loop is that feedback can be processed through an equalizer or filter to create a frequency damping effect. The echoes will be filtered during each cycle of the loop, making them sound thinner. High feedback levels, however, will cause the circuit to self-oscillate and overload. Also, note that if you've patched a PEQ-2 equalizer into the feedback signal path, increasing the gain on an EQ band will add to the amount of feedback.

Figure 4-14.
A secondary mixer
attenuates delay
feedback.

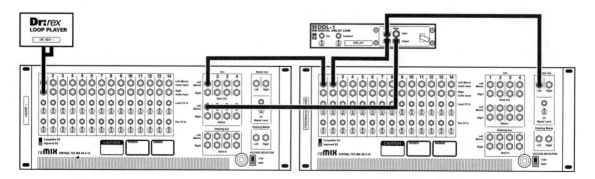

Chapter 5
Dynamics Effects

The amplitude of an audio signal determines its loudness, but this statement is somewhat misleading since other factors besides amplitude affect the perceived loudness. The actual amplitude of the signal is indicated with waveform or VU meter settings. The perceived loudness is determined by the amplitude and the type of sound, and two different sounds can appear to have different volumes even if they have the same measured amplitude. Generally, sounds with midrange and moderately high frequencies (up to 3kHz or so) sound subjectively louder than sounds that are restricted to the low frequency range. It's important to keep this difference in mind as we discuss the topic of dynamics. In some cases, what is heard will not always reflect what is measured. When it comes to a choice between the two, assuming you have a decent monitoring setup, you should always trust your ears rather than the meters.

Changes in loudness are referred to as *dynamics*, and processing devices that control loudness are commonly called dynamics effects. Included within this category are attenuators, compressors, limiters, and gates. Dynamics processors are typically named after the process they perform. A compressor squeezes down the dynamic range of an incoming signal. Limiters prevent incoming signals from exceeding a specified level. Gates, also called noise gates, allow signals above a certain level to pass through, while signals below the threshold are suppressed. Attenuators and amplifiers change the loudness of a signal.

Attenuators, which are found on every mixer, are the primary method of controlling dynamics. Reason also has a dedicated compressor/limiter device, the Comp-01. The Scream 4 Distortion Unit also can server as a compressor when the tape compression algorithm is selected. The RV7000 Advanced Reverb has a gate feature, and the mixer can be used to create "keyed" gating effects.

Headroom

Loudness is measured in units called decibels (dB), and the dynamic range of digital audio is measured between the full level maximum of 0dB, and silence $-\infty$ dB. Signals exceeding 0dB are called "overs" and cause clipping (a form of digital distortion). To prevent clipping, the levels of individual signals have to be attenuated so that when they're mixed (added together), their total level won't exceed 0dB. When overs occur, the Audio Out Clipping lamp glows on the Reason transport.

Most digital audio systems, including Reason, are designed so that normal signal levels are somewhat below 0dB. Some dynamic range is left over so that occasional peaks can be handled without clipping. This extra dynamic range is called headroom.

Compressors and limiters can be used to prevent clipping. They operate by reducing the level of the highest peaks in the signal. A compressor can be used as an insert effect to tame a drum track that has aggressive peaks, or it can be patched to the output of the main mixer to compress or limit the entire mix.

If you're running into clipping, try this technique for taming the signals going into the mixer. This technique is most effective when a piece of music has been fully sequenced, and all of the sound modules have been connected to mixer input channels. (It also assumes that you're using the individual modules' output level controls, not the mixer channel faders, to adjust their relative volumes.) Set the mixer master fader to 127. Solo a mixer channel and set the channel fader to 127. Run the sequence and watch the clipping indicator for overs. Adjust the sound module's master level control downward, if necessary, until no clipping occurs. Disable solo for that mixer channel and decrease the mixer channel fader to 100. Repeat this for each of the mixer input channels. When all of the modules' output levels are set, decrease the mixer's master fader level to 100. The levels of the incoming signals will peak at unity gain, leaving about 14dB of headroom to mix several loud signals without clipping.

Adjusting the maximum input signals from sound modules is one method of overload prevention, but this can lead to other signals being too low in the mix. This is where compressors become necessary. Compressors can confine the dynamic range between a specified range of levels to raise or lower signals while preventing overloads.

Compressor Basics

Compressors have become commonly used in audio production, because they are said to make a mix sound better. This doesn't mean that a compressor is necessary for every input channel, but using compressors in this way is not uncommon. Signal dynamics can be very erratic. A compressor is used to scale the range of level changes within certain limits, which smooths out the dynamic fluctuations. This keeps low levels from dropping too low and getting buried in a mix, and prevents loud peaks from getting too high and overshadowing a mix. A compressed audio signal is given more presence in the mix because its perceived loudness is more uniform.

The function of a compressor is simple. As long as the incoming signal remains below the *threshold* level, nothing happens: The output of the compressor is the same as the input. When the incoming signal rises above the threshold, the compressor reduces the gain of the signal passing through it. The amount of gain reduction depends on the *ratio* parameter. If the ratio is set to 2:1, the output signal is only allowed to increase by 1dB for every 2dB of increase in the input. When the ratio is set to 10:1, the output level increases 1dB above the threshold for every 10dB that the input rises above the threshold. High compression ratios provide protection against sudden spikes in audio levels that may clip. Compression ratios of 10:1 or greater are generally considered "limiting" since they prevent audio signals from exceeding a certain level.

When the input signal rises above the threshold level, compression is applied at the rate set by the attack and release parameters. Short attack times will apply compression quickly, which is handy for limiting unexpected signal peaks. Slow attack times will create a "squashed" sound, especially with drums. The initial hit is loud, and the compression effect gradually takes effect. Once the incoming signal drops below the threshold, the amount of compression backs off at the rate set by the release parameter. Moderately long release times are usually recommended for input signals with lots of dynamic variation.

A compressor can significantly reduce the levels of the incoming signals, so the decrease may need to be offset with a make-up gain control. If the compressed signal is 10dB lower, 10dB of gain is added to compensate for the loss. The Scream 4 has a dedicated level control for make-up gain compensation, and the Comp-01 Compressor/Limiter has an automatic make-up gain feature. Make-up gain sets the lower level of the compressed dynamic range so that very low signals are louder, and boosts compressed levels back up to higher levels.

Comp-01 Auto Make-Up Gain

The auto make-up gain makes the Comp-01 tricky to use since the processing is different than in a traditional compressor. The amount of make-up gain is determined by the values of the ratio and threshold settings. There are three rules to remember about the auto make-up gain. First, the ratio parameter determines the amount of gain added. Second, the threshold parameter will decrease the gain added by the ratio setting. Third, the amount of gain will not drop below 0.

The maximum amount of make-up gain added occurs when ratio is set to 127 and threshold is set to zero. Because make-up gain changes when these parameters are adjusted, the output signal level is sometimes unpredictable. When the compressor is used to reduce gain from an incoming signal, some settings will actually increase the output level.

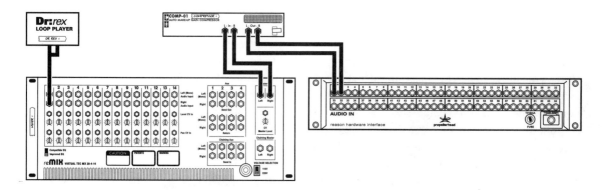

Figure 5-1.
Mixer inserted before
Comp-01 compressor.

A threshold of 64 and ratio of 80 are the optimal settings for attenuating the output level from a high incoming signal. This has nothing to do with the amount of compression or make-up gain, only amplitude reduction. If the threshold is adjusted to 0 or 127, the output levels start to increase as the parameter nears either extreme. A similar pattern of behavior occurs when the ratio is adjusted towards 0 or 127. When the output levels start to increase, reduce the fader level of the channel receiving signals from the compressor. As changes are made to the compressor settings, remember that the output levels will change, and subsequent fader changes may be needed to compensate for the change in output levels.

Increasing Input Signal Levels
Samples and ReCycle loops that have not been normalized may produce low-level audio signals, and the output levels may not be loud enough to cross the compressor threshold. The master level from a sampler or Dr.REX Loop Player should be set to maximum when feeding a compressor. A mixer can be inserted before the compressor if necessary to boost low signals. Connect the master outputs to the Comp-01 inputs, and connect the sound module to mixer channel inputs. Set the channel fader level above 100 to boost the signal, and if necessary increase the master fader above 100 to add still more gain. The Comp-01 seems to respond better with louder input signals when the ratio settings are between 40 and 80, so adding gain to the incoming signal will work wonders.

Setting the Comp-01 for Compression
This procedure works well in all applications where compression is required. Insert a compressor before the input of the mixer channel, and enable solo to monitor the input signals on that channel. If the signal uses the mixer channel EQ, disable

it. Equalizers change the dynamics of certain parts of the signal, and the compression cannot be properly assessed when the EQ is on.

- Set the attack and release parameters to 0.
- Set the ratio. For general compression the ratio should be between 2:1 (48) and 4:1 (82).
- Set the threshold to the same setting as the ratio. This minimizes auto make-up gain, and the gain meter should settle around 0.
- Run the sequence and observe the gain meter for changes in dynamics. If the gain meter doesn't move down at least two LED levels, gradually increase the level of the signal going into the Comp-01.
- Adjust the attack and release times to contour the sharpness of the compression. Short attack settings (0–30) will cut the transients down. Medium attack settings (30–80) are generally good when you want to keep the attack transients. Long attack settings (80–127) will make the initial hit sound louder, since the attack transients will not be compressed.

  Shorter release settings (0–32) will increase the perceived loudness, especially with drums and loops. Medium release settings (32–63) will create a "pumping" feel, useful for certain styles of dance music. Medium-to-long release settings (64–90) are the average settings for general compression. They are not too short to create a pumping feel, and not too long to emphasize the attack transients. Long release settings (90–127) will have the most gain reduction because the compression ratio is held, and the attack transient will be emphasized. The medium and long settings are best for smoothing out chaotic dynamics. The compression should sound slightly exaggerated when setting the attack and release settings.
- Increase the threshold amount by no more than 12. This will smooth out the compression. If the signal sounds too "squishy" (over-compressed), decrease the level of the input signal.
- Disable solo on the mixer channel, and adjust the fader level to balance the compressed signal with the rest of the mix.

"Pumping" Drum Loops

This effect setting works well with loops and Redrum drum patterns. However, it is not recommended to use these settings for an entire mix. These settings take advantage of the auto gain make-up feature and add a significant amount of level to the softer hits in the ReCycle drum sounds. It's an odd effect, because the Comp-01 behaves like a limiter on the louder drum hits and like an expander on the softer hits. The pumping sound is created by the quick release after each kick drum. The zero release time also makes the softer hi-hats of the loop sound louder.

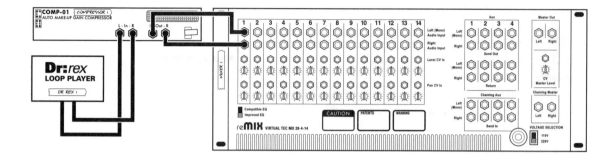

Figure 5-2.
Comp-01 inserted
between the Dr.REX
and mixer input.

- In an empty rack, create a mixer.
- Create a Dr.REX Loop Player.
- Load the ReCycle loop "Hse06_Strictly_130_eLAB.rx2" from the Reason Factory Sound Bank\Dr Rex Drum Loops\House directory.
- Copy the REX slice data to the Dr.REX 1 sequencer track.
- Set the Dr.REX output level to 127.
- Insert a Comp-01 Compressor/Limiter between the Dr.REX and the mixer input.
- Set the Comp-01 ratio to 92, threshold to 20, attack to 0, and release to 0.
- Run the sequence.

Limiter Settings

Limiter features are typically part of the standard features of a compressor because the two processes are closely related. A limiter is simply a compressor with a ratio of 10:1 or greater. The Comp-01 indicates a maximum ratio of 16:1. Again, using the Comp-01 for limiting can be rather tricky because the higher ratio settings increase the make-up gain.

Limiter ratio settings fall into the range between 100 and 127, and the best threshold setting is about 100. Higher threshold settings are useful for occasional spikes, but for general limiting 100 is the smooth break point. For best results, the input signal should be attenuated so that only the loudest peaks cross the threshold, and the make-up gain should be increased using a mixer input channel's gain.

Scream 4 Tape Compression Effect

The Scream 4 tape compression algorithm is quite useful for adding "colored" compression to an audio signal. The algorithm is intended to emulate the compression when audio is recorded to analog tape at very high levels. The Scream 4 tape

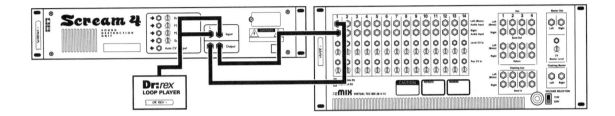

Figure 5-3.
Scream 4 inserted
between Dr.REX and
a mixer input.

compression algorithm is simple: The main parameters are Damage Control, which adds input gain, P2, which controls compression ratio, and the master level output, which controls make-up gain. P1 emulates a tape speed control by changing a lowpass filter. Setting P1 to 127 opens the filter.

Figure 5-3.
Scream 4 inserted
between Dr.REX and
a mixer input.

- Start with an empty rack and create a mixer.
- Set the song tempo to 140.
- Bypass auto-routing and create a Dr.REX.
- Load the ReCycle loop "Chm25_Winditup_140_eLAB.rx2" from the Reason Factory Sound Bank\Dr Rex Drum Loops\Chemical Beats directory.
- Copy the REX slice data to the Dr.REX 1 sequencer track.
- Insert a Scream 4 Distortion unit between the Dr.REX and the mixer.
- Program the following settings on the Scream 4: Damage on, Cut off, Body off, Damage control 88, algorithm Tape, P1 60, P2 88, Master level 65.
- Run the sequence.

Compressor Sidechain

The Comp-01 does not have a dedicated sidechain input like a typical hardware compressor/limiter, but a sidechain process can be imitated by processing mono signals through the right channel of the Comp-01 and using the left audio input as the sidechain input. This allows a separate audio signal to influence the compression. Audio signals connected to the inputs are not merged, so the output signals are discrete. This does not work exactly like a normal side-chain input, but with careful settings the results are very similar. The main trick is to keep the processed signal low so that it does not cross the threshold setting, while keeping the sidechain signal hot so that it does cross the threshold.

A sidechain routing is used for "ducking" and "de-essing." Ducking is a process

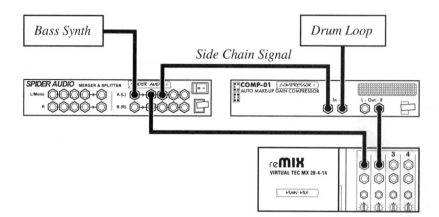

Figure 5-4.
Comp-01 left input used
as a sidechain input. The
bass synth signal modu-
lates the level of the
drum loop to create a
"ducking" effect.

where the dynamics of an audio signal are automatically lowered by an increased
level from another signal. For example, a drum loop is processed through a
compressor, with a signal tapped from a bass synth connected to the sidechain.
As the level of the bass synthesizer increases, the drum loop is compressed, causing the drum loop to "duck." De-essing is a type of frequency-dependent compression.
The audio signal being processed through a compressor is tapped and run
through an equalizer or filter. The equalizer is set to a very narrow frequency range,
which is then connected to the sidechain input. The audio signal is only compressed
when there are frequencies in the range dialed in by the equalizer.

Compressor De-Essing

De-essing is form of frequency-dependent compression. The signal at the sidechain
input is processed with a narrow equalizer curve to boost sibilance frequencies
(those found in the sound of the letter 's'). The boosted frequencies are connected
to the Comp-01 left input, and when the higher levels are sensed by the compressor,
the processing reduces the dynamics level of the output.

• Start with an empty rack and create a mixer.
• Set the loop locators to 1.1.1 and 3.1.1.
• Bypass auto-routing and create an NN19 Digital Sampler.
• Use the sample browser to load the sample "esses.aif" into the NN19 from the
  Power Tools for Reason CD Audio Samples directory.
• Set the NN19 master level to 127.
• On the NN19 1 sequencer track, view the key lane in edit mode.
• Enable the pencil tool, and draw a 2-measure event from 1.1.1 to 3.1.1.

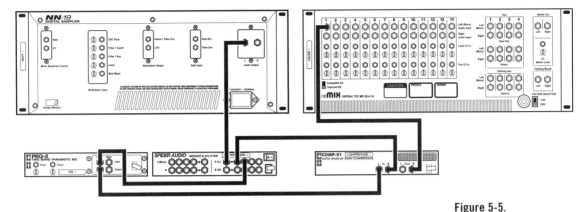

Figure 5-5.
The source signal is split and processed through an equalizer, then connected to the Comp-01 left input.

Compression Section

- Create a Spider Audio Merger & Splitter.
- Bypass auto-routing and connect the NN19's left audio output to the Spider Audio split A input.
- Bypass auto-routing and create a Comp-01 Compressor/Limiter.
- Connect the Spider Audio split A out 1 to the Comp-01 right input.
- Connect the Comp-01 right output to the mixer channel 1 left input.
- Set the Comp-01 ratio to 95, threshold to 24, attack to 0, and release to 18.

Side-Chain EQ Section

- Bypass auto-routing and create a PEQ-2 Parametric Equalizer.
- Connect the Spider Audio split A out 2 to the PEQ-2 left input.
- Connect the PEQ-2 left output to the Comp-01 left input.
- Set the PEQ-2 A frequency to 108, Q to 93, gain to 63.
- Enable EQ B and apply the same settings.
- Run the sequence.

    The sibilance levels are not necessarily louder than other signals. This is an example of "perceived" loudness, in which human hearing is more sensitive to certain frequencies. As the vocal sample plays, the compression is greater when "esses" are spoken, which reduces the level into a comfortable listening range. Equalization can be applied without de-essing, but this changes the harmonic content of the signal and makes it sound artificial. De-essing simply ducks the signal level instead of changing the frequency response.

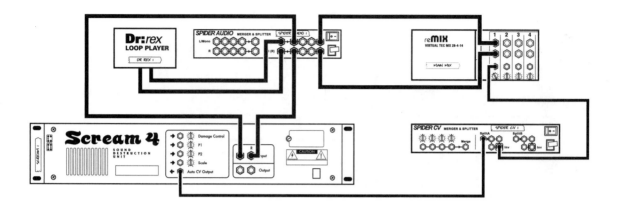

Figure 5-6.
Scream Auto CV
connected to Spider CV.
The inverted output
modulates the mixer
channel level.

CV-Based Dynamics Effects

All dynamics effects are based on circuitry that senses the levels of incoming audio signals. The sensing aspect of a compressor is, in essence, an envelope follower. The CV signal from the envelope follower is scaled by the ratio setting, and then modulates an amplifier circuit to control the output levels. With the envelope follower features in the Scream 4 Distortion unit and the BV512 Digital Vocoder, dynamics effects can be created by using the envelope follower CV output to modulate mixer level CV inputs.

Envelope Follower Limiter
Ideally, this example will result in silence. The control voltage signal generated from the Scream 4 Auto CV output is directly related to the loudness of the audio signal input. Using a Spider CV to invert the envelope follower CV value, the mixer level is attenuated based on the loudness of the source signal.

- In an empty rack, create a mixer.
- Bypass auto-routing and create a Dr.REX Loop Player.
- Load the ReCycle Loop "Chm22_Compress_135_eLAB.rx2" from the Dr Rex Drum Loops\Chemical Beats directory from the Reason Factory Sound Bank.
- Copy the REX slice data to the Dr.REX 1 sequencer track.
- Set the Dr.REX output level to 127.
- Split the audio output from the Dr.REX Loop Player using a Spider Audio Splitter.
- Connect one split signal from the Spider back into mixer channel 1.
- Bypass auto-routing and create a Scream 4 Distortion unit.

- Connect a second pair of signals from the Spider to the Scream 4 inputs. The distortion effect is not going to be used to process audio, so the outputs are not connected to any destination.
- Create a Spider CV Merger & Splitter.
- Connect the Scream 4 auto CV output to the Spider CV split A input.
- Connect the Spider CV split A inverted output to the mixer channel 1 level CV input.
- Set the mixer channel 1 level CV trim to a value of 2 or 3 for limiting. A value of 6 or 8 produces a severe pumping effect.
- Run the sequence.

When the audio signal is silent, there is no modulation of the mixer level. When the audio signal is loudest, the inverted CV signal value is –127, which modulates the mixer level down to zero. Decreasing the mixer level CV trim setting will scale down the modulation. Because the envelope follower tracks the changes quickly, this effect does not work as effectively as a compressor with controllable attack and release settings. The envelope follower on the BV512 may be more suited for this purpose.

Envelope Follower Ducking

This example builds on the inverted envelope follower configuration to modulate a different mixer input channel. The gain reduction induced by the envelope follower decreases the level of another signal, creating a ducking effect.

- Start with the song file you created in the previous example.

Figure 5-7.
Inverted envelope follower modulating a different mixer channel's level for ducking.

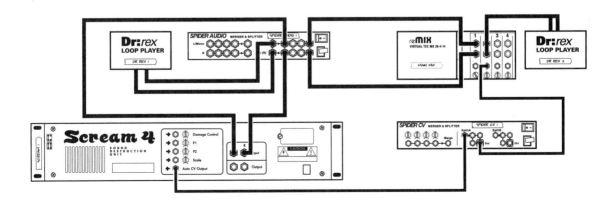

- At the bottom of the rack, add another Dr.REX Loop Player.
- Load the ReCycle Loop "125_OrganRiff_mLp_eLAB.rx2" from Music Loops\
  Variable Tempo (rex2)\Uptempo Loops directory from the Reason Factory
  Sound Bank.
- Copy the REX slice data to the Dr.REX 2 sequencer track.
- Set the Dr.REX 2 output level to 127.
- Re-route the Spider CV Splitter inverted output from mixer channel 1 to the chan-
  nel 2 level CV input socket.
- Set the mixer channel 2 level CV trim to 11.

Run the sequence and listen as the Dr.REX 2 signal is ducked by the inverted
modulation signal from the envelope follower receiving the Dr.REX 1 audio signal. Adjusting the mixer channel 2 level CV Trim to 0 will cut the modulation from
the envelope follower so the full level from Dr.REX 2 is heard.

This configuration is rather extreme, and acts more like a gate rather than a
ducker in the true sense of the word. Using very low trim settings and adjusting
the fader level to 127 will work best when this technique is used for ducking.

Vocoder Envelope Follower Compressor

The BV512 envelope follower has attack and release settings, which allows
smoother modulation of the mixer level CV. The attack and release settings
can be used to imitate the compressor's attack and release. With the vocoder set
to 4-band mode, the CV band levels are summed with a Spider CV Merger, and
the attack and release settings are set to "lag" the response of the modulation changes
on the mixer level CV.

- In an empty rack, create a mixer.
- Set the mixer's channel 1 fader to 127.
- Bypass auto-routing and create a Dr.REX Loop Player.
- Load the ReCycle loop "Chm22_Compress_135_eLAB.rx2" from the Reason Factory
  Sound Bank\Dr Rex Drum Loops\Chemical Beats directory.
- Copy the REX slice data to the Dr.REX 1 sequencer track.
- Set the Dr.REX master level to 127.
- Create a Spider Audio Merger & Splitter.
- Connect the Dr.REX audio outputs to the Spider splitter inputs A and B.
- Connect the Spider split A out 1 and split B out 1 to the mixer channel 1 inputs.
- Connect the Spider split A out 2 to the merger L/mono input 1.
- Connect the Spider split B out 2 to the merger L/mono input 2.
- Bypass auto-routing and create a BV512 Digital Vocoder.
- Set the Vocoder to 4-band mode.
- Adjust the Vocoder's attack setting to 0 and the decay setting to 83.

- Connect the Spider Audio merge L/mono output to the Vocoder modulator input.
- At the bottom of the rack, create a Spider CV Merger & Splitter.
- Connect the first four individual level band output sockets to the four Spider CV merger inputs.
- Adjust all four Spider CV merger input trim knobs to 24.
- Connect the Spider CV merger output to the split A input.
- Connect the Spider CV split A out 4/inv to the mixer channel 1 level CV input.
- Set the mixer channel 1 level CV trim to about 24.
- Run the sequence.

This configuration behaves very much like a compressor, but the compression ratio setting is not exact. Some trial-and-error tweaking is required with the CV input trim knobs to get good-sounding compression. Too much CV modulation of the mixer level will decrease the level to silence ($-\infty$ dB). Adjust the attack and decay settings on the BV512 Vocoder to contour the envelope response. A short attack time smooths transients, and a medium decay time creates a pumping effect.

Figure 5-8.
Vocoder bands merged and scaled to modulate mixer channel level.

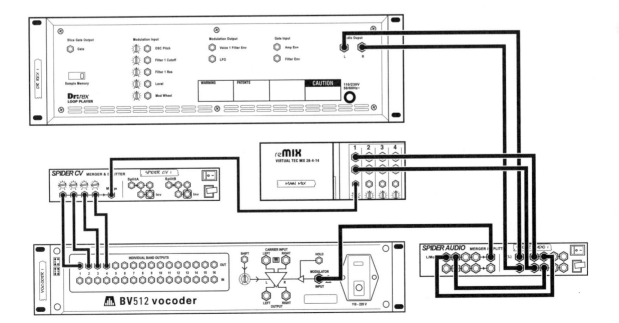

Gated Mixer Channel

Noise gates are used to automatically silence signals that fall below a threshold setting. These are typically used to prevent unwanted noise entering a mix, but noise is not usually a factor in Reason, so noise gates are unnecessary. A variation on the noise gate idea is called "keyed gating," which functions like a sidechain that opens and closes the gate. Keyed gating can be used as a production technique, allowing an audio signal to be chopped up in a rhythmic pattern. This example uses a Matrix curve CV signal to modulate a mixer channel between open and silence.

- In an empty rack, create a mixer.
- Create an NN19 Digital Sampler.
- Load the sample "BurstAway_eLAB.aif" from the Reason Factory Sound Bank\Other Samples\FX-Vox directory.
- Edit the NN19 sequencer track, drawing note events on C3 that are two measures long.
- Bypass auto-routing and create a Matrix Pattern Sequencer.
- Connect the Matrix curve CV output to the mixer channel 1 level CV input.
- Set the mixer channel 1 level CV trim to 100.
- Set the mixer channel 1 fader level to 0.
- Set the Matrix pattern to 32 steps and the resolution to 1/32.
- Draw maximum curve events on steps 1 through 17, 19, 21, 23, 25, 27, 29, and 31.
- Press Play and listen to the sample break up as the Matrix curve CV modulates the mixer level like a keyed gate.

Chapter 6
Filter & Equalizer Effects

Filter effects have become a common part of electronic music. It's hard to find a track that doesn't have drum loops, sweeping synth pads, or elastic acid leads processed by a filter. Filters are also an important aspect of subtractive synthesis in analog synthesizers and samplers. In Reason, they are found in all of the sound modules. Filters are devices that alter the frequency content of an audio signal, and equalizers are closely related since they are based on filtering principles. Filters remove frequencies from an audio signal, while equalizers can either boost or cut frequencies in an audio signal. Besides their standard use, filters are the basis for special processing effects such as vocoding.

The SubTractor Synthesizer, Dr.REX, NN19, and NN-XT have filters, which are used to shape the tone color of the sounds. The RV7000 has a parametric equalizer section that will contour the processed signals. The BV512 Digital Vocoder, Malström Graintable synthesizer, PEQ-2 Parametric Equalizer, and ECF-42 Envelope Controlled Filter are dedicated devices for filtering signals. These have audio input sockets, so signals from other devices can be processed through them. This chapter discusses a variety of applications for filters and equalizers, and covers a few key issues about using equalizers to balance frequencies in a mix.

Frequency Ranges

The pitch of a sound is measured in Hertz (Hz) — the number of oscillations that occur in one second. A person with normal hearing is sensitive to sound frequencies between 20Hz and 20kHz. This is considered the audible spectrum of sound. Human hearing is more sensitive in certain frequency ranges, and perceived loudness varies depending on the frequency. Filters and equalizers are used to balance the loudness of different ranges so that the sound appeals to our ears.

The audible frequency spectrum is usually divided into five regions: bass, low-mids,

mids (middle), high-mids, and highs. These ranges have generally accepted values in audio engineering, and many equalizers have fixed parameters based on these ranges. The notes of the scale are a subset of pitches, and are used as the standard for composition in Western music. It's important to understand the relationship between pitches and frequencies. Most equalizers use Hertz as a measurement increment, but musical pitch is measured in notes and octaves.

Frequency Range	Range Value (Hertz)	MIDI Notes	BV512 Bands (FFT)
Highs	8,000Hz–22,000Hz	C8–G8 and up	31–32
High mids	2,000Hz–8,000Hz	C6–B7	22–30
Middle	500Hz–2,000Hz	C4–B5	13–21
Low mids	100Hz–500Hz	G♯1–B3	5–13
Bass	20Hz–100Hz	E-1–G1	1–5

Filters

The filters on Reason devices usually have different modes, each mode corresponding to a specific type of filter. The standard filter types are lowpass, highpass, bandpass, and notch. Filters generally have two parameters, governing frequency (cutoff frequency) and resonance amount. These can be manually adjusted, but dynamic filtering effects can create exciting sounds, especially when the filter cutoff is modulated by a CV source. Other forms of dynamic automation come from using the module's own envelope, LFOs, and other modulation sources, automating the cutoff and resonance controls, and recording real-time MIDI controller data.

A lowpass filter rejects signals above the cutoff frequency while allowing frequencies below the cutoff to pass through. A highpass filter allows frequencies above the cutoff setting to pass. A bandpass filter allows frequencies at or near the cutoff frequency to pass through, while rejecting frequencies that are above or below the cutoff. A notch filter allows all frequencies to pass except for a range around the cutoff frequency.

With lowpass, bandpass, and highpass filtering, the resonance parameter produces a region near the cutoff where overtones are emphasized (boosted). With notch filtering, the resonance parameter controls the bandwidth of the notch: High resonance settings produce a narrower notch. With the lowpass, highpass, and bandpass filter modes, adding resonance can produce a significant amount of gain.

Reason has two devices that can be used for general filtering applications. The ECF-42 Envelope Controlled Filter is a multimode lowpass and bandpass filter, and the Malström Graintable Synthesizer has audio input sockets for processing

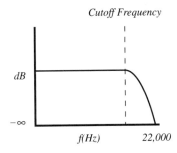

Lowpass Filter

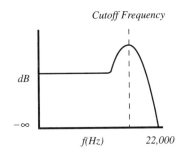

Resonant Lowpass Filter

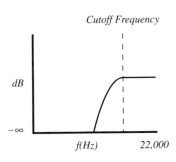

Highpass Filter

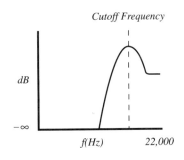

Resonant Highpass Filter

Figure 6-1.
Four filter response curves.

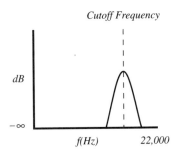

Bandpass Filter

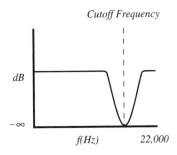

Notch Filter (Band Reject)

Figure 6-2.
The response curves of bandpass and notch filters.

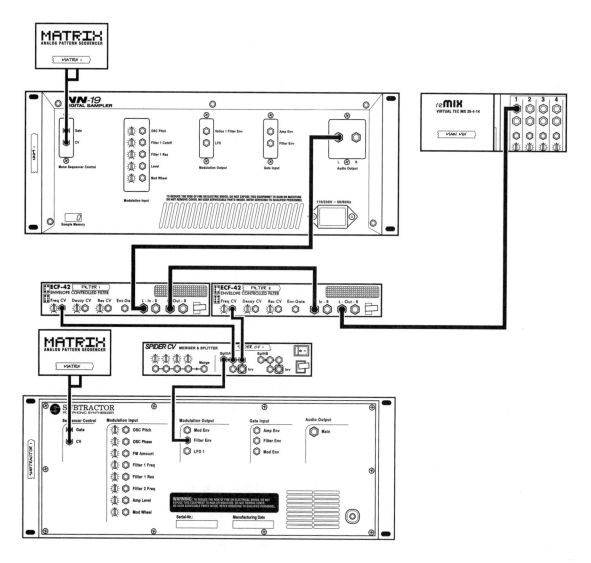

Figure 6-3.
A CV signal split to modulate the cutoff frequencies of two ECF-42 filters.

external signals through the filter section. Besides having the standard lowpass and bandpass types, the Malström has comb filter modes and an amplitude modulation (AM) mode. The comb filter is discussed in this section, but amplitude modulation is not exactly a filter, so it's discussed elsewhere.

Wah-Wah Effect

A simple wah-wah effect can easily be created using a bandpass filter on the synth sections of the sound modules in Reason, but the effect shown below differs since it uses two filters, a resonant 24dB lowpass filter connected in series with a 12dB resonant bandpass filter. The resonant lowpass filter adds a little extra body to the original tone and cuts off extraneous high frequencies that the bandpass filter does not cut. The effect is dynamic; it's only evident when the cutoff frequency is swept. Since two ECF-42 filters are required for the wah-wah, a real-time CV control section is necessary to modulate both filters with one control. Since the wah-wah pedal is originally a guitar effect, this example uses a guitar chord sample.

• Start with an empty rack, and create a mixer.
• Set the tempo to 75 BPM.

Signal Source Section
• Bypass auto-routing and create an NN19.
• Load the sample "Jh_DI_Guitar_chord.aif" from the *Power Tools for Reason* CD Audio Samples directory.
• Create a Matrix Pattern Sequencer connected to the NN19 sequencer control inputs.
• On the Matrix, program tied gate events from step 1 to step 15, all playing C3.

Filter & Distortion Section
• Bypass auto-routing and create two ECF-42 Envelope Controlled Filters. (The connections are all in mono for this configuration, so bypass auto-routing throughout.)
• Connect the NN19 left output to the filter 1 left input.
• Connect the filter 1 left output to the filter 2 left input.
• Connect the filter 2 left output to the mixer channel 1 left input.

• Program ECF-42 filter 1 with these settings:

ECF-42 Filter 1 Settings	
Freq	36
Res	48
Env. Amt	0
Velocity	0
Mode	LP 24
attack	0
decay	0
sustain	0
release	0

• Program ECF-42 filter 2 with these settings:

ECF-42 Filter 2 Settings	
Freq	26
Res	72
Env. Amt	0
Velocity	0
Mode	BP 12
attack	0
decay	0
sustain	0
release	0

Real-Time CV Control Section

The real-time control CV signal will be split to modulate the filter cutoff frequencies of both ECF-42 filters. Start by creating the real-time control section:

• At the bottom of the rack, bypass auto-routing and create a SubTractor Synthesizer.
• Enable the low BW button.
• Set the SubTractor polyphony to 1.
• Set the mod envelope ADSR settings all to 0.
• Set the filter envelope ADSR settings all to 0.
• Select the SubTractor, and then create a Matrix Pattern Sequencer.
• Set the Matrix pattern length to 1 step.
• On the Matrix, program a tied gate event on step 1.
• Bypass auto-routing and create a Spider CV Merger & Splitter.
• Connect the SubTractor filter envelope modulation output to the Spider CV split A input.
• Connect the Spider CV split A out 1 to the filter 1 ECF-42 Freq CV input.
• Connect the Spider CV split A out 2 to the filter 2 ECF-42 Freq CV input.
• Run the sequence.

As the guitar sample is triggered, change the value of the SubTractor filter envelope sustain level. This control opens and closes the filters, and periodic changes to the cutoff frequency create the sound made famous by the guitar pedal effect. Ideally this should be controlled by an expression pedal, but a knob or slider works fine. If these input options are not available, assign the modulation wheel from your keyboard controller to the SubTractor filter envelope sustain level using Reason's MIDI Remote Mapping feature.

96dB Lowpass Filter

Using a control scheme similar to the one used above for the wah-wah effect, several ECF-42 filters can be chained together to create an extreme 96dB lowpass filter. A single filter provides 24dB of stop-band attenuation, and when another filter is added with the same cutoff frequency, another 24dB is cut. Using four filters will create a very sharp filtering effect that literally cuts out the entire dynamic range above the cutoff. This effect becomes very interesting when resonance is added, but the results can easily be distorted. This example also employs a real-time CV control section to modulate the cutoff frequency and resonance of all four filters.

- In an empty rack, create a mixer.
- Create a Dr.REX Loop Player.
- Load the ReCycle Loop "Rnb14_Original_100_eLAB.rx2" from the Dr Rex Drum Loops\RnB HipHop directory from the Reason Factory Sound Bank.
- Copy the Dr.REX MIDI information to the sequencer.

Quad 24dB Filter Section
- Create four ECF-42 Envelope Controlled Filters. They should automatically be connected in series between the Dr.REX and the mixer.

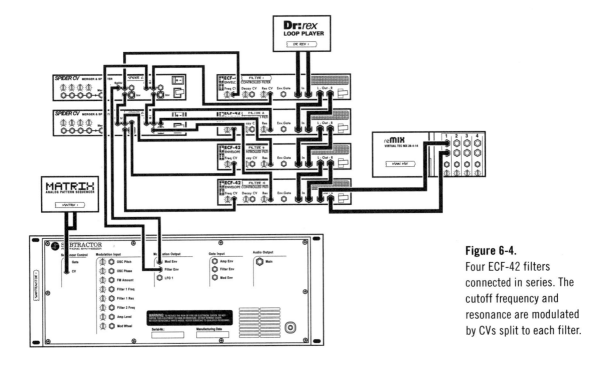

Figure 6-4.
Four ECF-42 filters connected in series. The cutoff frequency and resonance are modulated by CVs split to each filter.

• On all four ECF-42 filters, set the filter cutoff frequency to 0, the resonance to 0, the mode to 24dB/octave, and the envelope amount to 0. On the rear panel, set the freq and res CV trim knobs all to 127.

Frequency & Resonance CV Control Section
• Create two Spider CV Merger & Splitters — these should automatically be wired in series for a 6-way splitter.
• Connect the normal (not inverse) outputs from split A to the Freq CV input sockets on the ECF-42 filters.
• Connect the normal (not inverse) output sockets from split B to the res CV inputs on the ECF-42 filters.

Real-Time CV Control Section
• At the bottom of the rack, bypass auto-routing and create a SubTractor.
• Create a Matrix Pattern Sequencer.
• Connect the SubTractor modulation output mod env socket to the Spider CV split A input, and connect the filter env socket to the split B input socket.
• Set the SubTractor mod and filter envelope ADSR settings all to 0.
• Set the SubTractor polyphony to 1 and enable the low BW.
• Program a tied gate event on step 1 of the Matrix and set the pattern length to 1 step.
• Before playing the sequence, set the mixer master output to 36 and the channel 1 fader to 66. Turn your monitor levels down. The 96dB filter will result in some extreme sound levels, which can be unpleasant and potentially dangerous!
• Save the song file and run the sequence.
• Play with the SubTractor mod and filter envelope sustain levels to control the filter bank.

To avoid overloading the output, you may want to connect the resonance modulation to only two of the four ECF-42s. The sustain control on the SubTractor mod and filter envelopes modulate the cutoff frequency and resonance of the four ECF-42 filters, and these can be assigned to a continuous controller slider for direct control over the filterbank.

Screamin' Filterbank
This effect was inspired by a hardware filter device called the Sherman Filterbank. The configuration is based on the 96dB lowpass filter described above, but it adds several other features, including a Scream 4 Distortion and a dry/wet crossfade control, and it uses several Comp-01 compressors to govern the extreme output levels of the resonant filters.

• Start with the 96dB lowpass filter configuration previously described.

Dry/Wet Balance with Real-Time CV Control Section
- Select the mixer, and rename it "Crossfade."
- Create a Spider Audio Merger & Splitter.
- Connect the Dr.REX audio outputs to the Spider Audio Split A and Split B inputs.
- Connect the Spider Audio split A out 1 and split B out 1 to the Crossfade mixer channel 2 inputs.
- Set the Crossfade mixer's channel 1 fader level to 0, and the master level fader to 100.
- Create a Spider CV Merger & Splitter, and rename it "Xfade CV."
- Connect the Xfade CV Spider CV split A out 1 to the Crossfade mixer channel 1 level CV input.
- Connect the Xfade CV Spider CV split A out 4/inv to the Crossfade mixer channel 2 level CV input.
- Set the Crossfade mixer channel 1 and channel 2 level CV trim knobs to 64, if they aren't set to 64 already.
- Select the SubTractor and Matrix Pattern Sequencer, and duplicate them.
- Rename "SubTractor 1 Copy" "Dry/Wet CV."
- Connect the Dry/Wet CV SubTractor filter envelope modulation output to the Xfade CV Spider CV split A input.

Distortion Section
- Bypass auto-routing and create a Scream 4 Distortion unit.
- Move the Scream 4 up under the Dr.REX.
- Connect the Spider Audio split A out 2 to the Scream 4 Audio left input. Verify that the right channel is automatically cabled.
- Connect the Scream 4 left output to the Filter 1 left input. Again, verify that the right channel is automatically cabled.
- Set the Scream 4 Damage Control to 104, P1 to 84, P2 to 63.

96dB Filterbank Section
- Change the cutoff frequency to 32 on all four ECF-42 filters.
- Adjust the resonance CV trim to 64 on all four ECF-42 filters.

Filterbank Output Compression/Limiting Section
- Select the Filter 4 ECF-42 and create a Comp-01 Compressor/Limiter. This compressor is inserted after Filter 4.
- Set the Compressor 1 ratio to 117, threshold to 42, attack to 0, release to 60.
- Select the Compressor 1 Comp-01 and create another Comp-01.
- Set Compressor 2 ratio to 114, threshold to 64, attack to 0, release to 60.
- Select the Compressor 2 Comp-01, and create another Comp-01.
- Set Compressor 3 ratio to 85, threshold to 36, attack to 0, release to 16.

MIDI Control Section
- Assign the SubTractor 1 mod envelope sustain slider and filter envelope sustain slider to MIDI sliders or knobs.
- Assign the Dry/Wet CV SubTractor filter envelope sustain slider to a MIDI slider or knob.
- While running the sequence, move the control sliders.

The changes to the filterbank section limit the range of the filter cutoff frequency and resonance controls, but extreme sounds can still result. The compressors are a means of protecting the output signal (and ears) from overloads. The compressors will attenuate a lot of the output signal, and the auto make-up gain will also compensate for signals that are very low.

Figure 6-5.
Matrix CVs connected to the ECF-42 CV inputs to create a pattern-controlled filter.

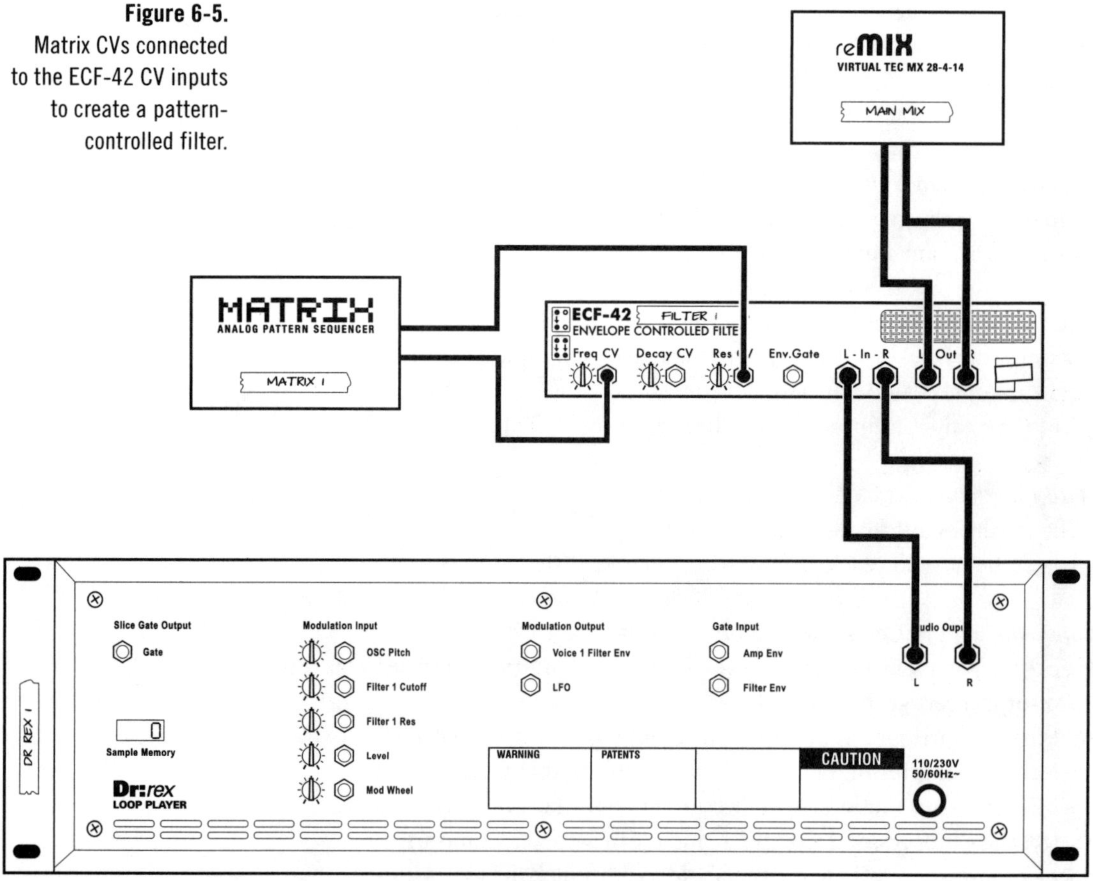

PCF: Pattern-Controlled Filter

Pattern-controlled filtering is a technique that is unique to electronic music, and Matrix curve CV patterns make it easy to produce this effect. This PCF configuration is similar to the PCF introduced in Propellerhead ReBirth RB-338.

- In an empty rack, create a mixer.
- Bypass auto-routing and create a Dr.REX Loop Player.
- Load the ReCycle loop "Chm04_Shag_125_eLAB.rx2" from the Dr Rex Drum Loops\Chemical Beats directory in the Reason Factory Sound Bank.
- Copy the REX slice data to the Dr.REX 1 sequencer track.
- Disable the filter on the Dr.REX.
- Insert an ECF-42 Envelope Controlled Filter between Dr.REX 1 and the mixer input channel 1.
- Set the ECF-42 cutoff frequency to 0, resonance to 30, envelope amount to 40, and velocity to 40, with envelope settings of A 10, D 0, S 127, R 70.
- At the bottom of the rack, create a Matrix Pattern Sequencer.
- Program the following in Matrix pattern A1:

Matrix Pattern

Step	1	2	3	4	5	6	7	8	9	10	11	12	13	14	15	16
Curve																
Note	C3	C3	C3	C3	C3	C3	C3	C3	C3	C3	C3	C3	C3	C3	C3	C3
Gate	H	M		M	TH	H	L	TM	M	L	L	M	H			

- Start the sequence to hear the pattern-controlled filtering of the drum loop.

Malström PCF

The independent filter section of the Malström synthesizer can also be triggered for pattern-controlled filtering effects. The envelope is triggered by the Matrix pattern sequencer, which triggers note events on the Malström. The Matrix gate CV can also be connected to the Malström's filter env gate CV input. This PCF takes advantage of the inverted envelope modulation as well as the velocity to filter amount modulation. The traditional PCF created using the ECF-42 filter and a Matrix only has positive envelope modulation.

- In an empty rack, create a mixer.
- Bypass auto-routing and create a Dr.REX Loop Player.
- Load the ReCycle loop "Chm04_Shag_125_eLAB.rx2" from the Reason Factory Sound Bank Dr Rex Drum Loops\Chemical Beats directory.

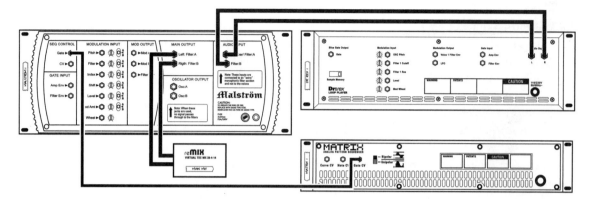

Figure 6-6.
Dr.REX connected to the
Malström audio inputs.
A Matrix gate CV triggers
the Malström filter
envelope.

• Copy the REX slice data to the Dr.REX 1 sequencer track.
• Disable the filter on the Dr.REX.
• Create a Malström Synthesizer.
• Connect the Dr.REX audio outputs to the Malström filter audio inputs.
• On the Malström, disable osc A, osc B, mod A, and mod B.
• Set the Malström velocity to filter envelope setting to 39.
• Set the Malström spread setting to 127.
• Set the cutoff frequency to 127 and resonance to 30 on the Malström's filter A
  and filter B.
• Enable the inverse setting on the Malström filter envelope and set the envelope
  as follows: A 18, D 36, S 127, R 42.
• At the bottom of the rack, create a Matrix Pattern Sequencer.
• Program the following on Matrix Pattern A1:

Matrix Pattern															
Step	1	2	3	4	5	6	7	8	9	10	11	12	13	14	15	16
Curve																
Note	C3	C3	C3	C3	C3	C3	C3	C3	C3	C3	C3	C3	C3	C3	C3	C3
Gate			H	H		H	H	H		H		H	H		H	

• Start the sequence to hear the pattern-controlled filtering of the drum loop.

Equalizers

Equalizers are devices that boost or cut problematic frequencies in an audio signal.
A common type of equalizer is the tone control on your stereo. These con-

trols, often called treble and bass, boost or cut high frequencies and low frequencies. Contouring the frequency response enhances certain ranges and balances a signal to fit in the mix. Reason has a variety of equalizers that can shape a signal's frequency response. The Mixer 14:2, the PEQ-2, and the RV7000 have parametric equalizers, and the BV512 Digital Vocoder has a graphic equalizer. Besides using equalizers with fixed settings to contour the frequency response, you can automate equalizer parameters with a sequencer track to create interesting time-varying frequency response effects. The PEQ-2 equalizer can also be modulated with CV signals from other devices like the Matrix for pattern-based equalization effects.

Parametric Equalizers

The PEQ-2 parametric equalizer has two bands, so you can shape two different frequency ranges at once. Each band has three controls: center frequency, bandwidth (Q), and gain. The center frequency is the highest or lowest point of the curve. The bandwidth control adjusts the width of the curve, and the gain control adjusts the amplitude of the curve.

The key to using any parametric equalizer is to find the ideal center frequency. This is the point where the gain change will be the greatest. Finding the ideal center frequency is quite easy. First, set the Q to a narrow bandwidth and set the gain to maximum. Adjust the frequency setting up or down until you hear the frequency levels suddenly spike. Lower the Q so that a broader range of frequencies is emphasized. Decrease the gain level to reduce the level of the troubling range.

Mixer EQ

The Mixer 14:2 has EQ control for bass and treble ranges. Unlike the PEQ-2, there is only one control that adjusts the cut or boost for the bass and treble. This is commonly called a "shelf" or "shelving" EQ because it has a fixed corner frequency. Signals above or below this frequency are boosted or cut.

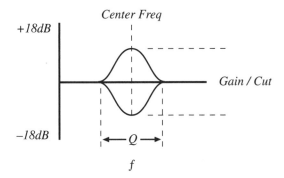

Figure 6-7.
The frequency response curve and parameters of the PEQ-2.

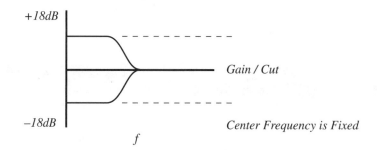

Figure 6-8.
Shelf EQ response curve
for the mixer's bass EQ.

The Mixer 14:2 EQ has two modes, which are controlled by a switch on the rear of the device. Compatible EQ is the same EQ found in early versions of Reason. The shelf EQ in compatible mode has a broad bandwidth, and when both treble and bass are reduced, it sounds more like attenuation than like EQ. Improved EQ has a narrower bandwidth, and the bass control distinctly affects frequencies in the 20Hz to 80Hz range. The improved EQ also has a more distinct bandwidth as it affects the high midrange and highs, with the most effect on the frequencies in the 6kHz to 20kHz range. The fixed bandwidths on the improved EQ leave the low midrange and mids unaffected.

Channel Strip

A channel strip is a feature found on a high-end mixing console, which has an extended equalizer and dynamics processor. This feature can be added to the mixer in Reason by inserting a PEQ-2 parametric equalizer and Comp-01 compressor/limiter in front of the mixer input channels. If the improved EQ setting is used on the mixer, using a PEQ-2 is important to shape the low-mid frequency range. Do not hesitate to insert parametric equalizers on as many channels as necessary to get the frequency balance just right.

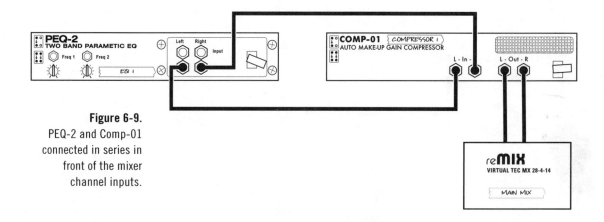

Figure 6-9.
PEQ-2 and Comp-01
connected in series in
front of the mixer
channel inputs.

• Start with an empty rack and create a mixer.
• Bypass auto-routing and create a PEQ-2 Parametric Equalizer.
• Bypass auto-routing and create a Comp-01 Compressor Limiter.
• Connect the PEQ-2 audio outputs to the Comp-01 audio inputs.
• Connect the Comp-01 audio outputs to the mixer channel 1 audio inputs.

This connection scheme can be duplicated for each mixer input that requires more EQ and dynamics control. When new devices are created at the bottom of the rack, the auto-routing feature will connect the audio outputs to free PEQ-2 inputs. It's very likely that equalization or compression is not required for every input, so the unneeded devices should be set to bypass mode.

Creating a separate PEQ-2 and Comp-01 for each input channel is rather excessive, but this example illustrates a basic way to connect devices in series.

PEQ-2 Sweeping Bands

This effect uses two PEQ-2 parametric equalizers with very narrow bands. An LFO CV source modulates the center frequency parameters of the bands to create a sweeping EQ effect. The effect almost sounds like a phaser without the actual shift in signal phase.

• In an empty rack, create a mixer.
• Bypass auto-routing and create a Dr.REX Loop Player.

Figure 6-10.
PEQ-2 center frequency CV inputs modulated by the Dr.REX LFO.

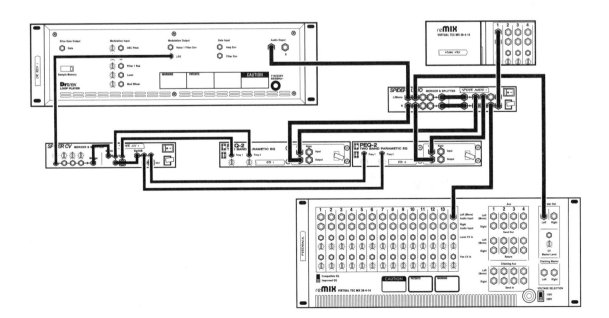

- Load the ReCycle loop "Trh08_HotValve_100_eLAB.rx2" from the Reason Factory Sound Bank\Dr Rex Drum Loops\Abstract HipHop directory.
- Copy the REX slice data to the Dr.REX 1 sequencer track.
- Enable sync on the Dr.REX LFO and set the rate to 8/4.

The Filter Section
- Create a Spider Audio Merger & Splitter.
- Bypass auto-routing and connect the Dr.REX audio output left to the Spider Audio merge L/mono input.
- Bypass auto-routing and connect the Spider Audio merge L/mono output to the split A input.
- Bypass auto-routing and create two PEQ-2 Parametric Equalizers.
- Bypass auto-routing and connect the Spider Audio split A out 1 to the EQ 1 left input.
- Connect the EQ 1 left output to the Spider Audio merge R input 1.
- Connect the Spider Audio split A out 2 to the EQ 2 left input.
- Connect the EQ 2 left output to the Spider Audio merge R input 2.
- Connect the Spider Audio merge R output to the split B input.
- Connect the Spider Audio split B out 1 to the mixer channel 1 input left.
- On EQ 1, enable EQ B. Set Freq A to 14, Freq B to 40, Q to 127 on A and B, and gain to 127 on A and B.
- On EQ 2, enable EQ B. Set Freq A to 58, Freq B to 73, Q to 127 on A and B, and gain to 127 on A and B.

CV Control Section
- Bypass auto-routing and create a Spider CV Merger & Splitter.
- Connect the Dr.REX LFO modulation output to the Spider CV merge input 1.
- Set the Spider CV merge input 1 trim to 46.
- Connect the Spider CV merge output to the split A input.
- Connect the split A outputs 1 and 2 to the EQ 1 Freq CV inputs.
- Connect the split A output 3 to the split B input.
- Connect the split B outputs 1 and 2 to the EQ 2 Freq CV inputs.

Feedback Section
- Bypass auto-routing and create a mixer.
- Rename this mixer "Feedback."
- Set the Feedback mixer channel 14 level to 32. (This step is important: If the channel fader is above 40 or so, runaway feedback will occur.)
- Connect the Spider Audio split B out 2 to the Feedback mixer channel 14 left input.
- Connect the Feedback mixer master out to the Spider Audio merge L/mono input 2.
- Run the sequence.

Graphic Equalizer

A graphic equalizer is an array of bandpass filters whose center frequencies are spaced at regular intervals. The vertical sliders provide a visual, or graphic, representation of how the equalizer is changing the frequency response. The bands of the filters usually overlap a bit, so that the entire frequency range is covered. Usually, graphic equalizers are better suited for contouring a range of frequencies rather than isolating precise frequencies, because the center frequencies of the bands are fixed. The BV512 bandpass filters can be swept using the shift parameter. Usually, graphic equalizers will boost and cut frequencies bands about 15dB, but the BV512 graphic equalizer will cut frequencies to $-\infty$ dB. These two features make the BV512 a useful device for dramatic filtering effects as well as for shaping frequency response.

There are some idiosyncrasies about the BV512 graphic equalizer. The first is that the band count modes 4, 8, 16, and 32 will color the signal. In some cases this is obvious, because certain frequencies seem obscured when processed through the graphic equalizer. This is caused by the nature of the bandpass filters' overlap. With some signals, the coloration actually sounds like resonating filters. The effect is less noticeable with lower band counts, but as the count is increased, the number of overlapping filters doubles. This should not discourage use of the BV512 graphic equalizer, because the filters can be used to virtually cut all frequencies in certain ranges. The 512-band FFT mode should be used if coloration is not desired.

FFT mode has 512 bands and does not induce the same coloration as the lower band counts, but FFT requires time to process, and the time window used by the FFT process will induce a noticeable delay in the signal. If you use the graphic equalizer between the mixer master outputs and the Reason Hardware Interface to shape the overall mixdown, then the processing delay is not significant. However, if the FFT graphic equalizer is used to process drums, the delay is long enough to influence timing. One solution to this is to run all of the instruments except the one to which you want to apply the FFT through a submixer, and then delay the output of the submixer using a DDL-1.

Figure 6-11.
The BV512 in 8-band equalizer mode.

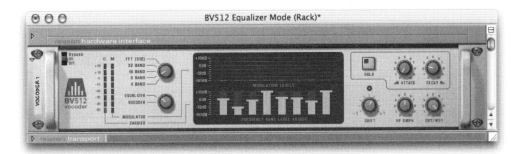

BV512 Filtering

The BV512 bandpass filters are useful if you want to completely strip a frequency range from a signal. This example demonstrates how the bass frequencies can be stripped from a drum loop. Using only four filter bands, the bass and low-mid frequency ranges are cut by setting the first two band levels to –InfdB (–∞ dB). The shift parameter is adjusted down to tune the filters with the signal.

• Start with an empty rack, and create a mixer.
• Create a Dr.REX Loop Player.
• Load the ReCycle loop "Trh18_OlSchool_100_eLAB.rx2" from the Reason Factory Sound Bank\Dr Rex Drum Loops\Abstract HipHop directory.
• Copy the REX slice data to the Dr.REX 1 sequencer track.
• Insert a BV512 Digital Vocoder between the Dr.REX and the mixer.
• Set the BV512 to these settings:

BV512 Settings		
Mode	Equalizer	
Band count	4	
Hold	Off	
attack		
decay		
Shift	–14	
HF Emphasis		
Dry/wet		
Band levels	1	–InfdB
	2	–InfdB
	3	0dB
	4	0dB

Figure 6-12.
BV512 equalizer inserted between Dr.REX and the mixer input.

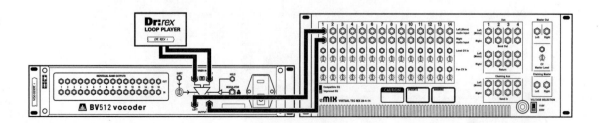

Run the sequence and hear how the BV512 Graphic Equalizer filters off all of the low and low-mid frequencies. This is an effective way of filtering elements from drum loops to layer with kick drums from a Redrum or a different ReCycle loop.

Multi-Band Effects

An audio signal can be split and filtered through several graphic equalizers. One equalizer might filter all except the low frequencies, while another filters out everything except the highs and a third only allows the mids to pass through. As a result, each frequency range can be isolated and sent down its own signal path. The split frequency signals can be processed with any effect device, then merged back together to create a multi-band effect. A typical example of multi-band processing is to use Comp-01 compressors with limiter settings, but you can use distortion units or delays to create some very interesting multi-band effects. This example

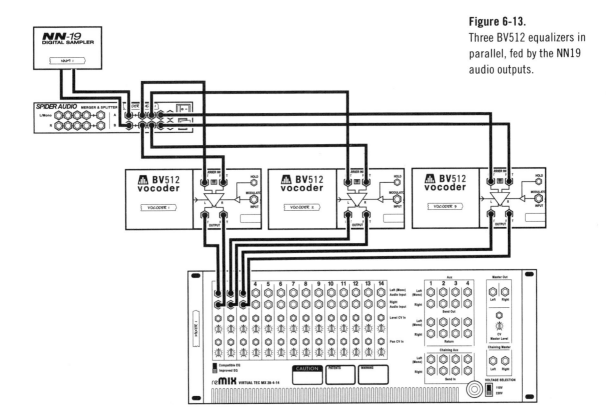

Figure 6-13.

Three BV512 equalizers in parallel, fed by the NN19 audio outputs.

demonstrates how to split a signal through three BV512 Graphic Equalizers in 8-band mode.

- In an empty rack, create a mixer.
- Bypass auto-routing and create an NN-19 Sampler.
- Load the sample "Peff_120BPMLOOP.aif" from the *Power Tools for Reason* CD Audio Samples directory.
- Enter edit mode on the NN19 sequencer track and view the key lane.
- Using the pencil tool, draw in a two-measure event on C3, and set the loop locators to 1.1.1 and 3.1.1.

Parallel Graphic EQ section
- Create a Spider Audio Merger & Splitter.
- Connect the NN19 audio outputs to the split A and split B inputs.
- Bypass auto-routing and create three BV512 Digital Vocoders.
- Connect a pair of Spider splitter outputs to each of the BV512 carrier inputs.
- Connect the BV512 carrier outputs to mixer channel inputs 1, 2, and 3.
- Set the BV512s as follows:

BV512 Multi-Band Graphic Equalizer Settings					
BV512 label	"Vocoder 1"		"Vocoder 2"		"Vocoder 3"
Mode	Equalizer		Equalizer		Equalizer
Band count	8		8		8
Shift	−10		0		14
Band levels	1 − 2	0dB	1 − 2	−InfdB	1 − 6	−InfdB
	2 − 8	−InfdB	2 − 6	0dB	7 − 8	0dB
			7 − 8	−InfdB		

Run the sequence and solo mixer channels 1, 2, and 3 to hear how the original loop is divided into low, mid, and high frequency ranges. Multi-band effects can quickly be created by inserting effects after each of the graphic equalizers. Scream 4 Fuzz and Overdrive algorithms work well with this particular loop.

Phase-Shifting Graphic EQs
This example uses CV signals to modulate the shift parameters of two BV512 Graphic Equalizers to create a stereo phase-shifting effect. The band filters' settings are offset between the two equalizers. Modulating the shift parameter creates movement in the stereo field.

- In an empty rack, create a mixer.
- Bypass auto-routing and create two BV512 Vocoder modules.

- Connect the Vocoder 1 left output to the mixer channel 1 left input.
- Connect the Vocoder 2 left output to the mixer channel 1 right input.
- Switch both vocoders to equalizer mode and set the band count to 32.
- On Vocoder 1, set all of the even bands to $-\infty$ dB.
- On Vocoder 2, set all of the odd bands to $-\infty$ dB.
- Create a Spider CV Merger & Splitter.
- Connect a Spider CV splitter A output to the Vocoder 1 shift CV input.
- Connect the Spider CV splitter A inverted output to the Vocoder 2 shift CV input.

- Bypass auto-routing and create a Malström Graintable Synthesizer.
- Connect the Malström mod A output to the Spider CV splitter A input.
- On the Malström, disable osc A, mod B, filter A, and filter B.
- Set the Malström mod A rate to 24.
- Bypass auto-routing and create a Dr.REX Loop Player.
- Connect the Dr.REX left audio output to the Vocoder 1 left input and the Dr.REX right audio output to the Vocoder 2 left input.
- Load the ReCycle loop "130_Clones_mLp_eLAB.rx2" from the Reason Factory Sound Bank\Music Loops\Variable Tempo (rex2)\Uptempo Loops directory.
- Copy the REX slice data to the Dr.REX 1 sequencer track.
- Run the sequence.

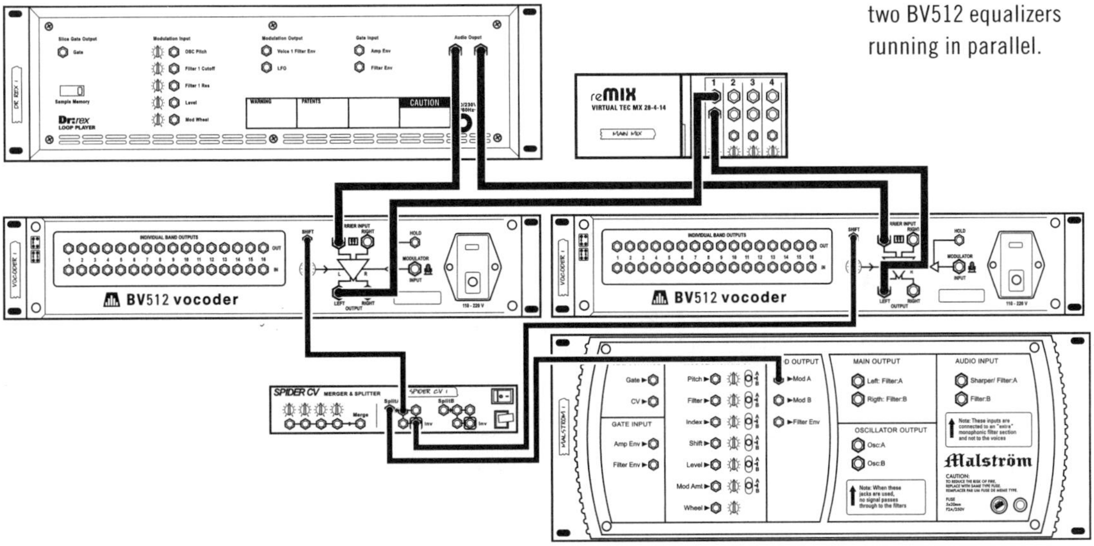

Figure 6-14.
Modulator CV output split
and inverted, connected
to the shift CV inputs on
two BV512 equalizers
running in parallel.

Comb Filters

C omb filters impose attenuation of certain frequencies like normal filters, but they're closely related to delays. A comb filter is a very short delay line with feedback. Because the delay time is short, certain overtones within the delayed signal will be out of phase from the original signal. When the delayed signal is combined with the original signal, some frequencies are cancelled out due to phase-shift.

DDL-1 Comb Filter

Using the DDL-1 Digital Delay Line, a basic comb filter effect can be created by setting the delay time to millisecond mode. This comb filter is limited, because feedback modulation is positive, and the delay times are set in one-millisecond intervals, but it demonstrates the properties of comb filters and the type of sounds they can produce. As the sequence plays, adjust the delay time to hear changes in the comb filter frequency. Because the delay time is fixed in millisecond increments, the actual frequencies are stepped, but some of the increments come close to chromatic notes. 3ms and 6ms settings are very close to the tuning in the key of E, and 1ms, 2ms, 4ms, and 8ms settings are close to tuning in the key of B.

- Start with an empty rack and create a mixer and a Dr.REX Loop Player.
- Set the tempo to 135 BPM.
- Load the ReCycle loop "Chm09_FatBoy_135_eLAB.rx2" from the Reason Factory Sound Bank\Dr Rex Drum Loops\Chemical Beats directory.
- Copy the REX slice data to the Dr.REX 1 sequencer track.
- Select the Dr.REX and insert a DDL-1 Digital Delay Line between it and the mixer.
- Set the DDL-1 delay time to 4ms, feedback to 108, and dry/wet balance to 38.
- Run the sequence.

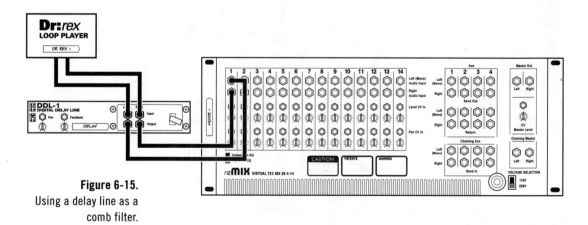

Figure 6-15.
Using a delay line as a comb filter.

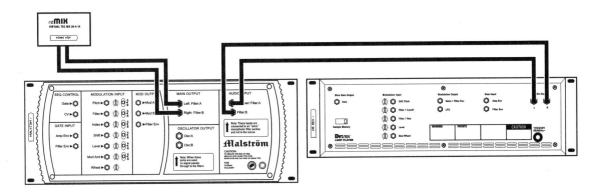

Figure 6-16.
Dr.REX connected into the
Malström's audio inputs.

Malström Comb Filter

The Malström filters have comb filter algorithms, which provide finer control than using the DDL-1. This configuration will demonstrate the differences between the two by using a Malström comb filter instead of the DDL-1. As the sequence plays, adjust the Malström filter A cutoff frequency knob to hear how much finer the resolution is with this comb filter effect.

• Start with the song file you created in the previous example.
• Delete the DDL-1.
• Bypass auto-routing and create a Malström Graintable Synthesizer.
• On the Malström, disable osc A, mod A, mod B, and filter B.
• Set Malström filter A mode to comb+, filter frequency to 2, and resonance to 99.
• Connect the Dr.REX left audio output left to the Malström shaper/filter A audio input.
• Connect the Malström main output left to mixer channel 1 left input.
• Run the sequence.

Modulator-Controlled Comb Filter

A modulation source can be used to create a pattern-controlled effect synchronized to the tempo of the track.

• Start with the Malström comb filter configuration described above.
• Set the Malström filter A frequency to 64.
• Enable mod B and turn on sync mode. Set the curve to 6, the rate to 1/8, and the mod B to filter modulation amount to 51.
• Run the sequence.

Chapter 7

Vocoder Effects

A vocoder is special filtering device, known for creating robot voices for science fiction films and countless songs in a variety of genres. Vocoding requires two audio signals, a carrier and a modulator. The frequency characteristics of the modulator signal are analyzed and then used to modulate a bank of filters processing the carrier signal. Both signals must be present in order for you to hear the effect.

There are two identical sets of bandpass filters in a vocoder. The modulator signal is processed through one set of filters, which separate the modulator signal into frequency ranges. (The multiband effect described in the previous chapter uses the BV512 Vocoder's bank of bandpass filters.) The output of each filter passes through an envelope follower, which generates a unipolar CV signal. The envelope follower CV signals modulate the output levels of the second set of filters, which process the carrier signal input.

In essence, the vocoder is simply a filter bank modulated by an audio signal, but the BV512 has extensive CV modulation features and MIDI control, which provide other options for controlling the filters. The modulator CV signals are also connected to sockets on the rear of the BV512, and this opens up the possibility of utilizing frequency-dependent CV modulations elsewhere in Reason.

Carrier Signal

F or an effective vocoding sound, the carrier signal must be rich in harmonics, with an ample amount of high frequency information. If the carrier signal has no high frequencies, when the high-frequency output filters are opened by the modulator signal, nothing will be heard. The following examples illustrate a few ideas for getting the best carrier signal for typical vocoding applications.

Classic Vocoder Effect

The typical vocoder sound uses a sawtooth wave from a synthesizer as a carrier signal.

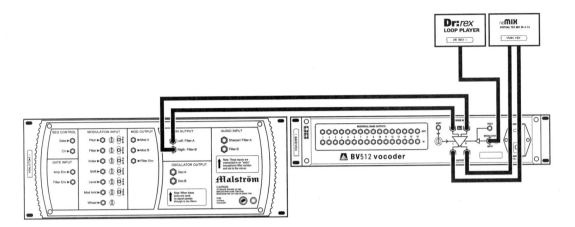

Figure 7-1.
Malström connected to
the BV512 carrier inputs,
and Dr.REX (with a vocal
ReCycle loop) connected
to the BV512 modulator
input.

This example uses a Malström Graintable as the source, but a SubTractor sawtooth wave will work as well. The ReCycle loop is a sliced sample of spoken dialog, used as a modulator signal for this example.

- In an empty rack, create a mixer.
- Set the tempo to 136 BPM.
- Create a Malström Graintable Synthesizer.
- On the Malström, enable osc B. Set the osc A graintable to Wave: Sawtooth*16 and the osc B graintable to Wave: Sawtooth. Set the osc B octave setting to 5.
- Insert a BV512 Digital Vocoder between the Malström audio outputs and the mixer inputs.
- Set the Vocoder band count to 16.
- Bypass auto-routing and create a Dr.REX Loop Player.
- Load the ReCycle loop "Peff_VocoderText.rx2" from the *Power Tools for Reason* CD Dr.REX Loops directory.
- Copy the REX slice data to the Dr.REX 1 sequencer track.
- Patch the Dr.REX left audio output to the BV512 modulator input.
- Enable MIDI through on the Malström 1 sequencer track, and run the sequence.

As the sequence plays the ReCycle loop slices, use a MIDI keyboard to play notes on the Malström to hear the classic vocoder sound of a sawtooth carrier wave. Try playing chords for more musical vocoding passages. For robot speech, play monophonic lines and play with the pitchbend.

Bell Labs Style Vocoder

One of the earliest forms of a vocoder used a noise generator as carrier signal to accentuate sibilance. This example is inspired by a technique devised at Bell Labs—where the vocoder was invented in the 1950s. Using the band level CV outputs, the modulation signal from one vocoder controls a second vocoder

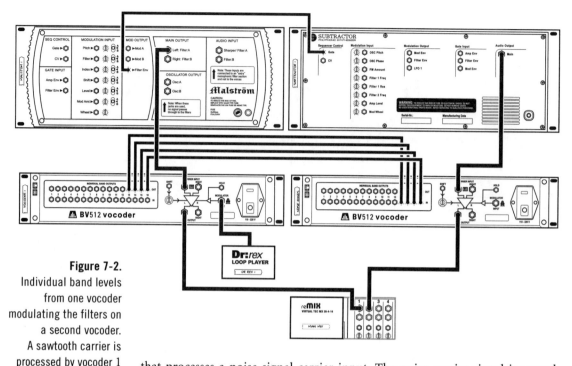

Figure 7-2.
Individual band levels
from one vocoder
modulating the filters on
a second vocoder.
A sawtooth carrier is
processed by vocoder 1
and a noise carrier by
vocoder 2.

that processes a noise signal carrier input. The noise carrier signal is passed when frequencies in the higher ranges are sensed by the main vocoder, which emphasizes sibilance and hard consonant sounds from speech.

• Start with an empty rack, and create a mixer.
• Set the song tempo to 136 BPM.

Dual Vocoder Section
• Bypass auto-routing and create two BV512 Digital Vocoders.
• Rename Vocoder 2 "Noise Bands."
• Set the band count to 16 on both vocoders.
• On Vocoder 1, set the frequency band level 13, 14, 15, and 16 to $-\infty$ dB. Set decay to 6.
• On Noise Bands, set the frequency band level adjustment 1 through 12 to $-\infty$ dB.
• Connect the left output of Vocoder 1 and left output of Noise Bands to mixer channel 1 and channel 2 left inputs.
• Connect the Vocoder 1 individual band level CV output 13 to the Noise Bands individual band levels input 13. Repeat this for bands 14, 15, and 16.

Sawtooth & Noise Carrier Signals
• Bypass auto-routing and create a SubTractor Synthesizer.
• Set the SubTractor polyphony to 1, enable the noise generator, set the noise color

to 127, osc mix to 127, filter frequency 1 to 127, amp envelope sustain to 127, and master level to 72.

- Connect the SubTractor audio output to the Noise Bands carrier left input.
- Bypass auto-routing and create a Malström Graintable Synthesizer.
- Set the Malström polyphony to 1 and set osc A graintable to Wave: Sawtooth.
- Connect the Malström left audio output to Vocoder 1 carrier left input.
- Connect the Malström filter envelope modulation output to the SubTractor sequencer control gate input. This chains note events from the Malström to the SubTractor.

Vocal Sample REX Loop Modulator
- Bypass auto-routing and create a Dr.REX Loop Player.
- Connect the Dr.REX left output to the Vocoder 1 modulator input.
- Load the ReCycle loop "Peff_VocoderText.rx2" from the *Power Tools for Reason* CD Dr.REX Loops directory.
- Copy the REX slice data to the Dr.REX 1 sequencer track.
- Route MIDI from a keyboard controller to the Malström, and run the sequence.

Start playing single notes on the MIDI keyboard to hear the effect. Vocoder 1 filters 13 through 16 are disabled, but the CV signals for these bands are unaffected. These bands modulate the same filters on the second vocoder, which is processing white noise generated by the SubTractor synthesizer. By patching one or two lower bands in the same way, you can give the vocoded sound a breathy quality.

Vocoded Crowd Noise
The process of vocoding is not limited to the classic style where a synthesizer signal is processed with vocals. Any sound can be used as a carrier signal. This

Figure 7-3.
The vocoder band level CVs are merged to modulate the mixer channel 2 level. Vocoder levels are used as an envelope follower to boost the dry signal of the crowd noise.

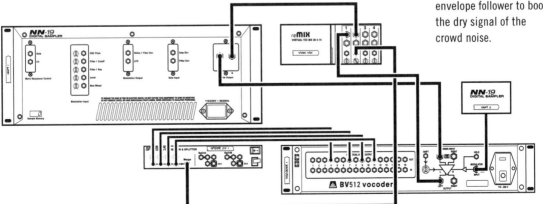

effect demonstrates using a loop of a crowd cheering in a stadium. The effect uses the vocoder to modulate the cheer so that it sounds like the crowd is chanting.

• Start with an empty rack, and create a mixer.

Crowd Noise Carrier Signal
• Bypass auto-routing and create an NN19 Digital Sampler.
• Using the sample browser, load the sample "Peff_Crowd.aif" from the from the *Power Tools for Reason* CD Audio Samples directory.
• Connect the NN19 audio output right to the mixer channel 2 left input.
• On the NN19 1 sequencer track, view the key lane and draw a note event on C3 from position 1.1.1 to position 9.1.1 (eight measures).

Vocoder Connections & Settings
• Bypass auto-routing and create a BV512 Digital Vocoder.
• Connect the NN19 audio output left to the BV512 carrier input left.
• Connect the BV512 carrier output left to the mixer channel 1 left input.
• Adjust the Vocoder parameters as follows:

Crowd Noise BV512 Settings	
mode	vocoder
band count	32
hold	off
attack	0
decay	60
shift	6
HF emphasis	72
dry/wet	119

In a large crowd of people, there's always a background din of noise, but when the crowd chants, there is a significant increase in loudness. To account for the dynamic changes, the vocoder is also used as an envelope follower to modulate the level of the dry crowd signal. Several of the vocoder's individual band level CV outputs are merged to create a modulator source for the dry signal mixer level control:

Envelope Follower for Dry Crowd Noise Level
• Create a Spider CV Merger & Splitter.
• Connect the BV512 individual band level outputs 4, 7, 9, and 11 to the Spider CV merger inputs.
• Connect the Spider CV merge output to the mixer channel 2 level CV input.
• Adjust the mixer channel 2 level CV trim to 56, and the fader level to 78.

Modulator Signal Source
- Bypass auto-routing and create another NN19 Digital Sampler.
- On NN19 2, load the sample "Peff_Vx_turnitup.aif" from the from the *Power Tools for Reason* CD Audio Samples directory.
- Set the NN19 2 filter mode to HP 12 and the filter cutoff frequency to 44.
- Connect the NN19 2 audio output left to the BV512 modulator input.
- On the NN19 2 sequencer track, view the key lane and draw note events on C3 from measure 1 through measure 8. Each note should be one measure long. These events will trigger the vocal sample to play in every measure.
- Run the sequence.

This effect works best if the chant vocal also sounds like a large crowd. The vocal sample used in this example was created by recording 24 different tracks of one person yelling the phrase in different ways and at different pitches. Some of the tracks were processed with a bit of pitch shifting and reverb, and then the tracks were bounced down to a stereo audio file. This is easy to accomplish with any digital audio workstation, or even a multitrack tape recorder. There are other ways to produce this sample using only Reason. Several layered audio files in an NN-XT sampler with slight pitch and filter variations on each key zone can be used to create the modulation source.

Vocoder Freeze

This effect is a variation on one of the suggestions in the Reason Operation Manual. A noise source is fed into the vocoder carrier input, and a Matrix Pattern Sequencer triggers the hold feature of the BV512. Hold modulation freezes the vocoder's modulation bands, filtering the noise generated from the SubTractor synthesizer and holding that curve until the gate event is released. This example also demonstrates using a drum loop as a modulation source. Drum loops vocoding a synthesizer carrier will create interesting rhythmic textures.

- In an empty rack, create a mixer.
- Set the tempo to 150 BPM.
- Bypass auto-routing and create a SubTractor Synthesizer.
- Set the SubTractor polyphony to 1, enable the noise generator, and set the noise color to 85, osc mix to 127, filter 1 frequency to 127, amp envelope decay to 0, and amp envelope sustain to 82.
- Create a Matrix Pattern Sequencer, and verify its connection to the SubTractor sequencer control inputs.
- Set the Matrix pattern length to 1 step.
- Program a tied note event on step 1 of the Matrix.
- Create a Spider Audio Merger & Splitter.
- Connect the SubTractor audio output to the Spider Audio splitter A input.

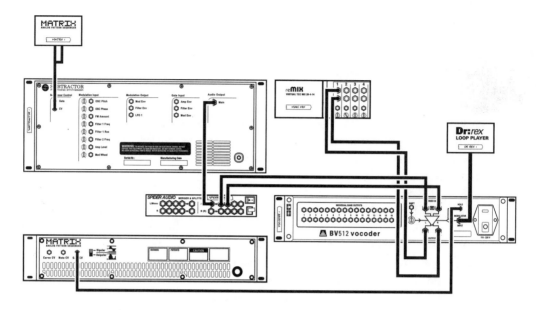

Figure 7-4.
A Matrix gate CV
triggering the vocoder's
hold feature.

• Bypass auto-routing and create a BV512 Digital Vocoder.

• Connect the Spider Audio splitter A outputs 1 and 2 to the Vocoder carrier inputs.

• Connect the Vocoder carrier outputs to the inputs on mixer channel 1.

• Set the Vocoder's parameters as follows:

BV512 Vocoder Settings	
mode	vocoder
band count	32
hold	off
attack	0
decay	18
shift	−14
HF emphasis	48
dry/wet	127

• Bypass auto-routing and create a Dr.REX Loop Player.

• Connect the Dr.REX left output to the Vocoder 1 modulator input.

• Load the ReCycle loop "Hco16_Piggy_150_eLAB.rx2" from the Reason Factory Sound Bank\Dr Rex Drum Loops\Hardcore directory.

• Copy the REX slice data to the Dr.REX 1 sequencer track.

• Bypass auto-routing and create a Matrix Pattern Sequencer.

• Connect the Matrix gate CV output to the Vocoder hold input.

• Program the following in Matrix pattern A1:

Matrix Pattern															
Step	1	2	3	4	5	6	7	8	9	10	11	12	13	14	15	16
Curve																
Note																
Gate		TH		TH		TH	TH	H		TH		TH	TH	TH	TH	TH

• Run the sequence.

While the sequence is playing, switch the Pattern on Matrix 2 to an empty pattern to hear the vocoding without the freeze effect.

Modulator Signals

As of version 2.5, Reason does not have an audio input, so there is no way to process vocals in real time. Speech samples must first be recorded using another application, then loaded into a Reason sampler. The sample can be sequenced to play back and used as the modulation signal for the vocoder. For musical applications, vocals should be synchronized with the tempo of the track. Ideally, a ReWire host application with recording features should be used, so the Reason song can be monitored while the vocal samples are being recorded. Once recorded, the audio track can be edited and saved as one or more samples that can be loaded into an NN19 or NN-XT sampler.

The process of recording custom vocal samples can be tedious if you don't have a ReWire host application that records audio. Render the track to an audio file and burn it to a CD or export it to a portable playback device. While listening to the track from the CD player or MP3 player, record the vocal samples, then edit them as needed. This takes a bit more time, but it's just as effective as recording to a ReWire host application.

It's important to keep modulator signal levels high. Low levels will still modulate the filters, but louder signals will make the vocoding effect more discernable. Since vocal samples must first be recorded and edited for use in Reason, the sampled phrases should be compressed and normalized. This will maximize the effect so the subtle nuances of speech clearly translate in the vocoding process. If compression is not available in your sample editor, process the vocal sample through a Comp-01 compressor/limiter or Scream 4 tape compression algorithm inserted between the sampler and the BV512 modulator input.

Processing vocal samples with ReCycle and saving them as REX files is useful, because the timing of each word can be adjusted to fit with the rhythm of the track. Even with vocal samples that are recorded with good timing, having the individual words sliced apart as segments adds flexibility if you want to remix the track or create stutter effects.

Although vocoders are primarily intended for use with speech sample modulation signals, other types of sounds can be directed to the BV512 modulator input. Drum loops are fantastic for modulating vocoder bands, because they usually have energy in all parts of the frequency spectrum — kick drums in the bass and low midrange, snare drums and claps in the high midrange, hi-hats and cymbals in the high frequency range, etc. The following examples illustrate various synthesis techniques for modulating the vocoder bands for unique filtering effects.

Vocoder Band Sweep

A sine wave is the purest type of audio signal. It contains no harmonics other than the fundamental. Using the sine wave as a modulator signal provides very precise filter modulation. This example uses a sine wave from a SubTractor Synthesizer. The pitch is controlled by sequencer events and the portamento sweeps the pitch from a low C to a very high G. As the pitch changes, the different bands of the vocoder open.

- Start with an empty rack, and create a mixer.
- Create a Dr.REX Loop Player.
- Load the ReCycle loop "125_FuzzyLogic_mLp_eLAB.rx2" from the Reason Factory Sound Bank\Music Loops\Variable (rx2)\Uptempo Loops directory.
- Set the Dr.REX master level to 127.
- Copy the REX slice data to the Dr.REX 1 sequencer track.

Figure 7-5.
SubTractor output connected to the vocoder modulation input.

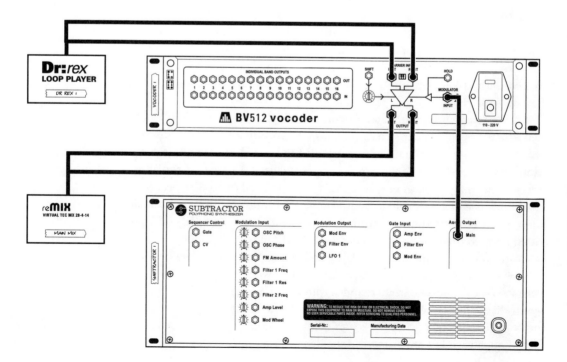

• Insert a BV512 Digital Vocoder between the Dr.REX audio outputs and the mixer inputs.
• Adjust the BV512 parameters as follows:

BV512 Vocoder Settings	
mode	vocoder
band count	FFT
hold	off
attack	70
decay	74
shift	0
HF emphasis	60
dry/wet	127

Sine Wave Carrier
• Bypass auto-routing and create a SubTractor Synthesizer.
• Set the SubTractor mode to legato, portamento to 127, and polyphony to 1, and enable low BW.
• Set the SubTractor osc 1 waveform to a sine wave (wave 3).
• Set the SubTractor filter 1 cutoff frequency to 127.
• Set the SubTractor amp envelope decay to 0, sustain to 127, and release to 34.
• Set the SubTractor master level to 83.
• Connect the SubTractor audio output to the BV512 modulator input.

Sequencer Control Track
• On the SubTractor 1 sequencer track, enter edit mode to view the key lane.
• Set the grid resolution to Bar.
• Use the pencil tool and draw a sustained event on C1 for the duration of the transport loop.
• Set the grid resolution to 1/4 and draw events of different durations on G8.
• Run the sequence.

The long portamento setting on the SubTractor will slowly slide the pitch from C1 up toward G8. As the pitch rises, the modulator signal will sweep through the vocoder bands. Because the sine wave has no added harmonic content, the sweep is fairly clean. Other waveforms can be used to create a different sweeping effect.

Formant-Controlled Vocoder
Vowel sounds created by the human voice are caused by frequency peaks called formants. Combinations of formants have distinct sounds like "ooh" or "aah." The Throat graintable in the Malström produces vowel formants, which can be

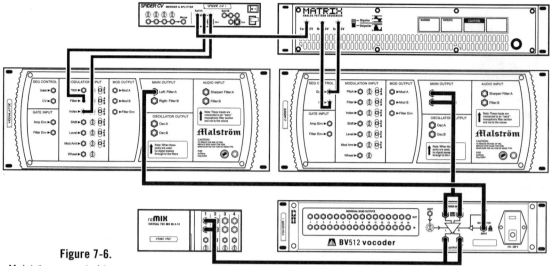

Figure 7-6.
Malström connected to BV512 modulator input. Matrix curve CV split to modulate the index and filter on the Malström.

accessed using the index parameter. The formant grains can be used as a vocoder modulator source to process carrier signals with voice-like filter characteristics.

• Start with an empty rack, and create a mixer.
• Bypass auto-routing and create a Malström Graintable Synthesizer. Rename the Malström "Modulator."
• Set the Malström polyphony to 1 and the portamento to 67.
• On osc A, select the graintable "Voice: Throat." Set motion to –64 and shift to 6, and enable routing into the shaper.
• Set the filter A resonance to 36 and cutoff frequency to 82.
• Set the filter envelope amount to 30.
• Create a Matrix Pattern Sequencer.
• Randomize pattern A1 by selecting the "Randomize Pattern" item from the Edit menu to randomize the curve CV settings.
• Program the following on Matrix pattern A1:

Matrix Pattern															
Step	1	2	3	4	5	6	7	8	9	10	11	12	13	14	15	16
Curve																
Note	C3	C3	C3	C3	C3	C3	C3	C3	G3	G3	G3	G3	G3	G3	G3	G3
Gate	TH	TH	TH	TH	TH	TH	TH	H	TH	TH	TH	TH	TH	TH	TH	TH

- Bypass auto-routing and create a Spider CV Merger & Splitter.
- Connect the Matrix curve CV output to the Spider CV splitter A input.
- Connect the Spider CV splitter A out 1 to the Malström filter modulation input.
- Connect the Spider CV splitter A out 2 to the Malström index modulation input, and set the index modulation trim to 127.
- Create a second Malström and rename it "Carrier."
- Enable osc B on the Carrier Malström, and Set the osc A and osc B graintables to "Wave: Sawtooth*16."
- Set osc A shift to –6 and cent tuning to 6.
- Set osc B shift to 6 and cent tuning to –6.
- Set the Carrier Malström spread to 83.
- Create a BV512 Digital Vocoder as an insert between the Carrier Malström audio outputs and the mixer channel 1 inputs.
- Connect the Modulator Malström's left main output to the Vocoder modulator input.
- Set the BV512 band count to FFT and the shift to 12.
- Set the MIDI enable on the Carrier Malström sequencer track, run the sequence, and play some chords from a MIDI controller.

Pattern-Controlled Vocoder Filtering

Pattern-controlled filtering is an exciting way to process signals, and using the vocoder for patterned-based filtering effects adds a dimension of multi-band filtering. Different bands of the frequency spectrum can be triggered by CV sources to create some bizarre filtering patterns.

Pattern-Controlled Vocoder

This effect could be created using a stack of Matrix Pattern Sequencers to trigger each of the individual band levels, but this would be tedious to edit. Instead, the individual channel gate CV outputs from a Redrum are connected to the BV512 band level inputs. This example only uses an 8-band vocoder to accommodate the limit of ten Redrum channels. Sixteen-band or 32-band mode could be used, but this would require more gate CV sources.

- In an empty rack, create a mixer.

Carrier Signal Source
- Create a Dr.REX Loop Player.
- Load the ReCycle loop "Tec15_Hause_130_eLAB.rx2" from the Reason Factory Sound Bank\Dr Rex Drum Loops\Techno directory.
- Copy the REX slice data to the Dr.REX 1 sequencer track.

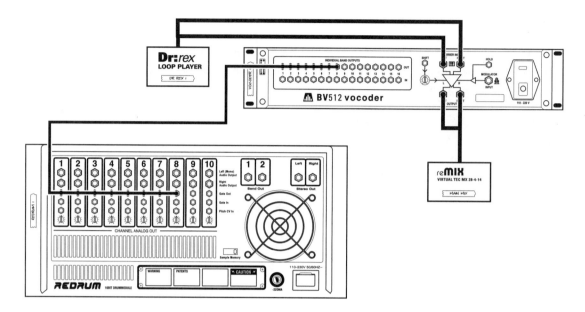

Figure 7-7.
Redrum gate CV outputs
connected to the BV512
individual band level CV
inputs.

Vocoder Section

• Insert a BV512 Digital Vocoder between the Dr.REX and the mixer.

• Adjust the BV512 parameters as follows:

BV512 Vocoder Settings	
mode	vocoder
band count	8
hold	off
attack	0
decay	40
shift	0
HF emphasis	48
dry/wet	127

Redrum Gate CV Section

• Bypass auto-routing and create a Redrum Drum Computer.

• Connect the Redrum channel 1 gate out socket to the Vocoder individual band level input 1. Repeat this for Redrum channels 2 through 8 and Vocoder bands 2 through 8.

• Set Redrum channels 1 through 8 to decay/gate mode 1 (gate mode) and set the length to 50.

• Program the following pattern into the Redrum pattern A1:

Redrum Pattern

	1	2	3	4	5	6	7	8	9	10	11	12	13	14	15	16
1	M				M				M				M			
2	M												M	M	M	
3	M								M							
4					M								M			
5					M								M			
6							M								M	
7				M	M						M		M			
8	S		M				M		S		M				M	
9																
10																

• Run the sequence.

As the drum loop plays, the Redrum pattern triggers the individual filter bands on the BV512. When no events are triggered, the vocoder bands stay closed, completely silencing the loop signal from the Dr.REX.

MIDI-Controlled Vocoder Filtering

The BV512 Vocoder responds to MIDI note events. To access these features, MIDI must be routed to the Vocoder from the Reason Hardware Interface or a sequencer track. The individual band levels are velocity-sensitive, and this example demonstrates a method of created keyed filtering events that synchronize with a ReCycle groove.

• In an empty rack, create a mixer.

Figure 7-8.
MIDI note events starting at C1 control the Vocoder band levels.

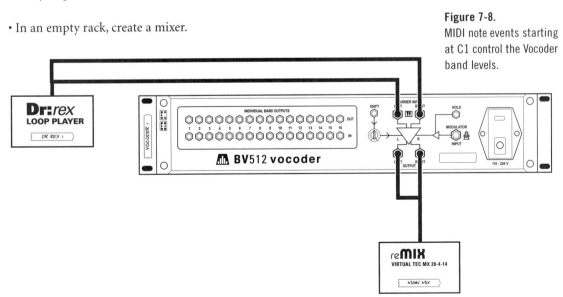

- Create a Dr.REX Loop Player.
- On Dr.REX 1, Load the ReCycle file "125_StopStart_mLp_eLAB.rx2" from the Factory Sound Bank from the Music Loops\Variable Tempo (rex2)\Uptempo Loops directory.
- Copy the REX slice data to the Dr.REX 1 sequencer track.
- In the sequencer arrange window, select the grouped regions of the REX slice data, and then click on "Get User Groove" from the Edit menu.
- Select the Dr.REX Loop Player and create a BV512 Vocoder.
- Adjust the parameters on the BV512 as follows:

BV512 Vocoder Settings	
mode	vocoder
band count	8
hold	off
attack	0
decay	0
shift	0
HF emphasis	0
dry/wet	127

- Create a sequencer track and route the MIDI to Vocoder 1.
- Enable MIDI input on the Vocoder sequencer track.
- On the sequencer, enable Quantize Notes During Recording and set the quantize amount to User.
- Enable the metronome and start recording notes to the vocoder sequencer track. The notes will be automatically quantized to the user groove, which has been set to match the REX note slices. In eight-band mode, the vocoder bands are triggered by playing notes between C1 and G1. In 32-band mode, the range extends up to G3.

These events could also be penciled in, but recording them in real time has a natural feel. The automatic quantization will synchronize the events in time with the ReCycle slice data. When manually programming note events in the sequencer, you can re-quantize the events so the filter pattern matches the quantization of the REX slices.

Vocoder Band CV Modulation

The individual band level outputs of the Vocoder can be patched to different inputs so that filter bands are linked to each other. This is useful if you wish to group bands together or create random associations between bands. The Bell Labs

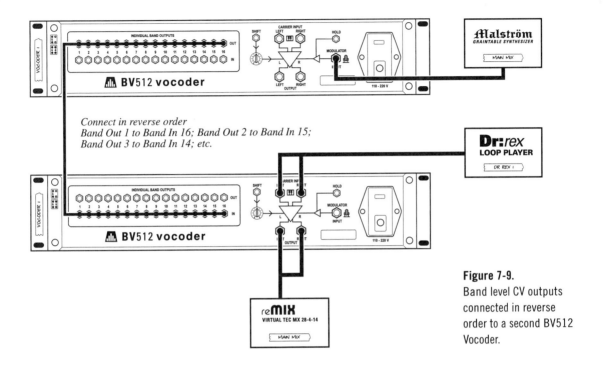

Connect in reverse order
Band Out 1 to Band In 16; Band Out 2 to Band In 15;
Band Out 3 to Band In 14; etc.

Figure 7-9.
Band level CV outputs connected in reverse order to a second BV512 Vocoder.

style vocoder example earlier in this chapter demonstrated one use of routing band CV signals, and the following examples demonstrate a few other applications.

Reverse Band Modulation

Using two BV512 Vocoders set to a band count of 16 or greater, a reverse band modulation can be configured by connecting the Band levels outputs in reverse order to a second BV512. The first vocoder analyzes the modulator audio and generates band level CV signals. The second vocoder filters are modulated by the incoming CV signals, and the carrier signal is processed in reverse.

- In an empty rack, create a mixer.
- Bypass auto-routing and create a Malström Graintable Synthesizer.
- Set the Malström osc A waveform to "Sawtooth*16."

Vocoder & Reverse Vocoder Sections
- Bypass auto-routing and create two BV512 Digital Vocoders. Rename them to "Reverse" and "Main."
- In reverse order, connect all 16 individual band level outputs from the Main BV512 to the individual band level inputs on the Reverse BV512. In other words, connect band out 1 to band in 16, band out 2 to band in 15, band out 3 to band in 14, etc.

• Adjust the Reverse BV512 as follows:

Reverse BV512 Vocoder Settings	
mode	vocoder
band count	32
hold	off
attack	0
decay	30
shift	10
HF emphasis	32
dry/wet	127

Adjust the Main BV512 as follows:

Main BV512 Vocoder Settings	
mode	vocoder
band count	16
hold	off
attack	0
decay	40
shift	0
HF emphasis	64
dry/wet	127

• Connect the Malström audio outputs to the Reverse BV512 carrier inputs.
• Connect the Reverse BV512 carrier outputs to the mixer channel 1 inputs.

Modulator Signal Source
• Bypass auto-routing and create a Dr.REX Loop Player.
• Load the ReCycle loop "Rnb29_Sweet_080_eLAB.rx2" from the Reason Factory
  Sound Bank\Dr Rex Drum Loops\RnB HipHop directory.
• Copy the REX slice data to the Dr.REX 1 sequencer track.
• Set the Dr.REX master level to 127.
• Connect the Dr.REX left audio output to the Main BV512 modulator input.
• Run the sequence.

The Malström is used as a carrier source which is processed by this configuration.
In order to hear the reverse band modulation, route MIDI to the Malström and
play some chords on a MIDI controller as the sequence plays.

Chapter 8
Delay Effects

Delays are traditionally used to generate echoes and induce a sense of space in a mix, but digital delays are the fundamental unit for a very large number of effects, ranging from simple echoing to flanging and complex reverberation effects. The DDL-1 Digital Delay Line, the CF-101 Chorus/Flanger, and the RV-7 and RV7000 reverbs are all time-based effects processors that use delay in some form. When using any time-based effect, keep in mind that the effect doubles whatever signal is already introduced into the mix. Delay effects can add density to a sparsely orchestrated track, but can overwhelm a mix that is already rich with sounds.

The DDL-1 Digital Delay Line is Reason's all-purpose digital delay. It's ideal for basic delay effects as well as tempo-synchronous effects. The RV7000 Advanced Reverb also has delay algorithms, which include features for making interesting stereophonic delay effects. This chapter will focus on some general applications of the delays. In a later chapter we'll go into more detail about delay used in reverberation.

The CF-101 Chorus/Flanger unit uses very short delays to create lush stereo effects. The principles behind short delays will be discussed below, but chorusing and flanging applications of the CF-101 will be described in a later chapter.

Phase Shifting

When signals are delayed by very short amounts — no greater than 1ms — a phenomenon called phase shifting occurs. When the shifted signal is combined with the original signal, it causes phase cancellation of certain overtones. Comb filters rely on this type of phase cancellation.

The concept of wave phase comes from trigonometry. It refers to the momentary position of a wave in relation to its total cycle (wavelength). Phase is measured in terms of angles (radians) of a circle, or in degrees of arc. A complete cycle around the circle represents a full cycle of the wave. A single cycle of a 250Hz sine wave is four milliseconds

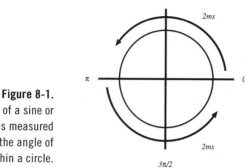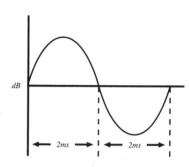

Figure 8-1.
The phase of a sine or cosine wave is measured in terms of the angle of arc within a circle.

long. At 0ms, the wave starts at 0 (2π) radians. At 1ms from the start of the wave, the cycle peaks at π/2 radians (90 degrees). At 2ms, half the cycle has passed, and the phase is π radians (180 degrees). After 3ms, the sine wave reaches the trough at 3π/2 radians (270 degrees), and the wave cycle completes at 2π radians after 4ms.

Normally, a wave will start at the beginning of the cycle at 0 (2π) radians, however a delay can offset the start time so that the phase is shifted relative to the original signal. Delaying the 250Hz sine wave by 2ms will offset the phase by π radians relative to the original, at which point the delayed signal will be out of phase. When the delayed signal is combined with the original, the two will cancel each other out, resulting in silence. Since most sounds consist of a number of partials (sine waves at various frequencies), some of the partials are likely to be out of phase while others are in phase.

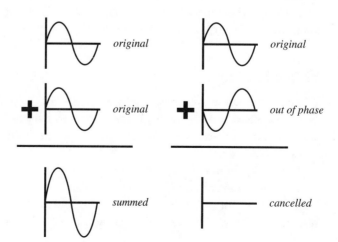

Figure 8-2.
A 250Hz sine wave summed with 2ms delay causes the waves to be out of phase, resulting in cancellation.

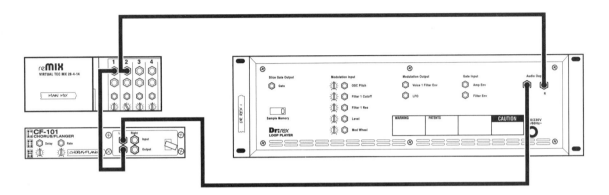

Figure 8-3.
An audio signal split into
parallel signals. One
signal is connected
directly to the mixer, and
the other is delayed
through the CF-101.

Very Short Delay

The heart of the CF-101 is digital delay. Chorusing and flanging effects are based on very short delay times, ranging from 1ms to 20ms. When the modulation and feedback parameters are disabled, the CF-101 becomes a digital delay. In the example below, a Dr.REX loop provides the audio which demonstrates this effect. Panning the input channels to the far stereo extremes demonstrates how the very short delay creates a subtle stereo widening effect.

• In an empty rack, create a mixer.
• Bypass auto-routing and create a Dr.REX Loop Player.
• Load the ReCycle loop "Trh22_Pharzyde_110_eLAB.rx2" from the Reason Factory Sound Bank\Dr Rex Drum Loops\Abstract HipHop directory.
• Copy the REX slice data to the Dr.REX 1 sequencer track.
• Connect the Dr.REX right audio output to the mixer channel 2 left input.
• Bypass auto-routing and create a CF-101 Chorus/Flanger.
• Connect the Dr.REX left audio output to the CF-101 left input.
• Connect the CF-101 left output to the mixer channel 1 left input.
• Set the CF-101 delay to 36 and LFO mod amount to 0, and enable send mode.
• Run the sequence.

Setting the delay time between 1 and 6 will create a comb filter effect, which is a normal phenomenon with short delays. With a delay time of 0 the output signal actually decreases, which indicates that phase cancellation is occurring. To hear more extreme comb filtering, mute mixer channel 2 and pan mixer channel 1 to 0. Adjust the feedback to below –60 or above 55.

Fattening

Delay times in the range between 1ms and 30ms can be useful to fatten up a sound. A dry signal and a delayed signal are usually panned hard left and right for really wide stereo placement, but these signals can be panned anywhere in between to control the width. Feedback should be set at zero when using the DDL-1 for fattening signals, as otherwise comb filtering will occur. The next few examples demonstrate how to use the DDL-1 to create the fattening effect.

Basic Fattening

This technique is useful for moving signals away from the center of a mix, and while it's most useful with signals with high frequencies, it can be used for bass fattening as well. As the sequence plays, switch the DDL-1 into bypass mode to hear the loop without the fattening. It's obvious that the original signal is monophonic, as the loop plays from dead center in the stereo field. Try panning the input signals to different positions, and keep the settings balanced — for instance, channel 1 pan to –33 and channel 2 pan to 32.

- Start with an empty rack, and create a mixer.
- Bypass auto-routing and create a Dr.REX Loop Player.
- Load the ReCycle file "130_Cycle_mLp_eLAB.rx2" from the Factory Sound Bank from the Music Loops\Variable Tempo (rex2)\Uptempo Loops directory.
- Copy the REX data to the Dr.REX 1 sequencer track.
- Bypass auto-routing and connect the Dr.REX left output to the mixer channel 1 left input.
- Bypass auto-routing and create a DDL-1 Digital Delay Line.

Figure 8-4.
Using a DDL-1 as an insert effect, the right audio output from a Dr.REX Loop Player is delayed by 12ms. The left output from the Dr.REX is connected directly to a mixer.

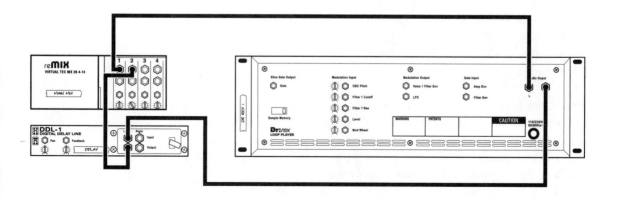

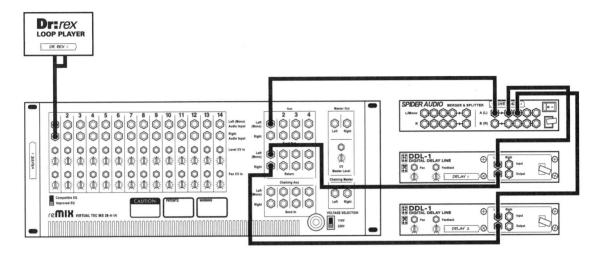

Figure 8-5.
An aux send split to two
DDL-1 delays. The delays
are connected to the aux
return inputs.

- Set the DDL delay time to 12ms and set feedback to 0.
- Connect the Dr.REX right output to the DDL-1 left input.
- Bypass auto-routing and connect the DDL-1 left output to the mixer channel
  2 left input.
- Pan mixer channel 1 to –64 and mixer channel 2 to 63.
- Run the sequence.

Stereo Fattening Send Effect

This example is a basic delay-based fattening technique implemented as a send
effect. A mono send signal is split and directed to two DDL-1 Delays with different
time settings. It's not quite as colored as using a chorus, yet the delayed signal creates a dense stereophonic effect. The signal is tripled by the use of two delays mixed
with the source signal.

- Start with an empty rack, and create a mixer.
- Create a Dr.REX Loop Player.
- Load the ReCycle file "130_Cycle_mLp_eLAB.rx2" from the Factory Sound
  Bank from the Music Loops\Variable Tempo (rex2)\Uptempo Loops directory.
- Copy the REX data to the Dr.REX 1 sequencer track.
- Bypass auto-routing and create a Spider Audio Merger & Splitter.
- Connect the mixer aux 1 send left output to the Spider split A input.
- Bypass auto-routing and create two DDL-1 Digital Delay Lines.
- Connect Spider split A out 1 to Delay 1's left input.
- Connect Spider split A out 2 to Delay 2's left input.
- Connect Delay 1's left output to the mixer aux return 1 left input.

- Connect Delay 2's left output to the mixer aux return 1 right input.
- Set Delay 1's delay time to 11ms and feedback to 0.
- Set Delay 2's delay time to 7 ms and feedback to 0.
- Run the sequence.

As the sequence plays, raise the mixer channel 1 aux 1 send to hear the loop processed with the fattening send effect.

Doubling and Slapback

Short delays become perceptible to the human ear as discrete events at about 20ms. At about 100ms they start sounding like distinct echoes. Doubling and slapback are useful delay effects that can be created with delay times that fall into this 20–100ms range. Doubling is more commonly created by recording two different performances of the same part, but a delay with a setting in the range of 20–50ms can be used to create the "doubled" track. Slapback is a common effect applied to vocal tracks, where the signal is processed through a delay with a setting of 60–100ms. Slapback delay times are usually tweaked so they fit with the groove of a track and occur close to a 32nd-note offset.

The DDL-1 can be used to calculate delay times in milliseconds based on the tempo of the track. First set the DDL-1 delay time to 1 step, then switch the units to ms. The number that appears on the time display is duration of a sixteenth-note in milliseconds. Useful slapback settings are usually half this amount.

The dry/wet balance is important when using slapback. The effect should be very subtle, so the delay sounds like a ghost note. Try experimenting with shifting the delay time up or down to change the feel of the groove.

Doubled Guitar

This example uses a multi-sampled guitar to demonstrate doubling. Doubling and slapback both are really effective with acoustic sounds because they create a synthetic feeling. Using these effects on synthesized sounds can easily muck things up, unless the synth envelopes have fast decay times and low sustain levels. Loud sustained synth sounds don't really benefit from doubling.

- Start with an empty rack, and create a mixer.
- Bypass auto-routing and create an NN19 Sampler.
- Load the patch "ACGUITAR.smp" from the Reason Factory Sound Bank\NN19 Sampler Patches\Guitar directory.
- Bypass auto-routing and connect the NN19 left output to the mixer channel 1 left input.

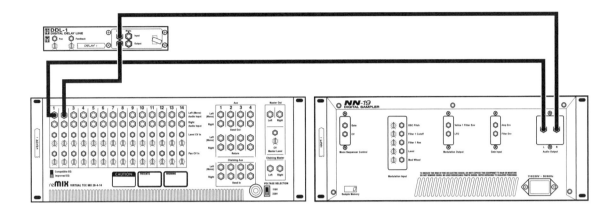

Figure 8-6.
NN19 left channel
connected to mixer
channel 1. NN19 right
channel processed
through a DDL-1 and
connected to mixer
channel 2.

- Bypass auto-routing and create a DDL-1 Delay.
- Set the delay time to 37ms and feedback to 0.
- Connect the NN19 right output to the DDL-1 left input.
- Bypass auto-routing and connect the DDL-1 left output to the mixer channel 2 left input.
- Set the mixer channel 1 pan to –64 and mixer channel 2 pan to 63.
- Play notes from a keyboard controller to hear the guitar samples doubled.

The guitar doubling effect is similar to fattening (described earlier), but the longer delay gives the impression of two different string plucks. The shorter delays for fattening still sound like one pluck. Try adjusting the delay to longer and shorter times to hear the difference.

Echoes

Delay times longer than 100 milliseconds used with a moderate amount of feedback can be used to create spatial effects and rhythmic delay effects. The delay algorithms in the RV7000 Reverb and the DDL-1 Digital Delay Line both have synchronization settings so that delay time can be set in relation to the song tempo. Usually tempo-synchronized delays are placed fairly high in the mix so that they are perceived as separate events. A single delay can be used with the dry signal panned to one channel and the delay panned to the other, but multi-tap and ping-pong delays can be created for more complex delay effects.

Multi-Tap Delay
A multi-tap delay is usually several delays in series. The connection between

each delay is tapped and routed to a mixer input channel. This example uses six DDL-1 delay lines connected in series. Each of the tapped delay signals can be attenuated and panned to create a cascading delay effect. The send effect is routed through the same mixer as the combined delay tap signals on the aux 4 bus. The aux 4 will provide feedback control from any of the incoming tap signals.

- In an empty rack, create a mixer.
- Set the mixer channel 1 aux send 1 amount to 68.
- Create a Redrum Drum Computer.
- On Redrum channel 1, load the sample "Clavinet_eLAB.aif" from the Reason Factory Soundbank\Other Samples\Chords-Phrases-Pads-Stabs directory.
- Select Redrum channel 1 and program a medium hit on step 1.
- Bypass auto-routing and create another mixer.
- Rename Mixer 2 "Multitap."
- Set the Multitap mixer channel 14 fader level to 0, aux 4 send to 100, and enable pre-fade for the aux send.

Figure 8-7.
Six DDL-1 delays connected in series. The right outputs are used as taps and combined in a mixer.

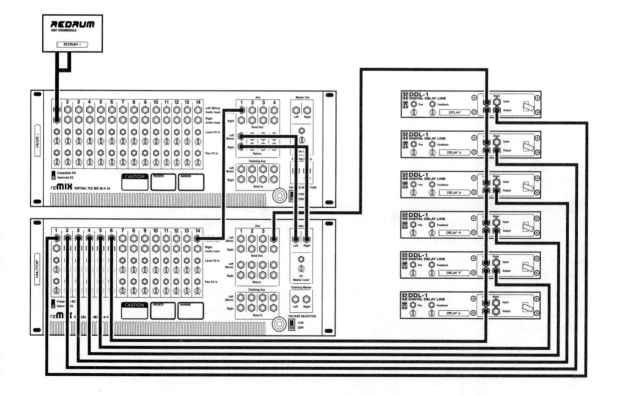

- Connect the Mixer 1 aux send 1 left socket to the Multitap mixer channel 14 left input.
- Connect the Multitap mixer master outputs to the Mixer 1 aux return 1 inputs.
- Bypass auto-routing and create a DDL-1.
- Set the delay time to 1 step and feedback to 0.
- Duplicate the DDL-1 five times. Rename the duplicates "Delay 2," "Delay 3," etc.
- Connect the Multitap mixer aux 4 send left to the Delay 1 DDL-1 left input.
- Bypass auto-routing, and connect the Delay 1 left output to the Delay 2 left input. Continue this procedure for each delay up to Delay 6.
- Connect the Delay 1 right output to the Multitap mixer channel 1 left input. Connect the Delay 2 right output to the Multitap channel 2 left input, and repeat through Delay 5. On the last delay, Delay 6, connect the left output to the Multitap mixer channel 6 left input.
- Set the pan on the Multitap mixer as follows: channel 1: –64; channel 2: –29; channel 3: –12; channel 4: 11; channel 5: 28; channel 6: 63.
- Set the Multitap mixer channel 5 aux 4 send to 49.
- Run the sequence.

Cross-Feedback Delays

This effect configuration is also known as a "ping-pong" delay because the delay signals move across the stereo field like a ping-pong ball skipping back and forth across a table. This effect uses the DDL-1 step delay mode to create a rhythmic ping-pong delay effect. Cabled feedback is attenuated and routed between two delay devices. The feedback signal from one delay is sent to the second delay, and the delay from the second delay is fed back to the first delay.

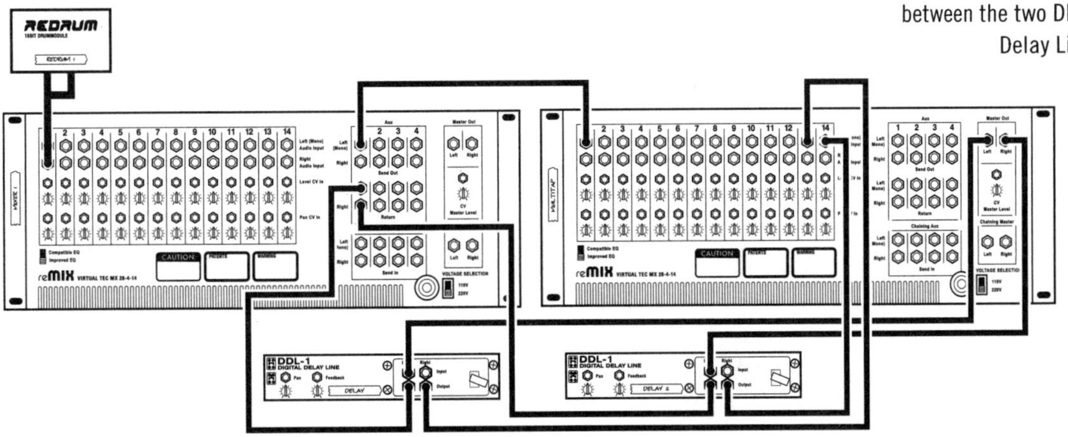

Figure 8-8.
Feedback cabled
between the two DDL-1
Delay Lines.

- Start with an empty rack.
- Create a mixer and a rename it "Main."
- Set the Main mixer channel 1 aux send 1 to 81, and pan to 63.
- Create a Redrum Drum Computer.
- On Redrum channel 1, load the sample "Clp_Beltram.wav" from the Reason Factory Soundbank\Redrum Drum Kits\xclusive drums-sorted\04_Claps directory.
- Select Redrum channel 1 and program a medium hit on step 1.
- Bypass auto-routing and create another mixer.
- Rename the second mixer "Cross FB."
- Pan the Cross FB mixer channel 1 to –64, channel 13 to 63, and channel 14 to –64.
- Set the Cross FB mixer channel 13 and channel 14 level faders to 63.
- Bypass auto-routing and create two DDL-1 Delays.
- Rename the DDL-1 Delays "Left" and "Right."
- Set the feedback to 0 on both the Left DDL-1 and Right DDL-1.
- Connect a mono signal from the Main mixer aux send 1 left to input channel 1 on the Cross FB mixer.
- Connect the Cross FB mixer master out left to the Left DDL-1 left input.
- Connect the Cross FB mixer master out right to the Right DDL-1 left input.
- Connect the Left DDL-1 left output to the Main mixer aux return input left.
- Connect the Left DDL-1 right output to the Cross FB mixer input channel 13 left input.
- Connect the Right DDL-1 left output to the Main mixer aux return input right.
- Connect the Right DDL-1 right output to the Cross FB mixer input channel 14 left input.
- Run the Redrum pattern.

Ping-Pong Delay

The RV7000 Advanced Reverb has a multi-tap delay algorithm that is different from using a series of DDL-1 delay modules. The multi-tap algorithm has damping and diffusion features that make the echoes decay naturally. Unlike the DDL-1, the RV7000 is a stereo effects processor, unless a monophonic signal is connected to the input. For this example, the ping-pong delay is more effective when the RV7000 is connected in mono.

- Start with an empty rack, and create a mixer.
- Set the mixer channel 1 aux send to 81, and pan to –64.
- Create an RV7000 Advanced Reverb.
- Disconnect the cable from the RV7000 right input.
- Open the RV7000 Remote Programmer.
- Set the RV7000 algorithm to multi-tap, turn tempo sync on, and set the diffu-

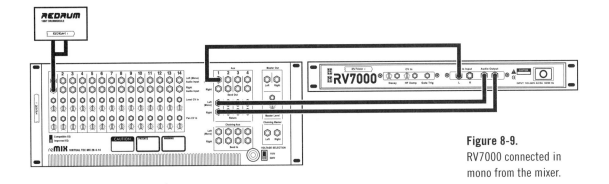

Figure 8-9.
RV7000 connected in mono from the mixer.

sion to 0, LF damp to 1,000Hz, tap 1 delay time to 6/16, tap 2 delay time to 3/16, and repeat tap repeat time to 6/16.

- Create a Redrum Drum Computer.
- On Redrum channel 1, load the sample "Clp_Photek.WAV" from the Reason Factory Soundbank\Redrum Drum Kits\xclusive drums-sorted\04_Claps directory.
- Select Redrum channel 1 and program a medium hit on step 1.
- Run the sequence.

Long Feedback Effects

With repeating echoes, the output levels increase as the feedback is combined with the input signal. The RV7000 decay parameter controls the feedback amount for the delay algorithms. A decay setting of 0 means no feedback, while a setting of 127 is 100% feedback. The next few examples use delays with high feedback settings. Delay parameters can easily be automated using sequencer tracks, but these examples use Matrix pattern sequencers to create rhythmic patterns of feedback control.

Gated Echoes

This effect uses a Matrix-controlled mixer channel to gate the effect send to a RV7000 echo delay. The echo delay effect has a long decay setting, and short keyed gate events will send bursts of signal to the RV7000. The master output from the "Send Gate" mixer is the source for the RV7000 echo. The effect send is going to be monophonic, so only use the master output left. The ReCycle drum loop provides the audio signal source for this example. The send signal on the aux send 1 bus will be connected to the Matrix-controlled gate.

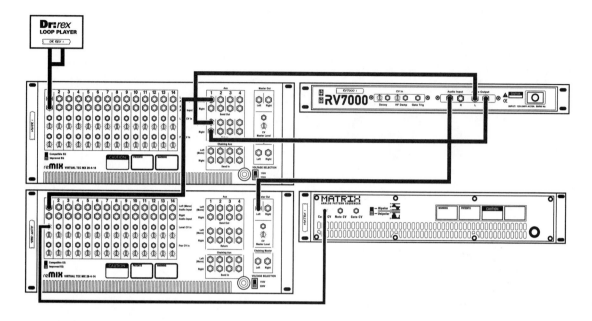

Figure 8-10.
A Matrix gate controlling the RV7000 input signal.

- Start with an empty rack, and set the tempo to 92 BPM.
- Create a mixer.
- Create a Dr.REX Loop Player.
- Load the ReCycle loop "Rnb14_Original_100_eLAB.rx2" from the Reason Factory Sound Bank\Dr Rex Drum Loops\RnB HipHop directory.
- Copy the REX slice data to the Dr.REX 1 sequencer track.
- Bypass auto-routing and create a second mixer.
- Rename Mixer 2 "Send Gate."
- Set Send Gate mixer channel 1 fader level to 0.
- Create a Matrix Pattern Sequencer.
- Connect the curve CV output to the Send Gate mixer channel 1 level CV input.
- Program a curve CV event on step 13 with a value of about 65%.
- Bypass auto-routing and create an RV7000 Advanced Reverb.
- Connect the Mixer 1 aux send 1 left to the Send Gate mixer channel 1 left.
- Turn Mixer 1 channel 1's aux send 1 up to 70.
- Bypass auto-routing and connect the Send Gate mixer master output left to the RV7000 audio input left.
- Connect the RV7000 audio outputs to the Mixer 1 aux return 1 inputs.
- Open the RV7000 Remote Programmer and set the parameters according to the following chart:

RV7000 Parameters	
EQ	Off
Gate	Off
Decay	108
HF Damp	0
Hi EQ	0
Dry/Wet	127
Algorithm	Echo
Echo Time	1/16
Diffusion	58
Tempo Sync	On
LF Damp	80
Spread	127
Predelay	0

• Run the sequence. The Matrix will gate the echo send, causing the snare on beat 4 to echo.

Feedback Hold Effect

The feedback parameter of a DDL-1 can be automated by a CV input. When the CV setting is 0 there is no feedback, and when the CV signal is 127, feedback is 100%. Full feedback can be used to create a repeating hold effect in which a sam-

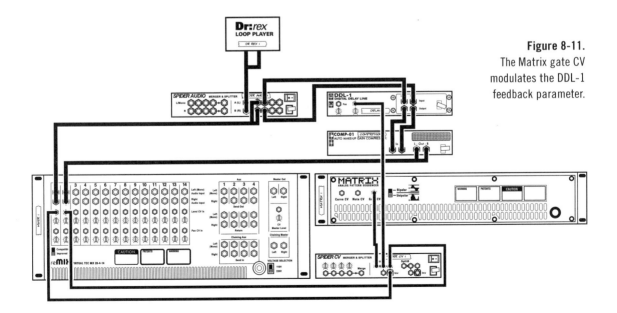

Figure 8-11.
The Matrix gate CV modulates the DDL-1 feedback parameter.

ple is looped. Using a gate CV signal from a Matrix, a feedback hold pattern can be used to create stuttering sample textures.

- Begin with an empty rack, and set the tempo to 75 BPM.
- Create a mixer and set the channel 2 fader level to 0.
- Bypass auto-routing and create a Dr.REX Loop Player.
- Load the ReCycle loop "Dub06_PercStix_070_eLAB.rx2" from the Reason Factory Sound Bank\Dr Rex Drum Loops\Dub directory.
- Copy the REX slice data to the Dr.REX 1 sequencer track.
- Set the Dr.REX master level to 128.
- Create a Spider Audio Merger & Splitter.
- Connect the Dr.REX audio outputs to the Spider Audio splitter A & B inputs.
- Connect the Spider splitter output 1 to the mixer channel 1 inputs.
- Bypass auto-routing and create a DDL-1 Digital Delay Line.
- Connect the Spider Audio splitter output 2 to the DDL-1 inputs.
- Connect the DDL-1 output to the mixer channel 2 inputs.
- Set the DDL-1 delay time to 50ms, and feedback to 0.
- Insert a Comp-01 Compressor/Limiter between the DDL-1 and mixer channel 2.
- Set the Comp-01 ratio to 94, threshold to 40, attack to 0, and release to 64.
- Create a Matrix Pattern Sequencer.
- Bypass auto-routing and create a Spider CV Merger & Splitter.
- Connect the Matrix gate CV output to the Spider CV split A input.
- Connect Spider CV split A output 1 to the DDL-1 feedback CV input.
- Set the DDL-1 feedback CV trim to 127.
- Connect Spider CV split A output 2 to the mixer channel 2 level CV input.
- Set the mixer channel 2 level CV trim to 30.
- Connect Spider CV split A output 4/inv to the mixer channel 1 level CV input.
- Set the mixer channel 1 level CV trim to 127.
- Program the following on Matrix pattern A1:

Matrix Pattern

Step	1	2	3	4	5	6	7	8	9	10	11	12	13	14	15	16
Curve																
Note																
Gate			TH	TH	TH		TH	TH			TH			TH	TH	

- Run the sequence.

Chapter 9
Reverb

Digital reverbs are used to simulate room acoustics. Reverb fills the gaps between notes with a little bit of sound, giving recorded music a more natural feel. The effect should be subtle and just loud enough to smooth out the gaps. Reverbs are also used as an element of sound design, to give a special character to single sounds within a mix. Using reverberation to enhance a mixdown or add a spatial element to a sound is ultimately a matter of taste.

There are some general rules when applying reverb, but breaking these rules can also be very interesting. It really depends on the style of the music being created. If reverb is applied to vocal samples, string sections, or acoustic drums, then using the traditional techniques for realistic ambience may be a good idea. If you're trying to create the sound of the listener floating in the middle of space, then atypical reverberation techniques would be more useful. An example of unconventional reverb can be found in dub and reggae styles, where the sound of a spring reverb goes hand in hand with the style of music.

Reason has two reverb devices, the RV-7 Digital Reverb and the RV7000 Advanced Reverb. The RV7000 is a far superior device to the RV-7, and given the choice between the two, most people will use the RV7000. On occasion, you might need a reverb that doesn't sound high-quality, in which case the RV-7 is perfect. Along with having a superior sound, the RV7000 is more complicated to program, having parameters for various aspects of reverberation. This section mainly covers the features of the RV7000, but many of the principles can also be applied to the RV-7.

The main parameter for both the RV-7 and RV7000 is the *algorithm* setting. The algorithm is the set of mathematical operations that control what happens to the signal. User inputs to the algorithm include such parameters as decay time, reflection diffusion, and so on, which create the reverberation effect. When approaching the mixdown of a track, it helps to have a feeling for the type of space you want your music to occupy. Algorithms are typically named after the space being simulated, and having a mental picture of the acoustic space will make algorithm choice simple.

Acoustic Space Simulation

The RV7000 has several algorithms that are used primarily for simulating the acoustics of various structures. The Arena algorithm creates the ambience of a very large empty structure with many reflective surfaces. The other extreme is the Small Space algorithm, which simulates the sound of a closet or even a metal box. The Hall algorithm emulates the characteristics of concert halls and other long spaces with high ceilings. The Room algorithm simulates the characteristics of rooms with lower ceilings and less volume than a hall. Hall and Room reverbs are the most common for acoustic space simulation, while Arena and Small Space reverbs are more suited for creating special ambient effects.

Reverberation effects incorporate dozens or even hundreds of delays to emulate the reflection of sounds of an acoustic space. Two types of echoes are created by the Hall and Room algorithms — early reflections and reverberation. Early reflections are short digital delays panned around the stereo field to simulate the echoes heard directly from surfaces in the room. Reverberation is the sound of echoes that bounce off of the surfaces many times before returning to the listener. The delay and pan patterns of early reflection and reverberation are controlled by the room shape parameter. Each shape has different delay characteristics. When you set the size to the maximum setting, the early reflection time and amplitude levels can be seen on the graphic time line representation on the RV7000 Remote Programmer.

Size & Decay

The size and decay parameters are analogous to the delay time and feedback parameters of the DDL-1 Digital Delay. The room size parameter determines the delay time of early reflections and the length of the reverberation. Higher size settings will have slightly longer delay times, and the time between early reflection echoes becomes a bit more distinct. The decay parameter controls feedback of the delays in the reverb algorithm to control the duration of the reverb tail. Just as with the DDL-1 feedback control, longer decay settings will increase the duration of the decay.

As a general rule for reverb applied to drum sounds, the size and decay para-

Figure 9-1.
The early reflections and reverberation parts of the hall algorithm.

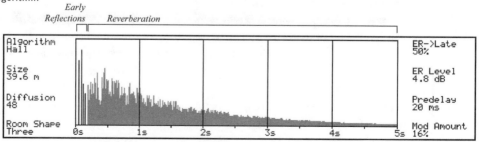

meters are usually adjusted so that the reverb tail from a snare hit does not overlap and obscure the attack of the next kick drum. This concept can be applied to vocals and solo instruments as well, so the reverb tail masks out silence between words and syllables or notes without intruding on the next word or note. This means the tempo of the track will affect the size and decay time of the reverberation that should be applied to drums.

Damping

The materials used in building construction have a tendency to filter high frequencies when sound is reflected. A harder wall surface will reflect more highs, while a softer surface will absorb highs. The damping parameter causes the algorithm to filter frequencies from the reflections. The HF Damp knob controls the rate at which high frequencies decay, which simulates the nature of reflections in acoustic spaces. If no HF damping is applied, the reflections and reverb will sound more metallic and have a bright sound. Some of the algorithms have low-frequency damping parameters, which cause low frequencies to decay faster than the high frequencies.

Predelay and ER->Late

Human perception defines space in terms of the delay time and attenuation — long delays should sound softer than short delays. The shorter and louder the delay, the smaller the acoustic space feels. Under normal atmospheric conditions at sea level, sound travels at 342 meters per second. This is the fundamental constant for calculating the initial reflection time of a reverb algorithm. The length of an echo from a wall 34 meters away is about 200 milliseconds — 100ms for the sound to travel to the wall, and another 100ms for the echo to return.

For natural-sounding reverberation, a slight delay occurs before the reverb is heard. This is controlled by the predelay setting. The predelay setting can control how far away a sound seems to be in a room. If the sound is distant from the listener, it will be heard only a few milliseconds ahead of the reverb, but if the sound is close, reverb will be heard later than the original sound.

The ER->Late parameter offsets the time between early reflections and the reverb. This controls the sensation of the proximity to the walls of a room. Sounds that are distant from the listener's perspective will be heard about the same time as the early reflections, and the offset should be set near 0%. Sounds close to the listener's position will have a slight delay between the early reflections and the reverberation, so the ER->Late parameter should be set higher.

Diffusion

The density of the reverb reflections is controlled by the diffusion parameter. Lower diffusion settings will make the reflections sound more distinct, while a higher diffusion setting will make the individual reflections less discernible and more dense. In most cases, high levels of diffusion are appropriate since the reflections are smoothed.

Setting the diffusion to zero is the best way to understand the different room shapes and the reflections in the algorithms. Set the decay to zero, HF Damp to zero, and size to maximum. Route a very sparse and slow drum loop through the reverb and start modifying the room shape parameter. With no diffusion applied to the reverb, the distinct echo characteristics of each room shape become very apparent. This is a good way to determine which room shape is appropriate for a track. Once the shape has been selected, the diffusion setting can be adjusted back up.

Modulation

The Mod Amount parameter controls a modulation feature that adds a chorusing character to the reverberation. Modulation seems to affect the reverb tail more than the initial delays of the algorithm and adds a variation that gives the reverb tail a smoother, more natural decay sound. With long sustained notes, the modulation can be heard, as if a subtle chorus effect has been inserted in front of the RV7000. Keep the mod setting low to minimize this effect. The effect is barely noticeable with drums and percussion.

Plate & Spring Reverbs

The plate and spring algorithms simulate electro-mechanical devices that themselves were used to simulate reverberation. A plate reverb is large sheet of metal suspended in an isolated room or box. Amplified signals are connected to a driver coil attached to the metal sheet, causing it to vibrate. A microphone or pickup would capture the sound of the vibration. The plate reverb is the descendent of the spring reverb, which works on a similar principle using a metallic spring. Audio signals would induce vibrations in the spring, which were captured by a pickup.

These types of reverb were used so often in the history of recorded music that their sound is often desired for productions. Plate reverb is often added to vocal tracks because it does not have the hard reflective characteristics induced by room and hall algorithms. The echoing effect of discrete reflections can add a type of chorusing that will distract the listener from an outstanding vocal performance. Because plate reverbs do not have early reflection characteristics, the effect is very smooth and ideal for long spatial effects as well.

Infinite Reverb

Using electronic reverberation, one can create acoustic environments not found in the real world. One example of this is the "infinite" reverb, which is a reverb with an infinite decay time. Any of the reverberation algorithms can be used for

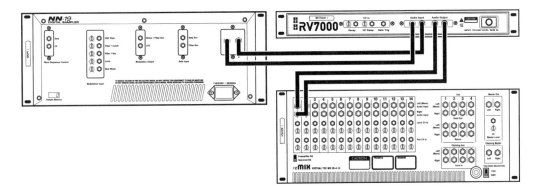

Figure 9-2.
In this patch, the
plate reverb decay is
set to 127.

this effect, but this example uses the plate reverb because it has a parameter to control low-frequency damping. Instead of using the decay, the high-frequency and low-frequency damping features will be used to attenuate the reverb tail.

- Start with an empty rack, and create a mixer
- Create an NN-XT Advanced Sampler.
- Load the NN-XT patch "InfiniteHit.sxt" from the *Power Tools for Reason* CD NN-XT Patches directory.
- Switch the sequencer to edit mode and view the NN-XT 1 track key lanes.
- Pencil in a C3 note event with a one-measure duration on measure 1, and do the same on measure 5.
- Insert an RV7000 Advanced Reverb between the NN-XT audio outputs and the mixer channel 1 inputs.
- Open the RV7000 Remote Programmer and set the parameters according to the following chart:

RV7000 "Infinite Reverb" Parameters	
EQ	Off
Gate	Off
Decay	127
HF Damp	0
Hi EQ	0
Dry/Wet	81
Algorithm	Plate
LF Damp	20Hz
Predelay	75ms

- Run the sequence.

As the sequence plays, you'll hear a dense lingering reverb tail from the initial sample hit. While the sequence plays, adjust the HF Damp parameter up to 127 and listen as high frequencies decay while the low frequencies continue to trail. This creates a dark and cavernous-sounding ambient space. HF Damp is similar to an equalizer or lowpass filter in that it cuts the high frequencies of the reflections in the reverb algorithm.

The LF Damp parameter of the plate algorithm is similar to HF Damp in that it filters low frequencies from the reverb tail. Set the HF Damp back to 0 and increase the LF Damp parameter to 93Hz. The density is gone, which gives the reverb an airy quality, as if it's ascending.

Dub-Style Spring Reverb

This effect uses a DDL-1 in combination with the RV7000 spring reverb algorithm to create a rhythmic echo and spring reverb effect. The eighth-note triplet delay time adds the syncopated rhythmic element found in dub and reggae music. One modification that can be made to this configuration is to connect the DDL-1 right output to the mixer aux return 2 input. Use the aux return knob to mix the level of the delayed signal.

Figure 9-3.
Delay inserted before the RV7000.

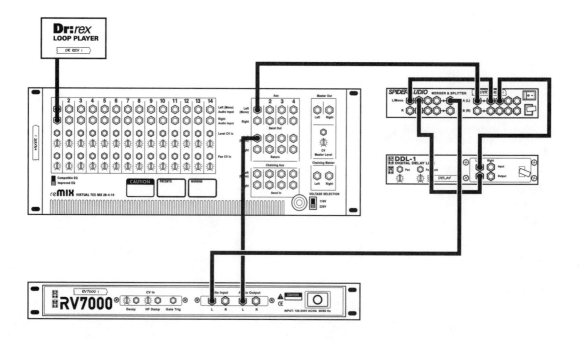

• Start with an empty rack, and set the tempo to 72 BPM.
• Create a mixer.
• Set the mixer channel 1 aux send 1 amount to 59.
• Create a Dr.REX Loop Player.
• Load the ReCycle loop "Dub04_Scientist_070_eLab.rx2" from the Reason Factory Sound Bank\Dr Rex Drum Loops\Dub directory.
• Copy the REX slice data to the Dr.REX 1 sequencer track.
• Create a Spider Audio Merger & Splitter.
• Bypass auto-routing and connect the mixer aux send 1 left output to the Spider Audio split A input.
• Connect the Spider Audio split A out 1 to the Spider Audio L/mono merge input 1.
• Bypass auto-routing and create a DDL-1 Digital Delay Line.
• Connect the Spider Audio split A out 2 to the DDL-1 left input.
• Connect the DDL-1 left output to the Spider Audio merge L/mono input 2.
• Set the DDL-1 delay time to 1 step, step length to 1/8T, feedback to 84, and dry/wet balance to 87.
• Bypass auto-routing and create an RV7000 Advanced Reverb.
• Connect the Spider Audio merge L/mono output to the RV7000 left input.
• Bypass auto-routing and connect the RV7000 left output to the mixer aux return 1 left input.
• Enable EQ on the RV7000 and set the decay to 82 and HF Damp to 18.
• Open the RV7000 Remote Programmer panel and program the following:

RV7000 Spring Reverb Parameters	
EQ	On
Gate	Off
Decay	82
HF Damp	18
Hi EQ	0
Dry/wet	127
Algorithm	Spring
Length	.37m
Diffusion	127
Disp Freq	873Hz
LF Damp	373Hz
Stereo	Off
Predelay	24ms
Disp Amt.	100%

• Switch the RV7000 Remote Programmer to EQ edit mode.

• Set the EQ parametric gain (not the low gain) to 8.9dB, parametric frequency to 1104Hz, and Q to 0.5.
• Run the sequence.

Gated Reverb

Reverb can add a lot of density to the sound of drums. By using the right algorithm settings you can create massive arena drums that have a lot of power. One problem with this technique is that the sound of the drums will overpower everything else in the mix, and the reverb tail from one hit will obscure the attack of the next drum hit. A method made popular with recordings in the '80s is to apply a noise gate after the reverb output. The noise gate threshold settings are set at a high enough level to cut off the tail of the reverb, while the dense reverberation in the early part of the decay is retained, giving a huge sound.

Typically, gated reverb should not be applied as a send effect for all devices. If certain sounds require gated reverb, a second reverb device should be added on a different aux effect bus on the mixer. The gate can be triggered in the conventional manner by carefully setting the threshold and envelope settings, or it can be triggered using gate CV signals from another device. This can be especially useful if you want to create the gated drum sound for Redrum patterns — the gate trigger CV output from a snare sample can be connected to the RV7000 gate trigger input. The reverb gate will open only when a snare drum hit occurs.

Gated Drums

This example demonstrates using the RV7000 as an insert device to create the gated drum sound effect. Using the RV7000 as a mono insert effect allows the effect to be panned in a specific position in the mix, and the sounds processed through the gated reverb will sound like they are down a hallway or a tube.

• Start with an empty rack. Set the tempo to 105 BPM, and set the pattern shuffle to 10.
• Create a mixer.
• Create a Redrum Drum Computer and load the patch "Groovemasters Rock Kit 3.drp" from the Reason Factory Sound Bank\Redrum Drum Kits\Rock Kits directory.
• Set the pan to 0 on Redrum channels 5, 6, and 7.
• Enable shuffle and set the Redrum flam amount to 108.
• Program the following on Redrum pattern A1:

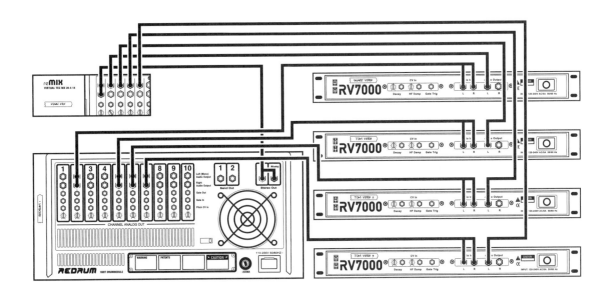

Figure 9-4.
RV7000 reverbs inserted between Redrum channels and mixer inputs.

Redrum Pattern

	1	2	3	4	5	6	7	8	9	10	11	12	13	14	15	16
1	M							M			S				S	
2				M									M			
3																
4																
5	M			M												
6							M			M						
7												S			M	
8	M		M	S	M	S	Sf		M		M	S	M	Sf	M	
9		S						S		S						S
10																

- Bypass auto-routing and create a RV7000 Advanced Reverb. Rename it "Snare Verb."
- Load the patch "ALL 1st Hall" from the Reason Factory Sound Bank\RV7000 Patches directory.
- Connect the Redrum channel 2 outputs to the RV7000 inputs.
- Connect the RV7000 outputs to the mixer channel 2 inputs.
- Set the RV7000 dry/wet mix to 54, and enable the gate.
- Open the RV7000 Remote Programmer and switch to gate edit mode.
- Adjust the gate threshold to −10.5dB and the gate release time to 100ms.

- Bypass auto-routing, create an RV7000 Advanced Reverb, and rename it "Tom Verb 1."
- Load the patch "ALL Small Room" from the Reason Factory Sound Bank\RV7000 Patches directory.
- Connect the Redrum channel 5 outputs to the Tom Verb 1 inputs.
- Connect the Tom Verb 1 left output to mixer channel 3 left input.
- Set the Tom Verb 1 dry/wet mix to 86, and enable the gate.
- Open the Tom Verb 1 Remote Programmer and switch to gate edit mode.
- Adjust the gate threshold to –12.6dB and the gate release time to 100ms.
- Make two duplicates of the Tom Verb 1 RV7000, and rename them "Tom Verb 2" and "Tom Verb 3."
- Connect the Redrum channel 6 outputs to the Tom Verb 2 inputs and the Redrum channel 7 outputs to the Tom Verb 3 inputs.
- Connect the Tom Verb 2 left output to mixer channel 4 left input and the Tom Verb 3 left output to mixer channel 5 left input.
- Set the mixer channel 3 pan to –56, channel 4 pan to –17, and channel 5 pan to 59.
- Run the Redrum pattern.

This patch can be edited in various ways. Try soloing each of the tom channels in the mixer and playing with the reverb settings for it. Switch the toms to gate mode 1 and shorten their length, so that the dry tom sound will also be gated.

Modulated RV7000 Gate & Decay

This example of a gated reverb uses a Matrix Pattern Sequencer to trigger the RV7000 gate. The gate threshold settings are disabled when the trigger source is switched to the MIDI/CV setting.

- Begin with an empty rack, and create a mixer.

Figure 9-5.
Matrix gate CV connected to the RV7000 gate trig CV input.

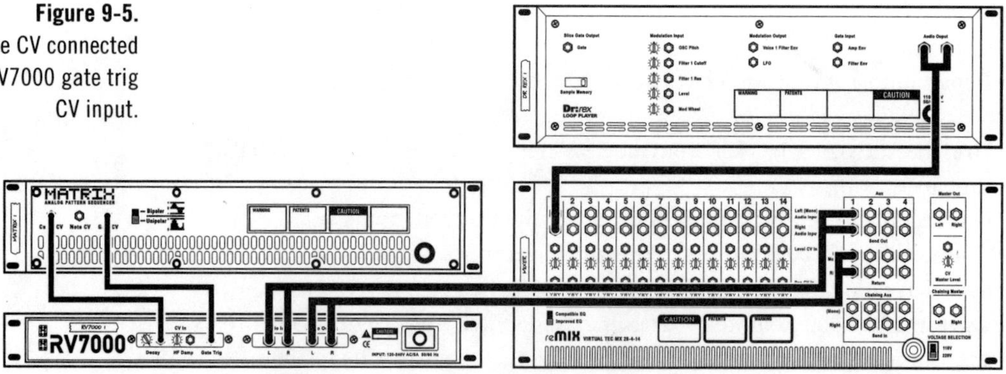

• Create an RV7000 Advanced Reverb and load the patch "DRM AMS PrcPlate.rv7" from the Reason Factory Sound Bank\RV7000 Patches directory.
• Set the RV7000 decay to 0, enable the gate, open the Remote Programmer, and set the gate trig source to MIDI/CV.
• Create a Matrix Pattern Sequencer.
• Verify that the Matrix curve CV is automatically cabled to the RV7000 decay input and that the Matrix gate CV output is connected to the RV7000 gate trig input.
• Set the RV7000 decay CV trim to 127.
• Program the following on Matrix pattern A1:

Matrix Pattern															
Step	1	2	3	4	5	6	7	8	9	10	11	12	13	14	15	16
Curve					128	72	48	0					64	48	32	0
Note																
Gate	TH	TH	TH		TH	TH	TH	TH			TH	TH	TH	TH	TH	

• Create a Dr.REX Loop Player.
• Load the ReCycle loop "Chm07_Skint_130_eLAB.rx2" from the Reason Factory Sound Bank\Dr Rex Drum Loops\Chemical Beats directory.
• Copy the REX slice data to the Dr.REX 1 sequencer track.
• Set the mixer channel 1 aux send 1 to 100.
• Run the sequence.

Reverse Reverb

Reverse reverb is an effect that originated in the '60s. It was originally produced by reversing the playback direction of a tape, sending the tape output (a guitar solo, for instance) into a reverb, and recording the reverb to a new track. Then the tape would be flipped over and played in its normal direction again, causing the reverb tail to appear before each note, growing from silence to a high level.

This effect can't be simulated perfectly in a digital reverb's "reverse" algorithm, but it can be approximated. In a reverse algorithm, the reverb tail gets louder rather than softer.

Reverse Drums

Using the reverse reverb as a send effect, the events from a ReCycle loop are ghosted and delayed by five steps to create an overlapping echo and reverse reverb pattern. As the pattern plays, adjust the RV7000 length parameter to hear the interesting rhythmic possibilities you can create with the reverse algorithm. Also, try setting the RV7000 decay to 127 to hear the full reverse hit rather than the crescendo. This works best with shorter lengths up to three sixteenth-note steps.

- Start with an empty rack, and create a mixer.
- Set the mixer channel 1 aux send 1 amount to 91.
- Create an RV7000 Advanced Reverb.
- Open the RV7000 Remote Programmer and set the parameters according to the following chart:

RV7000 Parameters	
EQ	Off
Gate	Off
Decay	97
HF Damp	20
Hi EQ	44
Dry/Wet	127
Algorithm	Reverse
Length	5/16
Density	127
Tempo Sync	On
Rev Dry/Wet	64

- Create a Dr.REX Loop Player.
- Load the ReCycle loop "Trh06_RZA_100_eLAB.rx2" from Reason Factory Sound Bank\Dr Rex Drum Loops\Abstract HipHop directory.
- Copy the REX slice data to the Dr.REX 1 sequencer track.
- Run the sequence.

Pre-Verb

The algorithm Dry/Wet parameter controls the level between the reversed reverb and delayed signal. The default setting of 64 mixes equal levels of the reverse and delayed signal, while a setting of 127 will only pass the reverse reverb signal. This example uses two identical samples. One sample, processed with a reverse reverb insert, is triggered four steps ahead of the second. The reverse reverb creates a build-up leading to the second sample.

- In an empty rack, create a mixer.
- Create a Redrum Drum Computer.
- On Redrum channels 1 and 2, load the sample "PianoStab2_eLAB.aif" from the

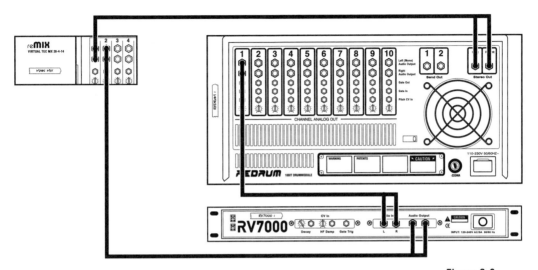

Figure 9-6.
Reverse reverb inserted
on Redrum channel 2.

Reason Factory Sound Bank\Other Samples\Chords-Phrases-Pads-Stabs
directory.

• Program the following on Redrum pattern A1:

Redrum Pattern

	1	2	3	4	5	6	7	8	9	10	11	12	13	14	15	16
1	M															
2					M											
3																
4																
5																
6																
7																
8																
9																
10																

• Bypass auto-routing and create an RV7000 Advanced Reverb.
• Connect the Redrum channel 1 outputs to the RV7000 audio inputs.
• Connect the RV7000 audio outputs to the mixer channel 2 input.
• Open the RV7000 Remote Programmer and set the parameters according to the
  following chart:

RV7000 Pre-Verb Parameters	
EQ	Off
Gate	Off
Decay	76
HF Damp	0
Hi EQ	0
Dry/Wet	127
Algorithm	Reverse
Length	4/16
Density	127
Tempo Sync	On
Rev Dry/Wet	127

• Run the Redrum pattern.

Equalization

Because many delays are summed in the process of creating a reverb effect, certain frequency ranges will be boosted. To balance the effect with the rest of the mix, it is often necessary to equalize the signal. For instance, string arrangements with cello parts that fall into the low midrange will cause a bellowing sound from the reverb. When combined with the rest of the mix, this creates muddiness. Using the RV7000's built-in EQ to roll off the bass and low mids will allow the reverb to sit above the string arrangement without overloading the mix.

The RV7000 has a shelving EQ control on the main panel. This is simply a treble control similar to the mixer treble EQ. There is also a dedicated EQ section, which has a low shelving equalizer and a single-band parametric EQ. Instead of using the RV7000 EQ, a PEQ-2 Parametric Equalizer can be inserted between the mixer aux send and the RV7000 inputs. Troublesome frequencies like the low midrange can be attenuated before processing. To pad down the low mids, set the PEQ-2 center frequency in the range between 22 and 50, Q set to 0, and a gain amount of between –10 and –22.

Feedback

Using reverb devices wired into feedback loops can create some very interesting effects that simulate the harmonic howling of a guitar pickup feeding back through an amplifier. A similar phenomenon occurs with a spring reverb pickup when the sound coming from an amplifier causes the spring to oscillate. The following examples demonstrate how to recreate these techniques using cabled feedback loops with reverbs.

RV-7 Feedback Resonance

In the world of hardware, it's common to find bits and pieces of odd gear sitting in the rack next to high-performance devices. One might wonder why a producer would choose to use an inexpensive reverb when a high-end reverb is available. Signal processing devices have their own characteristic nuances, which may be exactly what the mix calls for. Like using a spring reverb algorithm instead of a hall algorithm, choosing the RV-7 can be useful when you need to create a certain sound. This example shows how the RV-7 can be used to create a nice feedback effect. The feedback loop will be used as a send effect. The feedback resonance from the RV-7 algorithms sounds a lot like old science fiction film sound effects.

• Start with an empty rack, and create a mixer.
• Set the mixer channel 1 aux send 1 amount to 99.

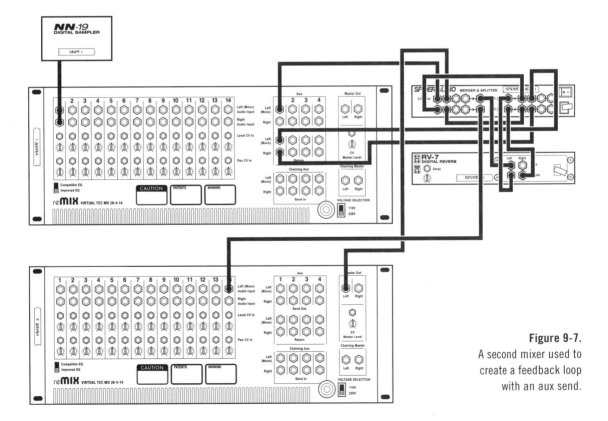

Figure 9-7.
A second mixer used to create a feedback loop with an aux send.

- Create an NN19 Digital Sampler.
- Load the sample "Guitarslide_eLAB.aif" from the Reason Factory Sound Bank\ Other Samples\Chords-Phrases-Pads-Stabs directory.
- On the NN19 sequencer track, use the pencil tool to draw two-measure note events on C3.

Reverb & Feedback Loop Section
- Create a Spider Audio Merger & Splitter.
- Bypass auto-routing and connect the mixer aux 1 send left to the Spider merge L/mono input.
- Connect the Spider Audio split A out 1 to the merge right input 1.
- Connect the Spider Audio split B out 1 to the merge right input 2.
- Connect the Spider Audio split A and split B out 2 sockets to the mixer aux return 1 input sockets.
- Bypass auto-routing and create an RV-7 Digital Reverb.
- Bypass auto-routing and connect the Spider Audio merge L/mono output to the RV-7 left input.
- Connect the RV-7 audio outputs to the Spider Audio split A and split B inputs.
- Bypass auto-routing and create another mixer.
- Set Mixer 2's channel 14 fader level to 50, EQ on, bass to –64.
- Connect the Spider Audio merge right output to the Mixer 2 channel 14 left input.
- Connect the Mixer 2 master output left to the Spider Audio merge L/mono input 2.
- Run the sequence.

The slight sound of metallic ringing is the circuit resonating through the feedback loop. As the pattern plays, mute Mixer 2 channel 14 to hear the effect without feedback. You can try playing with some of the RV-7 parameters, but this effect is so sensitive that most changes will create a feedback loop that overloads. Different algorithms will create interesting effects, especially "low density" and the "pan room" algorithms.

Chapter 10
Chorusing Effects

Stereo chorusing effects are used when you want to thicken up a sound. With the effects in this category, a monophonic signal from a SubTractor can be spread across the stereo field into a lush synthetic texture. The principles of comb filtering and fattening using delay modules were discussed using delay modules, and the concepts behind stereo chorusing effects are similar. The main difference with chorusing devices is that the delay time changes under the control of a modulation signal from a triangle wave LFO.

Reason has three devices for creating stereo effects based on the principles of short delay times. The CF-101 Chorus/Flanger and PH-90 Phaser use the principles of comb filtering, but the delay time is modulated with an LFO to produce variations. The UN-16 Unison module is another device used for creating stereo chorusing effects.

Chorusing

A chorus effect typically has a delay time between 15ms and 30ms, and it's very similar to using delays for doubling. The LFO modulation should be subtle, with a moderate amount of feedback to add density to the signal.

The CF-101 Chorus/Flanger can be used as either a send or an insert effect. The "send mode" button is like a dry/wet balance switch. When send mode is enabled, only the processed signal is routed to the outputs. When send mode is disabled, the dry signal and processed signal are mixed together. Since the device does not have a dedicated dry/wet balance control, it's easier to control chorusing when it's used as a send effect. The dry/wet balance can be adjusted using the effect send and return knobs.

Either monophonic or stereophonic signals can be processed through the CF-101. Unlike the DDL-1 Delay and RV-7 Reverb, the CF-101 processes stereo signals discretely. The stereo image that comes in remains unchanged at the output, and the CF-101 acts like two independent monophonic chorusing devices. This changes when only one input signal is connected to the left audio input: The CF-101 will take a monophonic input and create a stereo effect that spreads across the stereo field.

Simple Stereo Chorus

Stereo chorusing is enabled only when the CF-101 receives a mono input signal and the modulation amount is set greater than zero. There are really no set rules for creating a chorus effect, but this example gives the basic settings for an all-purpose stereo chorusing effect using the CF-101.

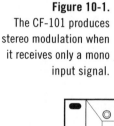

Figure 10-1.
The CF-101 produces stereo modulation when it receives only a mono input signal.

- Start with an empty rack, and set the tempo to 85 BPM.
- Create a mixer.
- Bypass auto-routing and create an NN19 Digital Sampler.
- Load the sample "170_Gated_mLp_eLab.aif" from the Reason Factory Sound Bank\Music Loops\Fixed Tempo (wave, aiff) directory.
- Bypass auto-routing, and create a CF-101 Chorus/Flanger.
- Set the CF-101 delay to 64, feedback to 10, LFO rate to 0, and LFO mod amount to 38.
- Connect the NN19 left audio output (mono) to the CF-101 left input.

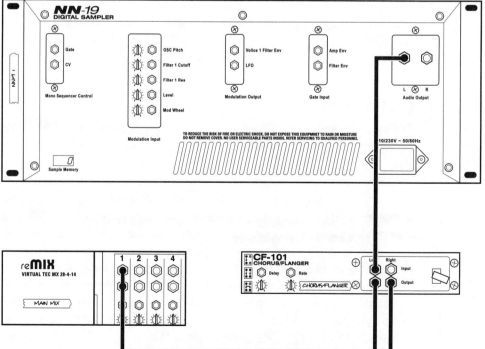

- Connect the CF-101 left and right outputs to the mixer channel 1 inputs.
- View the key lane on the NN19 sequencer track.
- Use the pencil tool and draw two-measure note events on C3.
- Run the sequence.
- Experiment with various settings of the CF-101's delay, feedback, rate, and mod amount knobs to get a feel for the sound of basic chorusing.

Flanging

Originally, flanging was created by running two synchronized tape machines that were playing the same audio signal. While the machines played the identical tracks, an engineer would press down on the flange of the tape reel on one machine, which would induce a slight pitch shift and delay. When the two signals were mixed, a comb filtering effect would be heard as the signals from the two machines fell slightly out of sync.

Signal processors like the CF-101 create a different type of flanging than the original tape technique. DSP flanging sounds more like a Doppler shift — a bit like the sound of a jet engine passing by the listener. A subtle phase shift created by delays with durations less than 10ms causes comb filtering. The LFO modulation sweeps the delay time, creating the Doppler shift sound. Unlike tape flanging, DSP flanging uses feedback to enhance the comb filtering to get a deeper resonating effect.

Stereo Flanger

This example demonstrates using the CF-101 stereo mode to create a lush stereo flanging effect. To hear the difference between the stereo flanging effect and the CF-101 used with stereo input signals, connect the right channel from the NN19 into the CF-101. This configuration is used as an insert device, so send mode should be disabled.

- Start with the patch you created in the chorusing example, above.
- Set the tempo to 130 BPM.
- Load the sample "130_PlanetE_mLp_eLab.aif" from the Reason Factory Sound Bank\Music Loops\Fixed Tempo (wave, aiff) directory.
- Set the CF-101 delay to 4, feedback to −42, LFO rate to 48, and LFO mod amount to 8.
- Select the NN19 sequencer track and enter edit mode to view the key lane.
- Set the sequencer resolution to Bar.
- Use the pencil tool and draw several four-measure events on C3.
- Run the sequence.

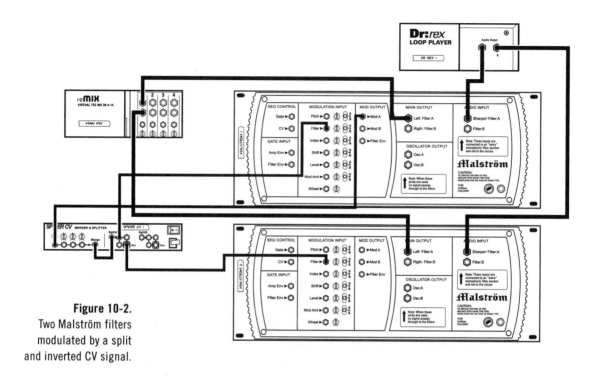

Figure 10-2.
Two Malström filters
modulated by a split
and inverted CV signal.

Malström Stereo Flanger

Once you understand that chorusing and flanging are created by comb filtering,
you can create a very nice stereo flanger using the comb filter mode in Malström's
filter section. The principle of this effect is to use two Malströms with the same
filter settings, then route a modulation curve signal through a Spider CV to
invert the signal. A direct modulation signal changes the filter frequency on one
Malström, while the inverted signal does the same on the second. The result is a
sweeping flange that rotates around the stereo field.

- Start with an empty rack and set the tempo to 135 BPM.
- Create a mixer.
- Bypass auto-routing and create a Dr.REX Loop Player.
- Load the ReCycle loop "Tec12_Cologne_135_eLAB.rx2" from the Reason
  Factory Sound Bank\Dr Rex Drum Loops\Techno directory.
- Copy the REX slice data to the Dr.REX 1 sequencer track.
- Bypass auto-routing and create a Malström Graintable Synthesizer.
- On Malström 1, disable all sections except mod A and filter A.
- Set modulator A curve to 1, enable sync, and set the rate to 8/4.
- Set filter A mode to comb+, resonance to 61, and frequency to 78.
- Connect the Dr.REX left output to the Malström shaper/filter A audio input.

- Connect the Malström 1 left:filter A main output to the mixer channel 1 left input.
- Bypass auto-routing and create a second Malström.
- On Malström 2, disable all sections except filter A.
- Set filter A mode to comb+, resonance to 61, and frequency to 78.
- Connect the Dr.REX right output to the Malström 2 shaper/filter A audio input.
- Connect Malström 2's left:filter A main output to the mixer channel 1 right input.
- Bypass auto-routing and create a Spider CV Merger & Splitter.
- Connect the Malström 1 mod A output to Spider CV merge input 1.
- Set the Spider CV merge input 1 trim to 46.
- Connect the Spider CV merge out to the split A input.
- Connect the Spider CV split A out 1 to the Malström 1 filter modulation input.
- Connect the Spider CV split A out 4/inv to the Malström 2 filter modulation input.
- Run the sequence.

The stereo sweeping caused by the inverted modulation sounds a lot like a phase-shifting effect, discussed later in this chapter. For a more subtle effect, change the mode to comb– and reduce the resonance settings on both Malströms. This configuration is also the basis for a large number of other stereo processing effects. Try changing the filter modes to lowpass and bandpass, and try using different modulation curves.

Phase-Shifting

The basic principle behind a phaser effect is the principle of phase shifting described in chapter 8. Phasers behave like notch filters, but they filter specific frequencies using phase cancellation. Phasers, such as hardware devices and the Reason PH-90, have stages that apply different amounts of phase shift to the signal to cancel several different frequencies. This is different from using a delay to create a phase-shift, because the delay has only has one stage.

Figure 10-3.

"Fake stereo" created by connecting a mono input to the PH-90 left input socket.

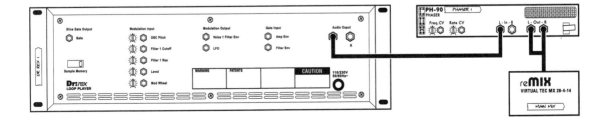

The PH-90 is a four-stage phaser, and in essence it behaves like a four-band notch filter. The frequency knob controls the base cutoff frequency of the first notch filter. The spacing between the center frequencies of the other three notch filters is determined by the split parameter. The width parameter controls the bandwidth: Higher width settings increase the bandwidth filtered by the notch filters — similar to the PEQ-2 Q parameter. The feedback parameter attenuates the feedback level of the filtered signal. Higher feedback settings will cause the phaser to resonate and increase the depth of the filters.

Classic Stereo Phaser

The PH-90 Phaser behaves differently depending on how it is cabled. Only connecting a signal to the left audio input will enable a special pseudo-stereo mode that creates the classic stereo phaser sound found on contemporary and vintage phaser devices. In order for the stereo effect to be enabled, the PH-90 must be wired in mono with a signal at the left audio input. The PH-90 modulates the right channel with an inverse phase to create the stereo effect. When the PH-90 is connected in stereo, both channels are modulated in the same manner.

• Start with an empty rack, and create a mixer.
• Create a Dr.REX Loop Player.
• On the Dr.REX, Load the Recycle file "135_TechChords_mLp_eLAB.rx2" from the Factory Sound Bank from the Music Loops\Variable Tempo (rex2)\Uptempo Loops directory.
• Copy the REX data to the Dr.REX sequencer track.
• Insert a PH-90 Phaser between the Dr.REX and the mixer channel 1 input.
• Disconnect the Dr.REX right output from the PH-90 right input.
• Run the sequence.

Pattern-Controlled Phaser

The PH-90 can be used as a pattern-controlled device like the ECF-42 Envelope Controlled Filter to create interesting pattern-based notch filtering. The pattern in this example sustains a fixed level for several steps. Phasers are commonly used as a filter device in the dub genre of music, and this example uses a DDL-1 inserted before the phaser to recreate the rhythmic syncopation induced by a 1/8T delay.

• Start with an empty rack, and set the song tempo to 70 BPM.
• Create a mixer.
• Bypass auto-routing and create an NN19 Digital Sampler.
• Open the NN19 Patch Browser, and open the ReCycle loop "090_DubStrat_mLp_eLab.rx2" from the Reason Factory Sound Bank\Music Loops\Variable Tempo (rex2)\Downtempo Loops directory.

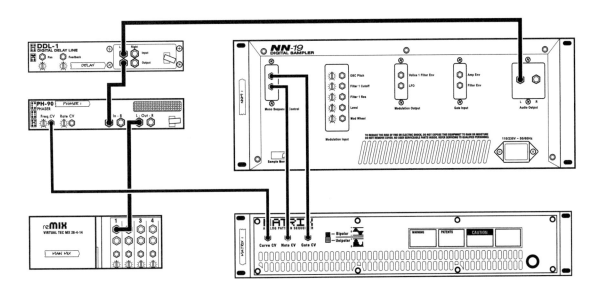

Figure 10-4.
The Matrix curve CV is cabled to the PH-90 frequency CV input. A DDL-1 is inserted before the phaser to create a dub style echo.

- Set the NN19 oscillator octave transpose to 3 and semitone to 10.
- Create a Matrix Pattern Sequencer.
- Program the gate and note events as follows:

Matrix Pattern

Step	1	2	3	4	5	6	7	8	9	10	11	12	13	14	15	16
Curve	50%	50%	50%	75%	75%	75%	40%	40%	40%	40%	20%	20%	20%	20%	80%	80%
Note	C3	C3	G2	C3	C3	C3	E2	C3	C3	C3	B2	C3	C3	C3	A2	C3
Gate		TH			TH			TH				TH				

- Switch to curve edit mode.
- Use the line tool (hold down the Shift key) and draw a flat line at 50% from step 1 through step 16.
- From step 3 to step 6, draw a line at 75%.
- From step 7 to step 10, draw a line at 40%.
- From step 11 to step 14, draw a line at 20%.
- From step 15 to step 16, draw a line at 80%.
- Bypass auto-routing and create a DDL-1 Digital Delay Line.
- Bypass auto-routing and connect the NN19 left output to the DDL-1 left input.

- Set the DDL-1 delay time to 1 step, step length to 1/8T, feedback to 88, dry/wet balance to 32.
- Bypass auto-routing and create a PH-90 Phaser.
- Bypass auto-routing and connect the DDL-1 left output to the PH-90 left input.
- Bypass auto-routing and connect the PH-90 left output to the mixer channel 1 left input.
- Connect the Matrix curve CV output to the PH-90 frequency CV input.
- Set the PH-90 frequency to 54, LFO F.Mod to 0, and feedback to 82.
- Run the Matrix pattern.

Unison

The UN-16 Unison module can be considered the ultimate chorus effect. While based on the same principles as chorus/flanging and delay doubling, the UN-16 Unison module works in a somewhat different way. The UN-16 splits the incoming signal from four to 16 times depending on the voice count parameter. Each of the duplicate signals is processed in parallel through delays and pitch shifters. Unlike a the CF-101, which uses a triangle wave to modulate the delay time, the UN-16 uses random noise to modulate the pitch shifting amount. The detune parameter scales the depth of the pitch modulation.

Like the CF-101 and PH-90, the UN-16 runs in mono, stereo, or fake stereo mode depending on the input and output cabling. The UN-16 can be used to thicken up any input signal, but it really shines as a stereo chorusing device. Cabled as either an insert effect or a send effect, a mono input signal on the UN-16 left input and stereo outputs will create a massive chorus sound.

Stereo SubTractor

This example describes a basic method of using the UN-16 as an insert device. Adjusting the Dry/Wet mix allows for some of the original mono signal to pass through, but for the widest possible stereo separation, set the Dry/Wet Mix to 127 (default). The UN-16 Detune setting seems to work best at 40 (the default), but this should be adjusted for taste.

- Start with an empty rack, and create a mixer.
- Create a SubTractor synthesizer.
- Load the patch "AnalogBrass" from the Reason Factory Sound Bank\SubTractor Patches\PolySynths directory.
- Select the SubTractor in the rack, and create a UN-16 Unison module to insert it between the SubTractor and the mixer channel 1 inputs.
- Play notes on a MIDI controller.

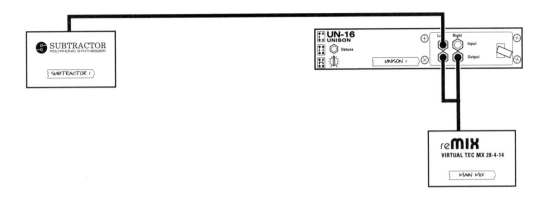

Figure 10-5.
UN-16 in fake stereo
mode with a mono input
signal connected to the
left input socket.

Big Brass Section

The UN-16 Unison module has a dry/wet balance control, which makes it very suitable as an insert effect. Signals processed through the UN-16 are dramatically different from the original, and getting the most out of the effect often requires careful balancing between processed and dry signals. This example demonstrates how subtle use of the UN-16 enhances a trumpet section multisample.

- Start with an empty rack, and create a mixer.
- Create a NN-XT Advanced Sampler.
- Load the patch "TRPS SfzC.sxt" from the Orkester Sound Bank\Brass\Trumpet Section (TRPS) directory.
- Insert a UN-16 Unison module between the NN-XT and the mixer.
- Set the UN-16 detune to 22, and the dry/wet mix to 89.
- Insert an RV7000 Advanced Reverb between the UN-16 and the mixer.
- Set the RV7000 decay to 30 and the dry/wet mix to 44.
- Open the RV7000 Remote Programmer.
- Set the RV7000 algorithm to hall, size to 26.5m, diffusion to 127, room shape to three, early reflection delay to 69%, early reflection level to 0.0dB, predelay to 30ms, and modulation amount to 42%.
- Play some notes on a MIDI controller keyboard.

Stereo Drum Processing

Most of the drum samples included in Reason Factory Sound Bank are monophonic, and the drum patterns usually end up as monophonic sources panned center in the mix. These sounds can be enhanced with a subtle bit of stereo processing through a UN-16 to spread the drum sounds across the stereo field.

- Start with an empty rack, and create a mixer.
- Create a Redrum Drum Computer.
- Connect the Redrum channel 1 outputs to the mixer channel 2 inputs.
- Load the Redrum patch "Electronic Kit 3.drp" from the Reason Factory Sound Bank\Redrum Drum Kits\Electronic Kits directory.
- Program the following on Redrum pattern A1:

Redrum Pattern

	1	2	3	4	5	6	7	8	9	10	11	12	13	14	15	16
1	M										M					
2							M									
3													M			
4			M									S				
5					M			S		S			M			S
6																
7																
8	M	S	S	S	M	S	S	S	M	S	S	S	M	S	S	S
9	M									M						
10															M	

- Insert a UN-16 Unison module between the Redrum stereo outs and the mixer channel 1 inputs.
- Set the UN-16 voice count to 8, detune to 18, and dry/wet mix to 90.
- Run the Redrum pattern.

The bass drum sample, which bypasses the UN-16, remains a mono sound in the mix, but the other samples processed through the UN-16 sound spread out between the left and right channels of the mix.

Chapter 11
Distortion Effects

Since the invention of electrified music instruments, the sound created by over-driven amplifiers has defined the music known as rock and roll. Electronic music has drawn upon the technical innovations created for rock, and distortion is commonly used to process synthesizers, drum loops, and vocals. In analog electronics, distortion is quite easy to achieve simply by overloading the levels in a circuit. In digital audio, overloading levels will result in clipping, which sounds nothing like analog distortion. Distortion is an effect that must be simulated using software algorithms that emulate analog circuits.

Reason has three distortion effects. The Scream 4 and D-11 are dedicated devices for distortion, and signals can be routed through the Malström Shaper section to distort them. The Scream 4 is the best distortion effect in the traditional sense, but the results differ on each device. In some cases the D-11 or Malström Shaper is most suitable. The Scream 4 parameters can be saved as patches, and there are number of presets available in the Reason Factory Sound Bank. Simply loading one of the presets will quickly get you started.

Distortion works best when used as an insert, and the examples provided below do not really explore special routing techniques like feedback. Some of the examples use distortion effects in parallel or several distortion units in series, but nothing more exotic. Distortion is normally a dramatic effect, but very subtle use of distortion can add slight harmonic changes to a signal to give a boring sound a little excitement. The Scream 4 can be used as a send effect, but this is really an unusual technique.

Instrument Distortion

Distortion is a dynamics-dependent effect, which means it's sensitive to signal level. The louder the incoming signal, the more distortion will be heard. The Scream 4 has two controls for adjusting levels, the damage control knob and the master output knob. Damage control is used to boost or cut the gain of the signal at the input of the effect. Adjusting this parameter to a high level is like overloading the input of an analog device to increase the distortion. Using a low damage control setting is useful to add subtle coloring to a signal. The master output control is a gain compensation control with which you can tame high levels. The master output knob functions like a mixer fader: Unity gain is 100, and settings above 100 will add gain to low signals.

The Scream 4 has several algorithms that simulate classic analog effects. The overdrive, distortion, and fuzz algorithms are the most suitable for simulating transistor-based distortion circuits. The tube algorithm does not have a strong distortion character, but the bias control is a useful feature to add harmonics to a signal.

Preamp & Distortion

Electric guitar rigs usually have several devices that can create distortion. Any guitarist will tell you that it's a combination of elements from the pickup to the right chain of effects to the right amplifier that creates a unique distortion sound. This example uses two Scream 4 units connected in series to create a fuller distortion tone. The first unit uses the tube algorithm to add density to the raw tone. The bias setting controls DC offset, a setting of 63 being zero offset. A slight upward offset shifts the waveform, adding harmonic content to the tone. The second unit distorts the signal with the distortion algorithm.

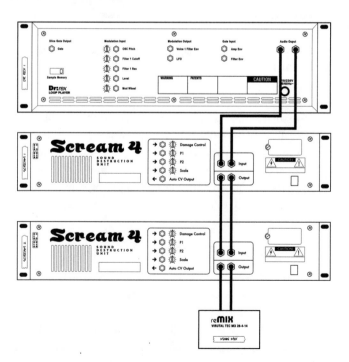

Figure 11-1.
Two Scream 4 units
connected in series.

- In an empty rack, create a mixer.
- Create a Dr.REX Loop Player.
- Load the ReCycle loop "Jh_DI_Guitar_heavyriff.rx2" from the *Power Tools for Reason* CD Dr.REX Loops directory.
- Copy the REX slice data to the Dr.REX 1 sequencer track.
- Insert two Scream 4 units in series between the Dr.REX and the mixer.
- Rename the first Scream 4 (connected right after the Dr.REX) "Preamp" and the second Scream 4 "Distortion."
- Program the following settings on the Preamp Scream unit:

Preamp Scream 4 Settings		
Damage: *on*	Damage control	62
	Algorithm	Tube
	P1	115
	P2	75
Cut: *off*	Lo	
	Mid	
	Hi	
Body: *off*	Reso	
	Scale	
	Auto	
	Type	
	Master	85

- Program the following settings on the Distortion Scream unit:

Distortion Scream 4 Settings		
Damage: *on*	Damage control	54
	Algorithm	Distortion
	P1	97
	P2	58
Cut: *off*	Lo	
	Mid	
	Hi	
Body: *off*	Reso	
	Scale	
	Auto	
	Type	
	Master	93

The Tube algorithm gives the signal a lot of body, and the combination of algorithms is useful for all types of input signal including synthesizers and drum loops. Try different algorithms on the Distortion Scream 4.

Acid Monosynth

Distortion has become as common with synthesizer as it is with electric guitar. The most common use of distortion with synthesizers is perhaps with bubbly acid-style monophonic synthesizer patterns. The Scream 4 can take a seemingly harmless monophonic synth line and turn it into an aggressive and ripping lead.

- In an empty rack, create a mixer.
- Create a Dr.REX Loop Player.
- Load the ReCycle loop "Peff_TB303Loop.rx2" from the *Power Tools for Reason* CD Dr.REX Loops directory.
- Copy the REX slice data to the Dr.REX 1 sequencer track.
- Insert a Scream 4 Distortion module between the Dr.REX and the mixer.
- Load the Scream 4 patch "Hollow303.scr" from the Reason Factory Sound Bank\Scream 4 Patches\Instrument Tweaks directory.
- Run the sequence.

Resonant filters make the distortion effect interesting. The resonant filter peak around the cutoff frequency is distorted the most, and sweeping the cutoff frequency creates a very dynamic distortion effect. Set the Dr.REX filter resonance to 80, then start sweeping the cutoff frequency as the loop plays.

Foldback Distortion

The D-11 Foldback Distortion unit creates a digital type of distortion based on clipping. When the foldback setting is 63, the output clipping is flat. Settings above 63 will engage the foldback process, in which the signal levels over the clipping threshold are subtracted from the threshold level. The result looks as if the peaks are folded back down. While the effect does cause distortion, it does not have the

Figure 11-2.
Sine wave (A) clipping (B) and foldback (C).

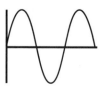

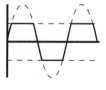

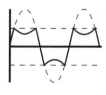

A   B   C

character of analog distortion. One useful application of the D-11 is with mono-phonic synthetic sounds, such as sine waves, which have little or no harmonic content. The clipping transforms the signal into a square wave.

• In an empty rack, create a mixer.
• Create a Malström Graintable Synthesizer.
• Set the polyphony to 1.
• Insert a D-11 Foldback Distortion module.
• Set the D-11 amount to 42, and foldback to 63.

Play a note on a MIDI keyboard, and adjust the foldback setting to hear how the parameter changes the harmonic content of the sine wave. As noted before, this works best with simple waveforms because the effect changes the harmonic content very drastically. Complex waveforms and polyphonic signals will often result in harsh digital-sounding noise. The Malström Shaper Saturation and Clipping algorithms simulate the clipping effect, but do not fold back the peaks. Saturation induces a DC offset like the Scream 4 tube algorithm, which sounds slightly warmer.

Speaker Cabinet Emulation

The Scream 4 Body section is designed to simulate the filter characteristics of a speaker cabinet. Body is a specialized resonant filter algorithm, and the parameters are similar to filter controls, but the results are quite different from the sound of a typical lowpass filter.

The Type switch selects among five different types of simulated cabinets. Types A, B, and C are smaller cabinets, and are ideal for simulating guitar amplifiers. Types D and E simulate large housings, like a bass cabinet. The Scale control determines the size of the cabinet, much like a room size parameter on a reverb, but the behavior is more like the cutoff frequency of a filter. As in a filter, higher resonance settings will make the cutoff frequency more noticeable. The Auto parameter is the scale modulation control from the envelope follower in the Scream 4.

Full Stack

This example uses two Scream 4 Distortion units running in parallel. The distortion algorithm and parameter settings are the same for both units, but different EQ and body parameters are used to simulate having two different speaker sources.

• In an empty rack, create a mixer.

D.I. Guitar Signal Source
- Bypass auto-routing and create a Dr.REX Loop Player.
- Load the ReCycle loop "Jh_DI_Guitar_finger lick.rx2" from the *Power Tools for Reason* CD Dr.REX Loops directory.
- Copy the REX slice data to the Dr.REX 1 sequencer track.

Bright Distortion & Speaker Simulator
- Bypass auto-routing and create a Scream 4 Sound Destruction Unit.
- Bypass auto-routing and connect the Dr.REX left audio out to the Scream 4 left audio input.
- Bypass auto-routing and connect the Scream 4 left audio out to the mixer channel 1 left input.
- Set the mixer channel 1 fader level to 82 and the pan to –3.
- Program the following settings on Scream 1:

Scream 1 Settings		
Damage: *on*	Damage control	72
	Algorithm	Distortion
	P1	75
	P2	99
Cut: *on*	Lo	17
	Mid	20
	Hi	13
Body: *on*	Reso	75
	Scale	81
	Auto	0
	Type	E
	Master	85

Dark Distortion & Speaker Simulator
- Bypass auto-routing and create a DDL-1 Digital Delay Line.
- Connect the Dr.REX right audio output to the DDL-1 left audio input.
- Set the DDL-1 delay time to 15ms and feedback to 0.
- Bypass auto-routing and create another Scream 4.
- Bypass auto-routing and connect the DDL-1 left audio out to the Scream 2 left audio input.
- Bypass auto-routing and connect the Scream 2 left output to the mixer channel 2 left input.
- Set the mixer channel 2 fader level to 74 and the pan to 9.
- Program the following settings on Scream 2:

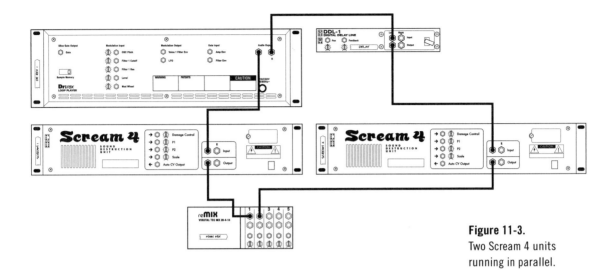

Figure 11-3.
Two Scream 4 units
running in parallel.

Scream 2 Settings		
Damage: *on*	Damage control	92
	Algorithm	Distortion
	P1	20
	P2	97
Cut: *on*	Lo	11
	Mid	24
	Hi	4
Body: *on*	Reso	78
	Scale	34
	Auto	8
	Type	C
	Master	85

• Run the sequence.

As the sequence runs, switch both Scream 4 devices into bypass mode to hear the raw signal. The difference is stunning. This full stack configuration makes use of the speaker simulator or "body" feature of the Scream 4 by creating two distinct cabinet sizes and placing them slightly off center in the stereo field. Try switching to different algorithms, making sure that both Scream 4 devices are using the same algorithm.

Tone Enhancer
This example demonstrates using only the body function of the Scream 4. The

specialized filter can be used in a subtle manner to add presence to a signal. Body algorithms D and E affect the bass and low-mid frequency ranges. Resonant settings using these body types will add fullness to the sound.

- In an empty rack, create a mixer.
- Create a Dr.REX Loop Player.
- Load the ReCycle loop "Rnb20_Vibey_090_eLAB.rx2" from Reason Factory Sound Bank\Dr Rex Drum Loops\RnB HipHop directory.
- Copy the REX slice data to the Dr.REX 1 sequencer track.
- Create a Scream 4 Sound Destruction Unit as an insert device between the Dr.REX and the mixer.
- Program the following settings on the Scream 4:

Scream 4 Tone Enhancer Settings		
Damage: *off*	Damage control	
	Algorithm	
	P1	
	P2	
Cut: *off*	Lo	
	Mid	
	Hi	
Body: *on*	Reso	81
	Scale	85
	Auto	0
	Type	E
	Master	85

- Run the sequence.

As the drum loop cycles, toggle the Scream 4 in and out of bypass mode to hear the difference between the original and processed signals. The subtle resonance from the body section adds fullness and color to the tone without drastically boosting the frequency range.

Low-Fidelity Effects

The Scream 4 "digital" algorithm simulates the sound of downsampling and bit-reducing digital audio. Downsampling occurs when the sample rate of a digital audio signal is decreased. The rate parameter controls the amount of downsampling. As the sample rate drops, artifacts are generated. A setting of 127 is the maximum sample rate. Bit reduction is the process of decreasing the size of the audio data word. The resolution parameter will decrease the data size from 16 bits down to 1 bit, with a resolution setting of 127 being the full bit depth.

8-Bit Audio

This example uses the Scream 4 digital algorithm to change a ReCycle loop into a drum loop that sounds generated from an old console video game or computer.

- In an empty rack, create a mixer.
- Create a Dr.REX Loop Player.
- Load the ReCycle loop "Trh19_KingBeat_125_eLAB.rx2" from Reason Factory Sound Bank\Dr Rex Drum Loops\Abstract HipHop directory.
- Copy the REX slice data to the Dr.REX 1 sequencer track.
- Insert a Scream 4 Distortion unit between the Dr.REX audio outputs and the mixer channel 1 inputs.
- Program the following settings on the Scream 4:

8-Bit Audio Settings		
Damage: *on*	Damage control	70
	Algorithm	Digital
	P1	31
	P2	76
Cut: *off*	Lo	
	Mid	
	Hi	
Body: *off*	Reso	
	Scale	
	Auto	
	Type	
	Master	85

- Run the sequence.

The two parameter controls on the Scream 4 control the bit depth and sample rate. Lowering the bit depth and sample rate creates quantization noise, which can be used to simulate video game noises from old hand-held game devices. To add a little more character to this downsample effect, insert a Malström between the Scream 4 and the mixer input channel, and use the Shaper set to "Quant." The Quant (quantize) algorithm also truncates a signal for creating low-fidelity digital effects.

Scream Auto CV Modulation

The Scream 4 envelope follower was described in detail in Chapter Three. The next examples further demonstrate uses of the auto CV modulation feature on the Scream 4.

Auto-Wah

Because the body section of the Scream 4 is a resonant filter, it can be used to create filter effects such as wah-wah. This example uses envelope follower modulation to dramatically control the scale parameter, which causes the body to filter like a wah-wah pedal.

- In an empty rack, create a mixer.
- Set the tempo to 86 BPM.
- Create a Dr.REX Loop Player.
- Load the ReCycle loop "Jh_DI_Guitar_finger lick.rx2" from the *Power Tools for Reason* CD Dr.REX Loops directory.
- Set the Dr.REX master level to 127.
- Copy the REX slice data to the Dr.REX 1 sequencer track.
- Create a Scream 4 Sound Destruction Unit as an insert device between the Dr.REX and the mixer.
- Program the following settings on the Scream 4:

Scream 4 Auto-Wah Settings		
Damage: *on*	Damage control	40
	Algorithm	Fuzz
	P1	70
	P2	50
Cut: *off*	Lo	
	Mid	
	Hi	
Body: *on*	Reso	111
	Scale	12
	Auto	111
	Type	B or C
	Master	85

- Run the sequence to hear the guitar riff distorted and processed with the auto-wah.

Auto CV Parameter Modulation

Using the auto CV output from the envelope follower on the Scream 4 is a great way to add dynamic parameter changes to the effect. This can easily be used to add similar changes to other effects.

- Start with an empty rack, and create a mixer.
- Create a Dr.REX Loop Player.
- Load the ReCycle loop "Chm28_TwoFour_125_eLAB.rx2" from the Reason Factory Sound Bank\Dr Rex Drum Loops\Chemical Beats directory.
- Copy the REX slice data to the Dr.REX sequencer track.
- Insert a Scream 4 Distortion unit between the Dr.REX audio outputs and the mixer channel 1 inputs.
- Program the following settings on the Scream 4:

Scream 4 Auto CV Modulate Settings		
Damage: *on*	Damage control	62
	Algorithm	Modulate
	P1	50
	P2	91
Cut: *off*	Lo	
	Mid	
	Hi	
Body: *off*	Reso	
	Scale	
	Auto	
	Type	
	Master	85

- Create a Spider CV Merger & Splitter.
- Connect the Scream 4 auto CV output to the Spider CV split A input.
- Connect the Spider CV split A out 1 to the Scream 4 P1 CV input.
- Connect the Spider CV split A out 4/inv to the Scream 4 P2 CV input.
- Run the sequence.

Chapter 12
Redrum Methods

When the first rhythm machines appeared, they were limited to a fixed number of sounds and patterns. Early beatboxes had very simple percussion sounds, and the patterns were named after the style of music: Machines with buttons labelled "Waltz," "Bossa Nova," and "Cha-Cha" were common. As technology progressed, rhythm machines became more flexible, allowing users to create their own patterns on a step sequencer interface. Today, programmed rhythms are a common part of many styles of music. The Redrum Drum Computer is the descendant of the original drum machines, and features an interface with which you can program patterns using buttons.

Redrum is a sample playback device, and an audio sample can be loaded directly into each of its ten channels using the sample browser. Alternatively, complete sample sets can be loaded from patch files. Patches do not contain audio sample information. Rather, they have file path information that tells Redrum to load a particular sample into a certain Redrum channel. Patches also contain parameter information such as pitch, panning, and envelope settings. Whether you choose to load individual samples or a patch that configures the entire machine, no sound will be heard from Redrum until samples are loaded into it.

Hardware drum machines have both a pattern mode and a song mode. Once several different patterns are programmed in the pattern sequencer, the patterns can be ordered into a song arrangement using the song mode. Redrum has no song mode of its own. Instead, patterns are arranged in the Reason sequencer. The switching of patterns can be recorded in real time, or edited by viewing the pattern lane in sequencer edit mode. Like hardware drum machines, patterns must first be programmed into a Redrum pattern. Once the patterns are programmed, they can be arranged using the sequencer track assigned to Redrum.

This chapter discusses various features of Redrum which can be used in combination with other devices to create intricate rhythm patterns.

Pattern Programming

Most Reason users are familiar with the standard methods of programming Redrum patterns using the 16-step pattern interface. Programmed rhythms do not have to sound like a metronome, however. The pattern shuffle feature can add a nice swing to a drum pattern. This section illustrates some unorthodox methods for programming Redrum to achieve exotic syncopated rhythms using a variety of methods, including gate CV triggering from other devices.

Vintage Drum Machine Swing

Some older drum machines did not have a "swing" or "shuffle" feature, and this technique was used to create patterns with a lively skip to the beat. Even though Reason has shuffle, the sound of a 16-step pattern with shuffle on does not quite capture the same feel as using sixteenth-note triplet steps.

- Start with an empty rack and set the tempo to 126 BPM.
- Create a mixer and a Redrum Drum Computer.
- Load the patch "House Kit 04" from the Reason Factory Sound Bank\Redrum Drum Kits\House Kits directory.
- Set the Redrum pattern length to 24 steps and the resolution to 1/16T.
- Set the Redrum edit steps to "1–16" and program the following pattern:

Redrum Pattern Steps 1–16

	1	2	3	4	5	6	7	8	9	10	11	12	13	14	15	16
1	M						S						S			
2							M									
3							M									
4																
5																
6																
7																
8			S			M						S			M	
9				M							M					M
10			S				M									

- Set the Redrum Edit Steps to "17–32" and program the following pattern:

Redrum Pattern Steps 17–24								
	17	18	19	20	21	22	23	24
1			S					S
2			M					
3			M					S
4								
5								
6								
7								
8		M			M			
9						M		
10						M		

This technique is widely used in producing house music tracks and is useful for other music styles that require a strong shuffle. The closed hi-hat hits take most advantage of this technique, but snare fills also have a nice feel when programmed in this manner. Try programming a snare roll from step 19 through 24.

Grooved Redrum Patterns

In reality, drum grooves are not fixed to perfect sixteenth-note quantization timing. While good drum programming can create some excellent grooves, it's not always possible to synchronize Redrum patterns with ReCycle loops. Redrum patterns can be converted to sequencer events, however, and these sequencer events can be quantized using a "user groove" established from the slice data sequence of a REX loop.

- Start with an empty rack, and set the tempo to 97 BPM.
- Create a mixer.
- Create a Dr.REX Loop Player.
- Load the ReCycle loop "Rnb08_Seductive_090_eLAB.rx2" from the Reason Factory Sound Bank\Dr Rex Drum Loops\RnB HipHop directory.
- Copy the REX slice data to the Dr.REX 1 sequencer track.
- Select a group in the Dr.REX sequencer track and click on "Get User Groove" in the Edit menu.
- Create a Redrum Drum Computer.
- Load the patch "Chemical Kit 03.drp" from the Reason Factory Soundbank\Redrum Drum Kits\Chemical Kits directory.
- Program the following on Redrum pattern A1:

Redrum Pattern

	1	2	3	4	5	6	7	8	9	10	11	12	13	14	15	16
1	M							M						M		
2																
3					M							M		M		
4																
5																
6																
7																
8	H	S	M	S	H	S	M	M	H	M	M	S	H	S	M	S
9		M														
10																

• Select "Copy Pattern to Track" from the Edit menu. The Redrum pattern will be converted to MIDI note events.
• On the Redrum, switch off pattern playback by clicking on the Enable Pattern Selection lamp.
• Select all drum lane events, then quantize them by clicking on the Quantize button. The quantization resolution should already be set to User.
• Run the sequence.

Matrix Multi-Quantization Patterns

Drum pattern programming is normally limited to the resolution and number of steps of the Redrum pattern. Using the Redrum gate inputs, however, a Matrix can be used to trigger the drum samples, and the Matrix can be set to an alternative pattern length and resolution. The basic rhythm pattern can be programmed on the Redrum, and variations with syncopated timing can be programmed on the Matrix using gate CV events.

Figure 12-1.
Matrix gate CV connected to the Redrum channel 3 gate CV input. The curve CV is controlling drum pitch.

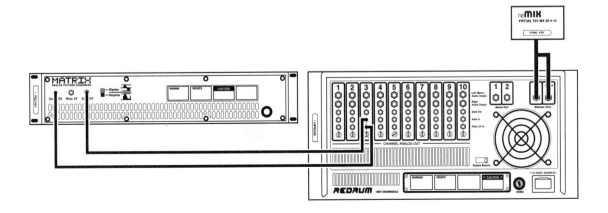

- Start with an empty rack, and set the tempo to 160 BPM.
- Create a mixer and a Redrum Drum Computer.
- Load the patch "DrumNbass Kit 04" from the Reason Factory Sound bank.
- Adjust the Redrum channel 3 level-to-velocity setting to 63.
- Program the following Redrum pattern in pattern A1:

Redrum Pattern

	1	2	3	4	5	6	7	8	9	10	11	12	13	14	15	16
1	S						S						S			
2					S								S			
3																
4																
5					S								S			
6	S										S					
7																
8	M		S		M		S		M		S		M		S	
9																
10																

- Bypass auto-routing and create a Matrix Pattern Sequencer.
- Switch the Matrix into bipolar mode.
- Connect the Matrix gate CV socket to the Redrum channel 3 gate in socket.
- Connect the Matrix curve CV output to the Redrum channel 3 pitch CV input.
- Set the Redrum channel 3 pitch CV trim to 8.
- Set the Matrix pattern length to 24 steps, and the resolution to 1/16T.
- On the Matrix, program gate events at steps 7, 13, 22, and 23. The gate event at step 7 should be the loudest, while the others should be less than 50%.
- Program curve events above and below the zero crossing on steps 7, 13, 22, and 23. The settings are arbitrary as long as they are different.
- Run the sequence.

While the Redrum pattern is based on 16 steps, the Matrix is playing a pattern through the Redrum based on 24 steps divided into sixteenth-note triplet increments. It's not practical to use a Matrix for every Redrum channel, but this is useful for snare samples where you want to create some intricate syncopation or flams. This technique is also useful where you want the flam to decrease in loudness on the second hit.

For drum 'n' bass patterns with a tempo around 160 BPM, try a 32-step pattern with 32nd-note resolution and enable shuffle. Set the master shuffle amount to 118. The shifted notes seem to syncopate nicely for ghosted snare hits.

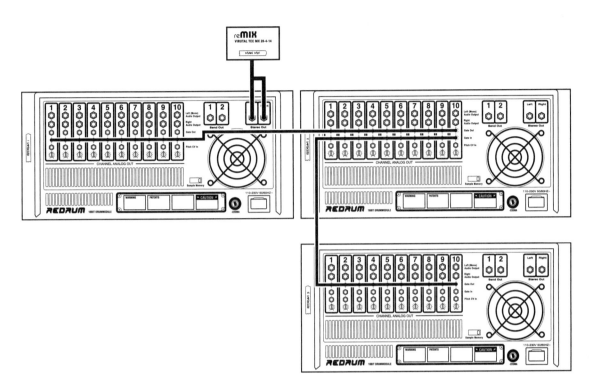

Figure 12-2.
Gate CV signals
daisy-chained from
Redrum 3 through
Redrum 2 into Redrum 1.

Layered Redrum Patterns

The Redrum can be used as a pattern-based gate CV source, and several Redrums can be daisy-chained with the gate signals connected between each other. This example illustrates how this configuration is created. Only one Redrum actually plays samples. The other Redrums simply send gate CV messages to the first Redrum. The main Redrum has a simple 16-step drum pattern, while the other Redrums have different resolutions and shuffle settings. The pattern events layered in this manner can easily create complex rhythms.

• Start with an empty rack.
• Set the tempo to 98 BPM and pattern shuffle to 99.
• Create a mixer and a Redrum Drum Computer.
• Load the patch "Dublab BrushKit2.drp" from the Reason Factory Soundbank\
  Redrum Drum Kits\Brush Kits directory.
• Program the following pattern on "Redrum 1" pattern A1:

Redrum Pattern

	1	2	3	4	5	6	7	8	9	10	11	12	13	14	15	16
1	M						M									
2					M								M			
3					M								M			
4																
5																
6																
7																
8	M		S		M		S		M		S					
9																
10																

- Bypass auto-routing and create a second Redrum.
- Connect all Redrum 2 gate out CV sockets to the corresponding Redrum 1 gate in sockets.
- Set the Redrum 2 pattern length to 12 steps and the resolution to 1/16T.
- Program the following on Redrum 2 pattern A1:

Redrum Pattern (Edit Steps 1–12)

	1	2	3	4	5	6	7	8	9	10	11	12
1							S		S			S
2												
3												
4												
5												
6												
7												
8										S	S	Sf
9												
10												

- Bypass auto-routing and create a third Redrum.
- Connect all Redrum 3 gate out sockets to the corresponding Redrum 2 gate in sockets.
- Set the Redrum 3 pattern length to 32 steps, resolution to 1/32, and enable shuffle.
- Switch to edit steps 17–32.
- Program the following on Redrum 3 pattern A1:

Redrum Pattern (Edit Steps 17–32)															
	17	18	19	20	21	22	23	24	25	26	27	28	29	30	31	32
1					S											
2																
3													S			
4																
5								S								
6												S				
7																
8																
9																
10																

Pitch CV Modulation

Each Redrum channel has a pitch CV input, which modulates the playback pitch parameter. The parameter is bipolar, so the sample can be pitched up or down. A slight amount of pitch modulation will add a lot of character to a drum sample. The following examples describe different methods for configuring Redrum channels to modulate pitch.

Velocity CV Pitch Modulation

This is a simple method of using the Redrum gate CV value to modulate the pitch. The value of the gate CV signal varies depending on the dynamics of the step, and connecting the gate CV out to the pitch CV in will alter the pitch of the sample as the dynamics change on a Redrum pattern. This technique can be applied to all of the Redrum channels and the amount of modulation can be scaled using the pitch CV trim knobs.

- Start with an empty rack and set the tempo to 126 BPM.
- Create a mixer and a Redrum Drum Computer.
- Load the patch "House Kit 02" from the Reason Factory Sound Bank\Redrum Drum Kits\House Kits directory.
- Enable Shuffle on Redrum 1.
- Connect the Redrum channel 1 gate out to the Redrum channel 1 pitch CV in.
- Set Redrum channel 1 to gate mode 1.
- Connect the Redrum channel 4 gate out to channel 4 pitch CV in.
- Set Redrum channel 4 to gate mode 1.
- In Redrum channel 1, set the level to 76, pitch to −24, and velocity-to-level to −26.
- Program the following pattern:

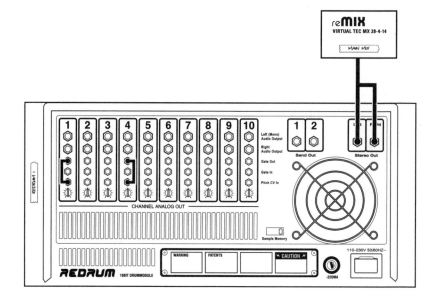

Figure 12-3.
Redrum gate CV outputs
connected to pitch CV
inputs.

Redrum Pattern

	1	2	3	4	5	6	7	8	9	10	11	12	13	14	15	16
1	S				M				M				M		H	H
2																
3																
4		M	H	S			S		S		S	H		S	M	S
5																
6																
7																
8																
9																
10																

• Run the Redrum pattern.

Global Pitch Control

Using several Spider CV splitters, a CV signal can be distributed to all of the Redrum channels. The pitch CV modulation is bipolar, so a Matrix pattern sequencer set in bipolar mode is a good choice to control the pitch of the Redrum samples.

• In an empty rack, create a mixer and a Redrum Drum Computer.
• Load the patch "RnB Kit 03" from the Reason Factory Sound Bank\Redrum Drum Kits\RnB Kits directory.
• Program the following pattern into Redrum pattern A1:

Redrum Pattern

	1	2	3	4	5	6	7	8	9	10	11	12	13	14	15	16
1	M															
2					M								M			
3																
4				M							M					
5																
6																
7	S	S	S		S	S	S		S	S	S	S	S	S	S	
8	M	M	M	M	M	M	M	M	M	M	M	M	M	M	M	M
9																
10																

- Bypass auto-routing and create a Spider CV Merger & Splitter.
- Connect the Spider split A output 3 to split B input.
- Duplicate Spider CV 1 and connect Spider CV 1 split B output 3 to Spider CV 1 Copy split A input.
- Duplicate Spider CV 1 Copy and connect the Spider CV 1 Copy split B output 3 to Spider CV 1 Copy 2 split A input.
- Bypass auto-routing and create a Matrix Pattern Sequencer.
- Set the Matrix to bipolar mode and connect the curve CV output to the Spider CV 1 split A input.
- The Matrix curve CV is now split 13 ways through the three Spider CV splitters wired in series. Connect free outputs from the Spider CV splitters to each of the Redrum pitch CV input sockets.

Figure 12-4.
Matrix curve CV split ten times with three Spider CV modules connected in series.

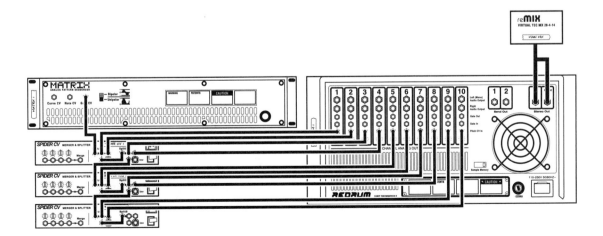

• Run the sequence, and adjust the Matrix curve CV to globally change the pitch on the Redrum channels.

Envelope-Controlled Pitch Modulation

This example demonstrates using a Redrum channel gate CV output to trigger the envelope generator on a SubTractor. The envelope generator CV signal is then routed back into the Redrum channel pitch CV input to modulate the sample pitch.

• Start with an empty rack, and set the tempo to 90 BPM.
• Create a mixer.
• Create a Redrum Drum Computer and load the patch "Dublab BrushKit2.drp" from the Reason Factory Soundbank\Redrum Drum Kits\Brush Kits directory.
• Set the Redrum channel 10 to gate mode 1.
• Bypass auto-routing and create a SubTractor Synthesizer.
• Connect Redrum channel 10 gate out to the SubTractor sequencer control gate input.
• Connect the SubTractor filter env modulation output to the Redrum channel 10 pitch CV input.
• Set the Redrum channel 10 pitch CV trim to 30.
• Set the SubTractor polyphony to 1, enable low BW, and set filter envelope attack to 55 and filter envelope decay to 80.
• Program the following on Redrum pattern A1:

Redrum Pattern															
	1	2	3	4	5	6	7	8	9	10	11	12	13	14	15	16
1																
2																
3																
4																
5																
6																
7																
8																
9																
10	H			M	S				S		M	M		S	H	

• Run the Redrum pattern.

The signal from the gate CV triggers the SubTractor filter envelope. The contoured control voltage signal generated by the envelope then modulates the pitch on the cymbal, creating a decaying pitch modulation. Some of the Redrum channels have pitch modulation features, but they don't have the flexibility of the SubTractor envelope generator.

Samples

Redrum is a 16-bit sample playback device, and 24-bit samples are reduced to 16-bit for playback when loaded into Redrum. If bit resolution is an issue, then you should consider using an NN-XT Advanced Sampler instead. The Redrum patterns can be converted to sequencer note events, and the sequencer track can be assigned to the sampler with the high-resolution drum samples mapped according to Redrum note values. Redrum channels 1 through 10 are triggered by note events on starting on C1 through A1. Mapping your sample zones accordingly will create a Redrum set with all of the features of the NN-XT.

Monophonic Redrum Channel

In the example below, the gate output from the Redrum channel 1 triggers the NN19 sampler. The same sample has been loaded on the NN19, and the parameters have been matched to settings from the Redrum patch. The difference is that the short bursts of 32nd-note drum hits are monophonic. On the Redrum these are polyphonic, and the sample decay overlaps over the next sample attack. This configuration produces a very sharp and clear rapid-fire drum pattern.

- In an empty rack, create a mixer and a Redrum Drum Computer.
- Load the Patch "Hardcore Kit 02.drp" from the Reason Factory Sound Bank\ Redrum Drum Kits\Hardcore Kits directory.
- Adjust the Redrum channel 1 level to 0.

Figure 12-5.
Redrum channel 1 gate CV out connected to the NN19 gate input.

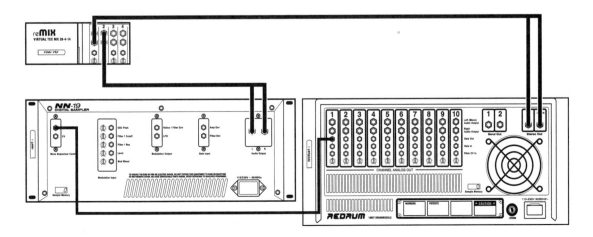

• Set the Redrum pattern A1 resolution to 1/32.
• Program the following on Redrum pattern A1:

Redrum Pattern

	1	2	3	4	5	6	7	8	9	10	11	12	13	14	15	16
1	M				M		M		M	M	M		M	M	M	M
2									M							
3																
4																
5																
6																
7																
8																
9																
10																

• Create an NN19 Digital Sampler.
• Use the NN19 sample browser to load "BD2_Anarchy.wav" from the Reason Factory Sound Bank\Redrum Drum Kits\xclusive drums-sorted\01_BassDrums directory.
• Set the NN19 polyphony to 1, velocity F.Env modulation to 16, and velocity amp modulation to 34.
• Set the NN19 filter cutoff frequency to 97 and the filter envelope sustain to 127.
• Set the NN19 amp envelope decay to 0, sustain to 127, and release to 88.
• Patch the Redrum channel 1 gate out to the NN19 mono sequencer control gate in.
• Run the Redrum pattern.

REX Slices

Besides standard audio formats such as WAV, AIFF, and SoundFonts, the sample playback devices in Reason can load individual sample slices from ReCycle loops. This is a great way to add programmed rhythms on top of a ReCycle loop playing on the Dr.REX Loop Player.

• Start with an empty rack, and set the pattern shuffle amount to 20.
• Create a mixer and a Redrum Drum Computer.
• Enable shuffle on Redrum pattern A1, and enable channel 8&9 exclusive using the small button in the lower left corner of the panel.
• Insert a Comp-01 Compressor/Limiter between the Redrum and the mixer.
• Set the Comp-01 threshold to 14, attack to 50, and release to 0.

Sample Loading Section
- Click on the sample browser button on Redrum channel 1 and open the file "Chm12_LoFi_125_eLab.rx2" in the Reason Factory Sound Bank\Dr Rex Drum Loops\Chemical Beats directory. The sample browser now lists the individual slices of the ReCycle file.
- Load slice "Chm12_LoFi_125_eLab.rx2 [0]" on Redrum channel 1.
- Channel 2: Chm12_LoFi_125_eLab.rx2 [5].
- Channel 3: Chm12_LoFi_125_eLab.rx2 [6].
- Channel 4: Chm12_LoFi_125_eLab.rx2 [2].
- Channel 5: Chm12_LoFi_125_eLab.rx2 [15].
- Channel 6: Chm12_LoFi_125_eLab.rx2 [14]. Set decay (length) to 32, pitch to −22.
- Channel 7: Chm12_LoFi_125_eLab.rx2 [6].
- Channel 8: Chm12_LoFi_125_eLab.rx2 [3]. Set velocity-to-level to 49, decay to 38.
- Channel 9: Chm12_LoFi_125_eLab.rx2 [7].
- Channel 10: Chm12_LoFi_125_eLab.rx2 [13].
- Program the following pattern on the Redrum:

Redrum Pattern

	1	2	3	4	5	6	7	8	9	10	11	12	13	14	15	16
1	M															
2											S				S	
3				S									S			
4				S												S
5			S					S			S			S		
6		S								S					S	S
7																
8	M	S	M	H	M	S	M	S	M	S	M	H	M	S		S
9															S	
10																

- Run the Redrum pattern.

This Redrum patch should be saved so the sample and parameter information can be quickly recalled.

Reverse Samples

Reversing the playback of a sample is handy trick to create little transitions between drum hits. The Redrum playback engine cannot reverse the playback of a sample, but a Redrum step can be used to trigger the NN-XT sampler. The drum sample can be loaded into the NN-XT, where the playback direction can be reversed.

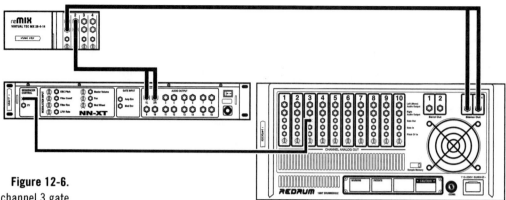

Figure 12-6.
Redrum channel 3 gate
CV output connected to
the NN-XT gate input.

- Start with an empty rack, and create a mixer.
- Create a Redrum Drum Computer and load the patch "Techno Kit 04.drp" from the Reason Factory Soundbank\Redrum Drum Kits\Techno Kits directory.
- Set Redrum channel 3 level to 0, length to 127, and decay/gate mode to 1.
- Create an NN-XT Advanced Sampler and open the Remote Editor.
- Load the Sample "Clp_Axis.wav" from the Reason Factory Soundbank\Redrum Drum Kits\xclusive drums-sorted\04_Claps directory.
- Set the sample end position to 44.8% and the play mode to BW.
- Adjust the NN-XT pmp envelope release to 7.04 seconds, the velocity level knob to 40%, and pitch semitone to 4.
- Connect the Redrum channel 3 gate CV output to the NN-XT gate input.
- Program the following on Redrum pattern A1:

Redrum Pattern															
	1	2	3	4	5	6	7	8	9	10	11	12	13	14	15	16
1																
2							M									
3	M															
4																
5																
6																
7																
8																
9																
10																

- Set the tempo to 135 BPM and run the Redrum pattern.

The gate message from Redrum channel 3 triggers the NN-XT, which plays the sample backwards. This is the same sample being played by Redrum channel 2.

Dynamics

The dynamics of a drum pattern are important for creating a groove. Even when the timing between steps remains perfect, changing the dynamics of the drum events will change the feel of the timing. Even with the limited variation between hard, medium, and soft dynamics, Redrum patterns have a more realistic feel when the dynamics vary. If higher resolution dynamics are necessary, the patterns can be converted to track notes and the velocity values can be edited in the sequencer.

One strategy of programming dynamics is to limit the basic pattern to soft and medium events. Even though the default event is set to medium, try programming the pattern using only soft dynamics. Go back through and change events on the downbeat and beat 3 to hard and events on beat 2 and beat 4 to medium. Once the base pattern is programmed, variations can be programmed using medium dynamics to create the feeling of hesitation or anticipation in a rhythm.

Redrum Accent Patterns

Many drum machines have a feature to accent a particular step in the pattern. The accent is a dynamic boost for the drum events on a particular step, and accents add dynamic change to static patterns. One way to add accents is to use Matrix gate events to trigger an envelope. This example uses only the Redrum itself, however, to create accents. The output of Redrum channel 10 gates a SubTractor envelope. The envelope's control voltage modulates mixer level to provide a slight increase in loudness. Keep in mind that this is not the way accents function in all drum machines. This technique is more like a pattern-controlled dynamic "bumper."

Figure 12-7.
Redrum channel 10 gate CV triggers a SubTractor envelope. The envelope CV modulates the mixer level to add an accent to a Redrum step.

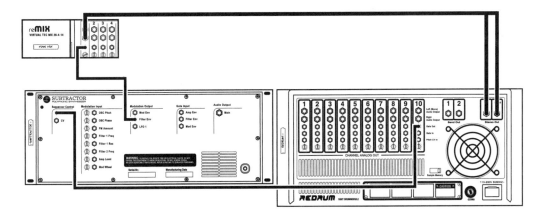

- Start with an empty rack, and set the tempo to 82 BPM.
- Create a mixer.
- Set the mixer channel 1 fader level to 84.
- Create a Redrum Drum Computer, and load the patch "Techno Kit 04.drp" from the Reason Factory Soundbank\Redrum Drum Kits\Techno Kits directory.
- Set the Redrum channel 10 level to 0. Channel 10 will be used to program accents.
- Program the following pattern on Redrum pattern A1:

Redrum Pattern

	1	2	3	4	5	6	7	8	9	10	11	12	13	14	15	16
1																
2																
3																
4																
5																
6																
7																
8	M	M	M	M	M	M	M	M	M	M	M	M	M	M	M	M
9																
10	M				M			M	M				M			M

CV Envelope Section
- Bypass auto-routing and create a SubTractor Synthesizer.
- Connect the Redrum channel 10 gate out to the SubTractor sequencer control gate in.
- Connect the SubTractor filter env modulation output to the mixer channel 1 level CV input.
- Set the mixer channel 1 level CV trim to 94.
- Set the SubTractor polyphony to 1 and enable low BW.
- Set the filter envelope attack to 0, decay to 0, sustain to 120, and release to 31.
- Run the Redrum pattern.

The SubTractor envelope decay and release values should be adjusted depending on the tempo of the track. Faster tempos will require shorter decay and release times, while slower tempos will need longer settings. The accent duration should not be longer than the duration of a step, but this may be compromised to emphasize long samples.

Instead of dedicating a Redrum channel to control the accents, the mixer level CV modulation can also be controlled from a Matrix Pattern Sequencer to trigger the SubTractor envelope. Using tied gate events on the Matrix can extend the dynamic boost over several steps rather than one step.

Chapter 13
ReCycle Loop Techniques

T he Dr.REX Loop Player is a specialized sample playback device specifically designed for loops created with Propellerhead's ReCycle software. In order to synchronize a normal sampled drum loop with a sequence, either the sample pitch must be changed so that the playback duration matches the tempo, or some sort of DSP must be used to change the length of the sample. But ReCycle loops automatically synchronize with the tempo of a track without affecting the original pitch of the drum sounds or adding undesirable time-stretching artifacts to the sound. Drum loops played from a Dr.REX will match any tempo without pitch changes, but it's not possible to load ordinary .WAV files into Dr.REX. The file must be processed through ReCycle, which is a separate product, not included with Reason. Fortunately, Reason ships with dozens of ReCycled REX files in various styles.

ReCycle takes a sampled drum loop, analyzes the locations of drum transients, and divides up the loop into smaller sample slices. The drum loop slices are mapped to the keys of a sampler. ReCycle also generates a MIDI sequence based on the timing of the segments. The MIDI sequence is a series of notes that start on C1 and ascend chromatically for each loop slice. Along with tempo and time signature information, the sample and sequence data is stored in the ReCycle format (REX, RCY, or RX2). RX2 is the most recent version of the ReCycle 2.x file format, which supports stereo audio data. When a sequencer plays the REX slice sequence at the original tempo, the slice events are triggered in the sequence from the first to last. Changing the sequencer tempo will trigger the events while keeping the same relative spacing.

Using the Dr.REX Loop Player is a two-step process. First, a ReCycle file must be loaded into the Dr.REX. Once the file is loaded, the MIDI sequence timing data must be exported to a sequencer track. Pressing the "To Track" button will copy the slice data to the selected MIDI sequence track, where it appears as one or more sequencer groups. The individual note events from the REX slice data can be inspected in the "REX lane" in sequencer edit mode.

REX Slice Modulation

The heart of the Dr.REX Loop Player is a sample playback device much like the Redrum and NN samplers. There are parameters to control relative pitch, level, decay, and pan for each of the slices. The Dr.REX also has global parameters that control the overall sample playback level, pitch, filtering, and envelope settings. The individual slice settings are relative to the global parameters, and the global parameters can be modulated by external CV signals.

Velocity-Sensitive REX Slices

By default, the Dr.REX does not respond to velocity messages from the slice data on a sequencer track. One of the most useful modulation adjustments is to set the velocity-to-amp modulation to about 40. This will make the individual slices respond to velocity changes. The output level from the Dr.REX will decrease as the velocity-to-amp modulation is increased, and the slice velocity values (some of them, at least, depending on what sort of accent pattern you want to create) will need to be increased to compensate for the decrease in level. The Change Events box, accessed from the Edit menu, has a feature that will allow you to quickly increase the velocities of all selected notes on the Dr.REX sequencer track. In sequencer arrange mode, select all of the REX data groups, set the velocity add amount to 36, and click on Apply.

REX Slice Parameters

Any type of sound can be processed using ReCycle and loaded into the Dr.REX Loop Player. This example demonstrates how a simple loop of bass notes can be manipulated in Dr.REX. The original sample is a series of 16 notes playing the same pitch. Using the Dr.REX slice parameters, the note pitches will be adjusted to create a melodic riff. The original audio file is also monophonic, and by modifying the slice pan parameters, the mono loop will acquire some stereo movement.

Figure 13-1.
The Dr.REX slice
parameter editor.

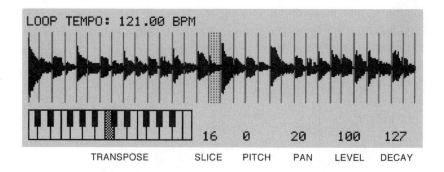

- In an empty rack, create a mixer and a Dr.REX Loop Player.
- Load the ReCycle loop "Peff_Moog_16.rx2" from the *Power Tools for Reason* CD Dr.REX Loops directory.
- Copy the REX slice data to the Dr.REX 1 sequencer track.
- Adjust the REX slice parameters as follows:

Dr.REX Slice Parameters

sce #	1	2	3	4	5	6	7	8	9	10	11	12	13	14	15	16
ptch	−12	0	0	−2	0	0	−2	3	−12	0	0	−2	0	12	−2	0
pan	0	0	−64	0	0	63	0	0	0	−64	0	0	0	0	0	63
level	127	100	100	100	127	100	100	100	127	100	100	100	127	100	100	100
decay	127	127	127	86	127	127	127	86	127	127	127	86	127	127	127	86

- Run the sequence.

This example was created for this specific synthesizer REX file, but it illustrates a technique that can be applied to any REX loop.

Note CV Pitch Modulation

Dr.REX parameters can also be controlled by various CV sources. This example illustrates using a Matrix pattern note CV to modulate the playback pitch of the Dr.REX. With the pitch CV sensitivity setting at 127, the note CV modulation is in chromatic increments. The note CV modulation requires a gate event on step 1 before the value.

- In an empty rack, create a mixer and a Dr.REX Loop Player.
- Load the ReCycle loop "090_RunningRhodes2_mLp_eLAB.rx2" from the Reason Factory Sound Bank\Music Loops\Variable Tempo (rex2)\Downtempo Loops directory.
- Copy the REX slice data to the Dr.REX sequencer track.

Figure 13-2.
Note CV connected to Dr.REX pitch CV modulation input.

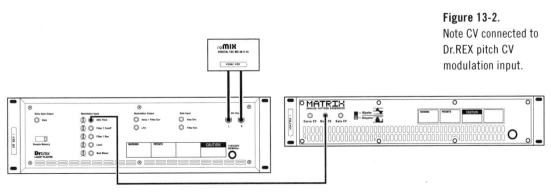

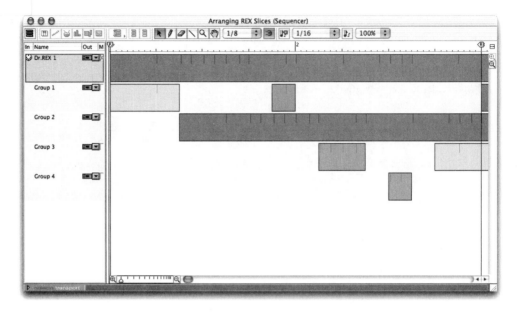

Figure 13-3.

A Dr.REX sequencer track has been duplicated, and sections of the REX data have been segmented into shorter sections.

• Set the Dr.REX transpose setting to −12 and the osc pitch octave to 0.
• Create a Matrix Pattern Sequencer.
• Connect the Matrix note CV output to the Dr.REX osc pitch modulation input.
• Set the Dr.REX osc pitch modulation input trim to 127.
• Draw F3 note events on steps 13 through 16, and draw a gate event on step 1.
• Run the sequence.

REX Slice Manipulation

Since Propellerhead introduced ReCycle, an entirely new method in electronic music production has evolved based on loop slices. The following examples demonstrate a variety of slice manipulation techniques useful for breakbeat and drum 'n' bass genres. These examples demonstrate a few ways the slice data can be manipulated in the sequencer to deconstruct and create completely different rhythms based on the original REX slice data.

Slice Rearrangement

This example demonstrates the basics of how complex drum 'n' bass loops are created using the Dr.REX Loop Player. The principle is to divide the REX data groups into smaller sections and move the sections around. Each of the smaller groups will contain a few slice events, and the timing among these events will not change, so in effect we'll be slicing the REX file into segments larger than a single slice.

- Start with an empty rack, and set the tempo to 157 BPM.
- Set the Loop Locators to 1.1.1 and 3.1.1.
- Create a mixer and a Dr.REX Loop Player.
- Load the ReCycle loop "Drb28_StartUp_155_eLAB.rx2" from the Reason Factory Sound Bank\Dr Rex Drum Loops\Drum N Bass directory.
- Copy the REX slice data to the Dr.REX 1 sequencer track.
- Make three duplicates of the Dr.REX 1 sequencer track.
- Rename the duplicate tracks "Group 1," "Group 2," and "Group 3." There should be four sequencer tracks, with the top track named "Dr.REX 1."
- Mute the Dr.REX 1 sequencer track. This will be kept as a reference containing the original REX slice data.
- Set the sequencer resolution to 1/8 and enable Snap to Grid.
- Enable the selection tool.
- Move the Group 2 region to start at position 1.2.3.
- Move the Group 3 region to start at position 1.3.3.
- Enable the pencil tool to draw new arrangement groups.
- On Group 1, draw a group from position 1.2.3 to 1.4.3, and delete this group.
- On Group 1, draw a group from position 2.1.1 to 3.1.1, and delete this group.
- On Group 3, draw a group from position 1.1.1 to 2.1.3, and delete this group.
- On Group 3, draw a group from position 2.2.3 to 2.4.1, and delete this group.
- Duplicate the Group 3 sequencer track, and rename it "Group 4."
- On Group 4, delete the region from 2.4.1 to 3.1.1.
- On Group 4, draw a group from position 2.2.1 to 2.2.3, and delete this group.
- On Group 4, select the region starting at 2.1.3, and change the start position to 2.3.1.
- Run the sequence.

Altering Notes

The Alter Notes feature, found in the Change Events window, is useful for creating variations of ReCycle loop sequences. This feature is different from randomizing note events, because the slice/note events are arranged in a different order. The feature only affects regions that are selected in either arrange mode or edit mode, so a small group of REX slices data can be altered rather than an entire loop.

- In an empty rack, create a mixer and a Dr.REX Loop Player.
- Load the ReCycle loop "Chm13_Boutique_125_eLAB.rx2" from the Reason Factory Sound Bank\Dr Rex Drum Loops\Chemical Beats directory.
- Copy the REX slice data to the Dr.REX 1 sequencer track.
- Select the REX slice groups in the Dr.REX sequencer track.
- Select Change Events in the Edit menu.
- In the Change Events box, find the Alter Notes function and click on the Apply button.

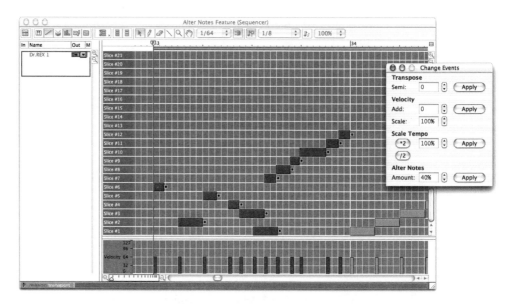

Figure 13-4.
The Change Events
window's Alter Notes
feature.

• Switch the sequencer to edit mode and view the REX slice data.
• Run the sequence.

Try experimenting with different selection ranges as well as alteration amounts. For example, select the last half measure of a REX slice sequence and apply the Alter Notes function. The first half will play normally while the second half plays a variation. Duplicate the Dr.REX sequencer track and experiment with the duplicate sequence. If the variations are a little too extreme, the original data can quickly be replaced.

Synchronizing ReCycle Grooves

Different REX drum loops will have different slice timings, especially when they originate from different styles of music. Slice data from one REX loop can be used as a quantization template to synchronize a different REX loop. Using the Dr.REX 1 REX data as a template, the Dr.REX 2 track can be quantized to conform and synchronize with the first track. Sometimes this function works flawlessly, but a lot has to do with the timing of the events and how close they are in relation to the other track. It works best if you use the track with more slices per measure as the template.

• Start with an empty rack, and create a mixer.
• Create two Dr.REX Loop Players.
• Set the loop locators to 1.1.1 and 9.1.1.

- In Dr.REX 1, load the ReCycle loop "Hse08_Armand_135_eLab.rx2" from the Reason Factory Sound Bank\Dr Rex Drum Loops\House directory.
- Select the Dr.REX 1 sequencer track, and copy the REX slice data to the track.
- In Dr.REX 2, load the ReCycle loop "Tec02_BoneHat_130_eLAB.rx2" from the Reason Factory Sound Bank\Dr Rex Drum Loops\Techno directory.
- Select the Dr.REX 2 sequencer track, and copy the REX slice data to the track.
- In the sequencer arrange view, select a group from the Dr.REX 2 track.
- Select Get User Groove in the Edit menu.
- Select group regions 2 and 4 on the Dr.REX 1 sequencer track.
- Click on the Quantize button.
- Run the sequence.

Selecting groups 2 and 4, but not groups 1 and 3, will allow you to compare the subtle differences in the quantization of the groove. Try listening both with the Dr.REX 2 track muted, and with it playing. Slowing down the tempo will make the differences easier to hear.

Matching grooves is not an exact science, but using REX slice data as a quantization template makes the process easier. The user groove can be applied to other parts of the sequence, such as a bass line sequence. This will tighten up the timing between the bass line and the drum loop.

Averaging Grooves
Sometimes straight quantization of REX slice data is so dramatically different that the second loop does not fit. By applying a 50% quantization from one REX track to the other, then using the quantized track as the new template, you can create

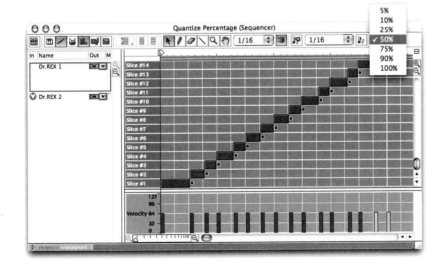

Figure 13-5.
Quantization percentage control on the sequencer button bar.

an average of the two grooves. Two REX loops with drastically different grooves will synchronize better with this technique. Applying the 50% quantization back and forth between the two different tracks will create an even smoother balance between the grooves, but it's always necessary to apply a 100% quantization to get the grooves in perfect sync.

• In an empty rack, create a mixer.
• Create two Dr.REX Loop Players.
• On Dr.REX 1, load the ReCycle loop "Hse10_Congas_125_eLab.rx2" from the Reason Factory Sound Bank\Dr Rex Drum Loops\House directory.
• Copy the REX slice data to the Dr.REX 1 sequencer track.
• On Dr.REX 2, load the ReCycle loop "Chm15_Funky_135_eLAB.rx2" from the Reason Factory Sound Bank\Dr Rex Drum Loops\Chemical Beats directory.
• Copy the REX slice data to the Dr.REX 2 sequencer track.
• In the sequencer arrange view, select a group from the Dr.REX 2 track.
• Select Get User Groove from the Edit menu.
• Select all groups on the Dr.REX 1 sequencer track.
• Set the quantization amount to 50%, and quantize the events on the Dr.REX 1 track.
• Select a group from the Dr.REX 1 sequencer track.
• Select Get User Groove from the Edit menu.
• Select all of the groups on the Dr.REX 2 sequencer track.
• Set the quantization amount to 100% and quantize all the groups on the Dr.REX 2 track.
• Run the sequence.

NN-XT REX Loop Player

The Reason samplers can load ReCycle loops, and the various modulation features of the NN-XT Advanced Sampler make it a very powerful ReCycle loop player. As in the Redrum, individual REX slices can be loaded using the sample browser, but an entire ReCycle loop can be loaded at once by selecting it in the NN-XT Patch Browser. When the ReCycle loop is loaded, the slices are automatically mapped across the keyboard.

NN-XT REX Playback Procedure

In order to extract REX slice data to the sequencer track, you still need to use a Dr.REX. Once this data is exported to the sequencer, the Dr.REX can be deleted. It's recommended that you keep the sequencer track even if the device is deleted. You may need to use this data for other purposes — as a user groove quantization template, for instance. The configuration below is no different from using a Dr.REX Loop Player, but there are features available on the NN-XT that allow you to manipulate the REX slices in ways not possible with the Dr.REX. The next few sections will illustrate the power of using the NN-XT as a ReCycle loop player.

• In an empty rack, create a mixer.
• Bypass auto-routing and create a Dr.REX Loop Player.
• Load the ReCycle loop "Chm19_Funkiest_130_eLAB.rx2" from the Reason Factory Sound Bank\Dr Rex Drum Loops\Chemical Beats directory.
• Copy the REX slice data to the Dr.REX 1 sequencer track.
• Create an NN-XT Advanced Sampler.
• Using the NN-XT patch browser, load the same ReCycle loop.
• Copy the REX slice groups from the Dr.REX 1 track to the NN-XT 1 track.
• Run the sequence, and save the file for use with the next example.

Reverse REX Slice Playback
By changing the play mode on certain slices of the ReCycle loop, some nice variations can result. Reverse hits can be used as little transitions between phrases, or as variations to the drum pattern. The sound of a reversed slice can also create elastic sounds with a completely different feel from the original loop.

• Start with the NN-XT REX player created in the previous example.
• Open the NN-XT Remote Editor panel.
• On the first slice, assigned to note C1, change the play mode to BW.
• Change the play mode to BW on slice 5 (E1) and slice 13 (C2).
• Run the sequence.

Looped REX Slices
The short loop times of the slices create a very distinctive sound, similar to granular synthesis. The loop length set by the Loop Start and Loop End parameters on each NN-XT zone can be either percussive for longer times, or harmonic with very short times. Building ReCycle slice loops in this manner requires quite a bit of work, but the unique results are well worth the effort. The results are very esoteric and are the roots of new electronic styles of music.

• Start with the NN-XT REX Player described above.
• Set the loop markers in the sequencer to loop only one measure, from 1.1.1 to 2.1.1.
• Open the NN-XT Remote Editor panel.
• On the NN-XT, make the following edits to the REX slice zone parameters (empty = no change):

Slice # / Root Key	Loop End	Play Mode
1 / C1		
2 / C#1	5.5%	FW-LOOP
3 / D1	5.6%	FW-LOOP
4 / D#1		
5 / E1		
6 / F1	28.6%	FW-LOOP
7 / F#1	14.4%	FW-LOOP
8 / G1	5.9%	FW-LOOP
9 / G#1		
10 / A1	4.4%	FW-LOOP
11 / A#1		
12 / B1	0.8%	FW-LOOP
13 / C2		
14 / C#2		BW

• Run the sequence.

This technique is similar to the drum programming used to create "drill" rhythms. Using looped drum samples in conjunction with a fast sequence containing 64th-notes will create completely new textures.

Velocity-Switching REX Slices
The ReCycle loop sample zones in the NN-XT can be quickly duplicated and layered. The layered zones can be assigned to respond to different velocities so that forward and reverse samples can be changed by changing the velocity in the sequence.

• Start with the NN-XT REX player described above.
• Set the loop markers in the sequence to loop two measures from 1.1.1 to 3.1.1.
• Open the NN-XT Remote Editor panel.
• Select all NN-XT slice zones by clicking on the group (G) area of the editor window.
• Adjust the group low velocity to 64.
• In the Edit menu, click on Duplicate Zones, and then select Group Selected Zones.
• Scroll to the bottom of the NN-XT Remote Editor window and select the second group of zones if it isn't already selected.
• Adjust the low velocity to 1 and high velocity to 63 for the second group.
• Change the play mode to BW on all of the zones in the second group. You must do this individually for each zone. There is no group adjustment for this parameter.

• Change the sample end (not loop end) markers for each of the second group zones according to the following chart. This must be done manually for each zone.

Slice #/Root Key	End
1 / C1	42.0%
2 / C♯1	75.6%
3 / D1	78.1%
4 / D♯1	82.6%
5 / E1	49.7%
6 / F1	81.4%
7 / F♯1	76.8%
8 / G1	69.1%
9 / G♯1	56.8%
10 / A1	73.7%
11 / A♯1	75.4%
12 / B1	68.4%
13 / C2	30.4%
14 / C♯2	74.4%
15 / D2	68.6%
16 / D♯2	76.1%
17 / E2	63.4%
18 / F2	69.9%
19 / F♯2	34.5%
20 / G2	60.0%
21 / G♯2	76.0%
22 / A2	42.1%
23 / A♯2	83.5%
24 / B2	86.5%
25 / C3	69.8%
26 / C♯3	67.2%
27 / D3	73.7%
28 / D♯3	40.0%
29 / E3	59.1%

• Switch the sequencer to edit mode and enable the REX and velocity lanes.
• Enable the pencil tool, and modify the velocity values to less than 64 for the following slices: 2, 4, 6, 8, 10, 14, 18, 22, 27, and 29.
• Save the NN-XT patch, and then run the sequence.

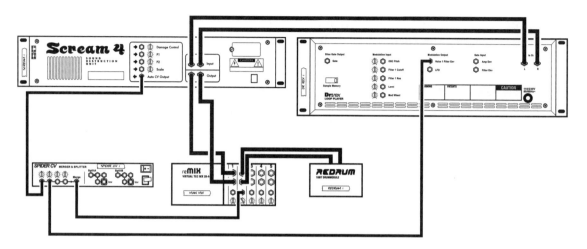

Figure 13-6.
Dr.REX output passing
through a Scream 4 on its
way to the mixer. The
Scream 4's auto CV
output is merged with the
Dr.REX filter envelope CV.
The merged CV modulates
the level of the Redrum
mixer channel input.

Groove Tools

f there were a method of consistently creating a solid rhythm on any track, then
the art of creating music would be a lot easier. Drum tuning, timbre, timing, and
dynamics are the elements that create a solid groove. If one of these elements is
not right, then a loop will lack that sparkle that moves a listener. This is why drum
loops are so popular. Rather than painstakingly recreate grooves, they can be called
upon in an instant with the Dr.REX Loop Player. The following examples are a
little different from the standard audio processing tools because they are designed
to take advantage of the natural feel found in sampled drum loops.

Groove Follower

This examples uses an envelope follower on the Scream 4 to create a control voltage based on the dynamics of a ReCycle loop. The envelope follower signal is merged
with the Dr.REX envelope CV to modulate the levels of a mixer channel. Using
the envelope signal is optional, but without it, quiet sections of the loop will not
open the mixer level CV enough for you to hear the Redrum pattern.

• In an empty rack, create a mixer and a Dr.REX Loop Player.
• Load the ReCycle loop "Chm09_FatBoy_135_eLAB.rx2" from the Reason
  Factory Sound Bank\Dr Rex Drum Loops\Chemical Beats directory.
• Copy the REX slice data to the Dr.REX 1 sequencer track.
• Set the Dr.REX filter envelope sustain to 64 and the master level to 78.

Envelope Follower Section
• Insert a Scream 4 between the Dr.REX and the mixer.

- Disable Damage.
- Create a Spider CV Merger & Splitter.
- Connect the Scream 4 auto CV output to Spider CV merge input 1.
- Connect the Dr.REX voice 1 filter env modulation output to the Spider CV merge input 2.
- Connect the Spider CV merger output to the mixer channel 2 level CV input.
- Set the mixer channel 2 level CV trim to 58 and the fader level to 0.

Drum Pattern Section
- At the bottom of the rack, create a Redrum Drum Computer.
- Load the patch "House Kit 03" from the Reason Factory Sound Bank\Redrum Drum Kits\House Kits directory.
- Program the following pattern:

Redrum Pattern

	1	2	3	4	5	6	7	8	9	10	11	12	13	14	15	16
1	M															
2					M								M			
3																
4				M							M					
5																
6																
7	S	S	S		S	S	S		S	S	S	S	S	S	S	
8	M	M	M	M	M	M	M	M	M	M	M	M	M	M	M	M
9																
10																

- Run the sequence.

The groove follower can be especially effective if the Redrum pattern is copied to the sequencer track and quantized based on the Dr.REX slice data. In many cases, the quantization will completely change the groove, and averaging the grooves will be more successful.

Beat Juggler

This technique was inspired by watching a DJ cut up beats on two turntables playing the same loop at different start times. The delay line creates a duplicate delayed signal of the original beat, and the Matrix modulates the mixer channels like a cross-switcher. Try adjusting the delay time to find different grooves, and then try creating different switching patterns on the Matrix. This is a fantastic way to give a simple drum loop new life and the energy of being cut by a live DJ.

- Start with an empty rack, and create a mixer.
- Set the fader levels on mixer channel 1 and channel 2 to 0.
- Bypass auto-routing and create a Dr.REX Loop Player.
- Load the ReCycle loop "Chm06_Bold_130_eLAB.rx2" from the Reason Factory Sound Bank\Dr Rex Drum Loops\Chemical Beats directory.
- Copy the REX slice data to the Dr.REX 1 sequencer track.

- Create a Spider Audio Merger & Splitter.
- Connect the Dr.REX audio outputs to the Spider splitter A and B inputs.
- Connect the Spider splitter A out 1 and splitter B out 1 to the mixer channel 1 inputs.

- Bypass auto-routing and create a DDL-1 Digital Delay Line.
- Set the DDL-1 delay time to 5 steps and set the feedback to 0.
- Connect the Spider splitter A out 2 and splitter B out 2 to the DDL-1 audio inputs.
- Connect the DDL-1 audio outputs to the mixer channel 2 inputs.

- Create a Matrix Pattern Sequencer.
- Set the Matrix to bipolar mode.
- All of the curve settings in Matrix pattern A1 should be at minimum. Program maximum (63) curve settings on steps 1, 5, 11, 12, and 13.

- Create a Spider CV Merger & Splitter.
- Connect the Matrix curve CV output to the Spider CV splitter A input.
- Connect the Spider CV splitter A out 1 to the mixer channel 1 level CV input.
- Connect the Spider CV split A out 4/inv to the mixer channel 2 level CV input.
- Set the mixer channel 2 level CV trim to 36.

- Run the sequence.

Rather than using a Matrix curve CV, create a real-time CV configuration using a SubTractor, as explained in Chapter Three, and route the envelope CV connection into the Spider CV splitter A input. Once the real-time CV control is set up, assign the slider to a MIDI controller to do some real-time crossfades between the loop and the delayed loop. Not only is this a lot of fun, it's a great technique to use in a live situation.

Chapter 14
Synthesizers

Software synthesis requires a lot of computing power and speed, so it has only been within the last few years that advances in computer technology have made software synthesis accessible to owners of personal computers. The technology behind Reason's SubTractor and Malström synthesizers would not be possible without a computer's ability to perform complex processes in a fraction of a second.

Synthesis is the process of creating sound electronically. A musician programming a synthesizer patch is like a painter developing his or her own colors and brushes for a work of art, or a composer building instruments exclusively for a new composition. The SubTractor and Malström are the main devices for synthesizing sounds in Reason, but the Redrum, NN-XT, NN19, and Dr.REX also have functions similar to those found on synthesizers. The main difference is that the latter group of devices uses audio samples as the source of sound waves.

This chapter discusses the practical side of adjusting parameters on the SubTractor and Malström synthesizers, and discusses some theoretical aspects of how sounds are generated in these devices. Some people will pick up the basics by learning the process of creating patches, while others need a conceptual framework to understand how the devices work.

Sound Deconstruction

A friend passed on a bit of wisdom from her grandmother, who said, "If you can imagine every quality about a rose — the fragrance, the texture of the petals, the gentle colors — you have the skills to be a good cook." Synthesizing sounds should be approached in this manner. Imagine the sound with as much detail as possible. With the sound in your mind, deconstruct it into its basic qualities: pitch, timbre, dynamics, modulation, and effects. These aspects provide the blueprint for programming a synthesizer. Once the basic parameters have been set, the fine details can be adjusted. Further adjustments can be made once you hear how the sound fits into the piece of music you're working on.

Pitch

Pitch is an easy quality to isolate, since it's usually categorized in frequency regions such as bass, midrange, and treble, which are relative to the position of the note C4 (Middle C). A synth bass patch will have definite low frequency characteristics. A flute sound falls in the treble range, so the pitch settings will be high. The Reason synthesis and sampler devices have pitch controls with slightly different labels. The Malström and SubTractor have pitch transposition controls labeled "oct," which transposes the pitch up and down in octave increments, "semi," which transposes the pitch up in semitones, and "cent," which adjusts the pitch in cents (increments of $\frac{1}{100}$ of a semitone).

As you create a patch, it's a good idea to play notes on a MIDI keyboard to audition the sound. You should play notes in the region that reflects the pitch characteristics you want. If you're creating a bass patch, play keys in the bass region. If you're creating a pad sound, play chords in the range they'll occupy in the music.

Timbre

The term timbre (pronounced "tam-br") refers to the tone of the sound, which is determined primarily by the waveform chosen in the sound generator (oscillator). A way of thinking about timbre is to compare the sound you want to create to one that's familiar. Decide if you want your patch to sound like strings, like a voice, like a tuba, etc. This will determine the type of waveform you need to create the patch, and may also suggest which type of sound generator to use. Synthetic timbres are easiest to create using the SubTractor oscillators. A Malström or an NN-XT multisample is more suited for complex timbres like voice or piano. The Malström has a unique waveform synthesis system, which is fantastic for timbres that change over time.

The complexity of the waveform determines the harmonic content. Dull sounds have limited harmonic content, while bright sounds are more complex and have more harmonic content. A sine wave is the simplest of all waveforms because it contains only one harmonic, the fundamental. This is the frequency or pitch of the sine wave. At the opposite end of the spectrum is white noise, which contains equal levels of all frequencies.

Another important component of timbre is created by filtering. Like the tone controls of an equalizer, the filter sections on the various Reason sound modules shape the tone. Overtones from complex waveforms can be filtered out. This process is known as subtractive synthesis, because harmonics are being removed from the original waveform. In theory, a resonant filter can reduce a complex waveform to a sine wave.

The timbre of a sound usually changes over the duration of the note as the filter envelope applies modulation to the filter cutoff frequency. This modulation is important for any synthesizer patch. Sometimes a static filter setting is appropriate, but in most cases some type of filter envelope modulation is necessary.

Dynamics

Dynamics are changes in the amplitude (loudness) of a sound. The main parameters for controlling the dynamics are the amp envelope ADSR settings. Basic sounds have simple gate dynamics: They are either on or off. Short staccato sounds like synth bass and drums work well with a gate envelope. Soft string sections and synth pads require envelopes that glide in softly, linger, and slowly fade away. These sounds use slower envelope attack and release settings, so that the volume changes over a note's duration. With your sound in mind, you can quickly determine the envelope settings needed to shape the dynamics of the patch.

Modulation

Most sounds change depending on how long they are played and on how loudly they are played. These transformations are controlled by modulation routings. Dynamic changes are easily recognized, but changes in pitch and timbre are also key elements in any patch. Each of the synthesis devices and sampler devices has modulation sources such as envelopes and LFOs, which are used to create variations in pitch, timbre, and dynamics. The SubTractor has an extensive set of velocity modulation routings, allowing several different parameters to be changed based on the velocity of an incoming note message. The Malström modulators can be routed to several different parameters to create complex LFO-type modulations. With any modulation routing there is a parameter to scale the amount of change applied to pitch, filter cutoff, or other parameters.

Modulation routings are key to creating unique patches. The variations in pitch, timbre, and dynamics created by modulation routings add character to the patch. More modulations add more texture to the sound and make the sound more expressive.

Effects

Contemporary synthesizers incorporate effects processing to further modify the sound of a patch. The synthesizer devices in Reason don't have dedicated effects processors, but effects modules can be quickly added to provide stereo chorusing, distortion, or reverberation for the patch. Some sounds don't require effects processing, but if the sound you have imagined is a lush stereo synth pad, then inserting a UN-16 Unison module and perhaps an RV7000 Reverb is critical for getting the desired result. Because effects change the character of a patch so drastically, it's often best to program the patch before inserting the effect device. After the effect is inserted, the dry/wet balance should be adjusted to a suitable position. Further parameter modifications can be made by moving back and forth between the patch and the effect device.

Patch Programming

Some people have an innate talent for programming synthesizer patches, while others find the task a bit daunting. Most of the time, synthesizer programming is a trial-and-error process in which one sets a few parameters, plays some notes, and then adjusts the parameters until the sound is just right. This section describes a basic methodology for approaching patch programming.

Polyphony, Pitch & Amp Envelope

Polyphony, pitch, and dynamics are the easiest qualities to isolate in a sound, and these parameters should be adjusted before anything else. If the final sound is polyphonic, then determine how many voices are necessary. Each voice of polyphony will require more CPU processing resources. Eight to 12 voices should be plenty for most musical parts.

Pitch transposition is relative based on incoming note events. If the synthesizer is being driven by a Matrix pattern, then using the pitch transpose parameters is easiest. If a MIDI keyboard is used to trigger the synthesizer, then playing notes in the appropriate range is best. If the range is not high or low enough when the sound is played on a keyboard, then octave transposition should be applied.

The amp envelope parameters should be adjusted to reflect the dynamics of the sound. The envelope parameters should reflect how the sound is going to be played. If the sound is a short percussive or bass sound, then the attack should be zero and the release time should be less than 32. If the sound is a long drone or pad sound, then the attack should be long and the release time should be long as well. For plucked sounds, the attack and decay should both be fairly fast, and the sustain level should be set low so the attack sounds louder than the sustain.

Oscillator & Filters

Next the oscillator waveform should be selected, as this provides the basis of the timbre of the sound. Once the waveform is selected, the type and amount of filtering should be applied accordingly to shape the harmonic content of the waveform. Besides selecting waveforms, there are a number of ways to synthesize timbres on the SubTractor. Both the SubTractor and Malström have two oscillators, so two waveforms can be layered. Layering two different waveforms will create even more harmonic content. Detuning one oscillator from the other and applying SubTractor FM are also important techniques.

Filter envelope settings should be programmed next so that the timbre changes over time. As a basic starting point for filter envelope settings, match the ADSR parameters with those set by the amp envelope settings. Play a few notes and start adjusting the filter envelope modulation amount.

At this point, people often go back and try different waveforms to see how they respond through the filter and filter envelope modulations. The waveform previously chosen might be good for the sound desired, but there might be a different waveform that works better. Often, one stumbles across a waveform or combination of layered waveforms that sounds really amazing.

Modulation

The basic patch is now structured, so it's time to apply modulation routings to give the patch more expressive character. Modulation routings work in the same manner as routing CV cables between Reason devices. They have a source, such as LFO/mod, envelope, velocity, or MIDI Control Change (CC) messages, a destination such as filter cutoff frequency or oscillator pitch, and an amount control, which scales the modulation.

LFO/mod and envelope modulation routings should be familiar since they function the same way as the CV patch connections discussed in Chapter 3. These are fixed modulation routings, which means they're part of the synthesizer patch. Velocity and MIDI CC messages are performance modulation routings: The modulation changes depending on how the note is played or what MIDI CC value is received. Velocity is the equivalent of a gate CV signal, and a MIDI CC message is the equivalent of a real-time unipolar curve CV.

The velocity value is determined by how hard or soft a note is played on a velocity-sensitive MIDI keyboard controller. This value can be used to modulate dynamics so that playing the note softly will decrease the volume level, while playing hard will increase the volume level. In some patches, which will be discussed below, velocity messages can be used to change the waveform so that the timbre changes depending on how hard a note is played.

The filter sections on the SubTractor and Malström have a keyboard modulation input that allows keyboard tracking modulation of the filter cutoff frequency. When keyboard tracking is enabled, the filter cutoff frequency is modulated based on the incoming note value. Higher notes will raise the filter cutoff frequency and lower notes will decrease it.

Real-time MIDI control messages like mod wheel and aftertouch can be used to modulate various parameters. For example, the filter cutoff frequency can be modulated from the mod wheel so that filter sweeps can be controlled by the wheel while notes are played with the right hand. This is far more convenient than playing a solo passage with the left hand and trying to change the filter cutoff frequency using a mouse.

Modulation of Modulation Amounts

Imagine if the CV sensitivity knob could be modulated so that the amount of modulation could be controlled. CV signals could be faded in so that the amount of modulation increased gradually rather than staying fixed at the sensitivity setting. While the CV trim pots can't be automated in Reason, several of the modulation routings in the synthesizers have a similar feature, which is usually controlled from note velocity messages or the mod wheel.

On both the SubTractor and Malström, note velocity can scale the filter envelope modulation amount, so that filter envelope modulation is greater when a note is played harder. Adding velocity modulation to a patch will give the sound more character and expressiveness. Velocity modulation can be inverted so that higher velocity values decrease parameter values. The amp envelope attack time can receive an inverse velocity modulation so that higher velocity values will decrease the duration of the amp envelope attack time.

Vibrato is a common modulation routing in which the LFO alters the pitch of the oscillator. The mod wheel can be used to control the amount of LFO pitch modulation so that it can be added during a performance. When the mod wheel is set to zero, no vibrato occurs, and as the mod wheel is raised, the intensity of the vibrato increases.

Oscillators

The basic synthesizer features of the SubTractor and Malström are very similar, but the method of generating waveforms is dramatically different. In the process of programming a synthesizer patch, some may find it helpful to understand how the oscillators function on these devices. The SubTractor oscillators play digital waves that consist of single cycles, reading them from a memory area called a wavetable. The Malström oscillators use a combination of wavetable and granular synthesis, which the developers call graintable synthesis.

SubTractor Oscillators
To get a better idea of the timbral resources offered by the SubTractor oscillators, try these experiments.

• In an empty rack, create a mixer and a SubTractor.
• Set the frequency slider of Filter 1 to 127.
• Use the osc 1 waveform selector to audition the 32 basic waves while playing a
   MIDI keyboard.

The oscillator mode switch adds far more timbres to this basic palette. When the mode is switched to '–' or 'x', two copies of the oscillator waveform are combined, using either subtraction or multiplication. With these settings, the phase knob will have a major impact on the sound of the oscillator. In addition, the phase can be controlled in real time.

- Select either the '−' or 'x' mode.
- Turn the osc 1 phase knob to 0.
- In the left-hand control section, turn the phase modulation amount knob up to 63.
- Choose various waveforms (other than the sine wave), play the keyboard, and move the mod wheel.

The mod wheel allows you to hear both the variety of waveforms available and the sounds you can create by modulating the phase. If you like one of the sounds, but you don't like the real-time modulation, turn the osc 1 phase knob so that this sound is produced when the mod wheel is at zero.

To experiment with FM (frequency modulation) timbres, proceed as follows:

- Turn the oscillator mix knob to 0.
- Click on the red button in osc 2 to activate it.
- Set both oscillators to sine waves (wave 4), and set their mode to 'o' (no phase processing).
- Turn the FM amount knob up gradually while playing the keyboard.
- Try various octave settings of the two oscillators.

The amount of FM can be controlled from the mod wheel, from LFO 1, or from the mod envelope. Envelope-controlled FM is especially useful for certain types of sounds. The sine wave is a good choice for FM, because the FM process will turn the upper harmonics in most of the other waveforms into noise.

Starting from the patch you've created in the previous examples, try these steps:

- Set the FM amount knob to about 24.
- Switch the mod envelope so that its destination is FM. Increase the decay time to about 64.
- In the velocity section, increase the mod envelope velocity amount to about 40.

Playing the keyboard will add more FM to the tone of osc 1 depending on how hard you play.

Malström Graintable Oscillator

Granular synthesis is a method of sound generation that uses small portions of a sample. The sample is divided into segments called grains. The duration of a grain is variable: It can be as short as a single cycle, or as long as 100ms. Individual grains can be looped to generate a short waveform, several grains can be sequenced in a successive or random pattern, or short bursts of grains can be triggered to create unique timbres.

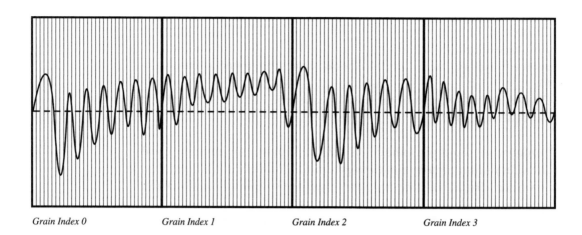

Grain Index 0	*Grain Index 1*	*Grain Index 2*	*Grain Index 3*

Figure 14-1.
Each grain is, in effect, a separate wavetable. Grains are ordered in a sequence like ReCycle loops.

The Malström graintables can be longer than a single cycle of a waveform. Some of the graintables, like the sine, square, and sawtooth, are single-cycle waveforms, but most of the others have longer durations and are composed of hundreds of grains.

Each grain is affected by pitch changes in the same manner as a SubTractor oscillator. The grains are ordered like a sequence of wavetables, similar to the way ReCycle loops function. The speed of the grain sequence is independent of the pitch of the individual grains. For example, the graintable "303Loop" can be played as a chord, and the sequence of notes stay in time even though each note is playing a different pitch.

When MIDI or CV note events trigger the oscillator, the graintable sequence starts at the position indicated by the index slider. The actual number of grains varies depending on the original sample, so the index parameter is a relative control rather than a precise indicator of the actual grain position.

The tempo of the graintable sequence is controlled by the motion parameter. The default setting of 0 plays the grain sequence at the original tempo. Increasing the motion parameter will trigger the grains at a faster rate, and the length of each grain will shortened. When the motion parameter is less than 0, each grain is looped until it's time for the next grain to be triggered. In some wavetables you'll also hear what sounds like crossfading from grain to grain. Setting the motion parameter to –64 will stop the sequence and loop the grain at the current position of the graintable sequence. With the motion sequence stopped, new note events will loop the grain pointed to by the index parameter.

The nature of the motion sequence varies depending on the graintable. Some motion sequences repeat through the grain indices from index 0 to index 127 and back to index 0. Some loop back and forth bidirectionally between index 0 and index 127. Several motion sequences behave like sample loops: The sequence first plays through from index 0 to index 127 and then loops starting from an index point in between. Graintables like sine, square, sawtooth, and triangle are unaffected by the motion parameter.

Altering the shift amount may sometimes sound like a pitch change, especially with a fixed waveform such as a sine wave. Regardless of the graintable selected, the shift parameter will dramatically alter the harmonics.

Example Patches

This section provides some examples to show how synth patches are created using the techniques described above. The parameter settings are ordered in a deliberate manner to illustrate how a patch takes shape as each setting is changed. After each adjustment, play a few notes from a MIDI keyboard or a sequence to hear how the tone has changed. The parameter settings start with the initial patch settings on a SubTractor or Malström when it's first created in the rack.

Monophonic Square Wave Bass

Synthesized bass is one of the staples of every electronic music style. A bass sound has a quick, loud attack and settles down to a relatively low sustain level. Synth bass sounds are usually lower in pitch, and don't have much in the way of high-frequency harmonics, so a lowpass filter is used to eliminated all but the low-frequency harmonics from the SubTractor square wave. This patch has a simple, almost generic sound, but it can be processed through a Scream 4 to yield a variety of solid tones.

Polyphony:	1
Osc 1 octave:	3
Osc 1 waveform:	square (2)
AMP envelope:	A 0, D 50, S 67, R 24
Filter 1:	
Type:	LP 24
Freq:	44
Res:	18
Kbd:	64
Filter envelope:	A 0, D 50, S 26, R 24, amount 0
Velocity modulation:	
Amp:	32
F. Env:	32

24dB Bandpass Filter Sweep

The filter sweep synthesis patch is another common sound found on almost every synthesizer. The filter sweep is a slowly evolving sound in which a long attack and long release create an ethereal motion. The sawtooth oscillator generates a waveform with a lot of harmonics, and a bandpass filter slowly moves upward from a low center frequency, only letting a few harmonics pass through at a given moment. This example uses one Malström oscillator and both filters in series to create a 24dB bandpass filter that sweeps the overtones produced by a sawtooth graintable.

Polyphony:	8
Osc A octave:	4
Osc A envelope:	A 100, D 116, S 127, R 96
Osc A waveform:	Sawtooth*16
Osc A to shaper:	off
Osc A to filter B:	on
Filter B:	
Type:	BP 12
Freq:	14
Res:	0
Env:	on
Kbd:	off
Filter B to shaper:	on
Filter A:	
Type:	BP 12
Freq:	14
Res:	0
Env:	on
Kbd:	off
Filter envelope:	A 116, D 100, S 64, R 98, amount 111

Synth Pad with Effect Inserts

A synth pad patch is usually polyphonic, so that chords or bass octaves can be played to create a rich drone. The sound is not too deep, so the oscillator is not transposed downward. To vary the harmonics, a type of modulation called pulse width modulation (PWM) is usually applied to a square wave. Pulse width modulation shortens and lengthens the duration of the square wave's "duty cycle," which changes the harmonics. The changing harmonics created by PWM can be recreated in the SubTractor by using a sawtooth waveform using phase subtraction mode and modulating the phase from an LFO. A lowpass filter is used to cut off the high harmonics, and a slight amount of keyboard tracking modulation is used to modulate the filter. No envelope modulation is applied to the filter of the synth pad. The signal from the SubTractor is fed through a UN-16 unison and a RV7000 Reverb to add the atmospheric texture normally associated with pad sounds.

Polyphony:	8
Osc 1 octave:	4
Amp envelope:	A 75, D 100, S 101, R 73
Osc 1:	
Waveform:	sawtooth (1)
Mode:	–
Phase:	64
LFO 2	
Dest:	Phase
Rate:	52
Amount:	34
Filter 1:	
Type:	LP 24
Freq:	65
Res:	36
Kbd:	42
Velocity modulation:	
Amp:	14
F. Env:	0

Insert a UN-16 and set the dry/wet mix to 52. Insert an RV7000 and set the dry/wet mix to 36.

Stereo Female Choir

The "Voice: FemaleChoir" Graintable on the Malström Synthesizer is a lovely oscillator source for creating lush polyphonic vocal pads. Because this a pad sound, the patch has a slow attack and release, and should be played as long sustained notes. This patch will not use filtering, taking advantage of the full harmonic content of the female voice graintables. This example uses both oscillator A and B using the same graintable. A slight pitch adjustment and a slight index shift will generate a subtle stereo effect when the spread parameter is adjusted. When the filters are switched off, the spread control is like a mix level between osc A and osc B. Zero spread means the two signals are merged and the output is monophonic, and a spread of 127 completely isolates the outputs so that only osc A is routed to the left output and only osc B to the right output.

Polyphony:	8
Osc A & B octave:	4
Osc A & B envelope:	A 70, D 100, S 127, R 86
Osc A & B waveform:	Voice: FemaleChoir
Osc A & B:	on
Osc A:	
index:	0
cent:	−3
Osc B:	
index:	4
cent:	3
Filter A & B:	off
Spread:	127
Velocity modulation:	
level A:	16
level B:	16

This is a foundation for creating interesting stereo Malström patches. The subtle pitch difference and offset indices create the variation between the left and right channels. Try experimenting by selecting different graintables with this patch. Both oscillators must be using the same graintable.

Amplitude Modulation Organ

Ring modulation is a process that requires two oscillator signals. The two signals are multiplied by one another to create new harmonics, whose frequencies will depend on the input frequencies. Amplitude modulation is similar to ring modulation except that the original tones are combined with the new harmonics; a true ring modulator outputs only the sum and difference tones, not the original waveforms.

This example uses SubTractor sine waves set at different octaves. The output from the ring modulator is balanced with the oscillator 1 signal using the mix knob: A setting of 127 will only pass the ring modulation output and a setting of 0 will only pass the oscillator 1 signal. An LFO is used to modulate the filter cutoff frequency to simulate a rotating speaker effect found on old Hammond organs with Leslie speaker cabinets. The Init Patch amp envelope, filter, and filter envelope modulation settings are used in this patch.

Polyphony:	8
Osc 1:	
Waveform:	sine (4)
Oct:	4
Osc: 2	on
Waveform:	sine (4)
Oct:	5
Semi:	7
Ring modulation:	on
Osc mix:	67
LFO 1:	
Dest:	F.Freq
Rate:	62 (80 for fast Leslie sound)
Amount:	22

Try out different waveforms to hear how the ring modulation works with oscillators that generate more complex harmonics. Adding mod envelope pitch modulation to this patch will create an interesting special effect. Set the mod envelope decay to 90, the mod envelope amount to 100, and the destination to osc 1. The harmonics sweep as the pitch of the oscillator is modulated by the envelope.

FM Electric Piano
Frequency modulation (FM) is a process that requires two oscillators, which are called a carrier and a modulator. The carrier oscillator is the one we listen to. The modulator changes the frequency of the carrier to create new harmonics, whose frequencies are based on the frequencies of the harmonics in the two waveforms. Vibrato is a basic form of frequency modulation: The LFO changes the pitch of an oscillator. But FM synthesis requires a modulator that can make tones in the audio range (above 20Hz) and track the keyboard.

The Yamaha DX7 was a popular synthesizer released in the mid-1980s that used FM synthesis to create complex synthetic timbres. FM synthesis can generate very complex harmonics very easily, so using sine waves, as the DX7 did, is ideal for creating useful timbres. The modulator oscillator (osc 2 in SubTractor) can be set to subtract (−) mode to add a bit more harmonic content. Other waveforms are not recommended for SubTractor FM, because the interactions of the overtones will cause aliasing (non-harmonic artifacts). However, you might want to try other waveforms for a special effect.

The example below uses velocity to control the amount of the frequency modulation. This adds expressive depth as different velocity values change the initial timbre. Mod envelope and LFO modulation are also used to alter the pitch, adding slight amounts of character of the overall tone. A lowpass filter is used in moderate amounts to cut off some of the high-frequency noise generated by the FM process.

Due to some limitations with the SubTractor's FM synthesis features, this patch changes character in the lower registers, but the higher range is still useful for solo electric piano parts.

Polyphony:	8
Amp envelope:	A 0, D 72, S 0, R 36
Osc 1:	
Waveform:	sine (4)
Oct:	4
Osc 2:	on
Phase:	19
Mode:	(−)
Waveform:	sine (4)
Oct:	7
Semi:	4
FM amount:	4
Osc mix:	0
Mod envelope:	A 0, D 58, S 30, R 44, amount 26, destination: phase
Filter 1:	
Type:	LP 24
Freq:	91
Res:	0
Kbd:	36
Filter envelope:	A 0, D 30, S 0, R 0, amount 12
LFO 1:	
Dest:	Osc 2
Rate:	68
Amount:	4
Velocity modulation:	
Amp:	27
Filter env:	0
FM:	29
Filter env decay:	12
Mod env:	20

The extensive velocity modulation of this patch makes it very expressive when notes are played with different dynamics levels. Velocity changes the timbre by modulating the FM amount and by modulating mod envelope phase modulation. This makes the timbre more complex when notes are played harder.

Synthesized Bass Drum

Many vintage drum machine devices were not sample-based like the Redrum. They used analog subtractive synthesis and oscillators to generate percussion sounds. These sounds are typically monophonic and have a fast attack and short decay. The pitch of a bass drum sound is usually modulated by an envelope so the initial attack is a higher pitch.

This example uses a Malström, which does not have an envelope that modulates pitch. Mod A can be used as an envelope curve when it's set to one-shot mode, however. This will cycle through the modulator curve only once when a note event is received. The rate knob will control the duration of the pitch envelope, and the modulator's pitch amount knob will scale the amount of pitch modulation. Mod A controls the pitch of both oscillators in this example. Oscillator B is detuned by 50 cents, causing an effect known as beating, where a small amount of phase cancellation between the two oscillators creates a rhythmic pattern.

Polyphony:	1
Osc A & B octave:	2
Osc A & B envelope:	A 12, D 68, S 0, R 32
Osc A & B waveform:	Sine
Osc B:	On
Cent:	50
Mod A:	
Curve:	10
1-Shot:	On
Rate:	86
Pitch:	51
Velocity modulation:	
Level A:	12
Level B:	12
Master level:	106

For a kick drum sound, play at the bottom of the keyboard. For a thicker sound, try turning on the Shaper and routing oscillator 1 into it.

A similar patch can be created using the SubTractor, but the pitch modulation envelope will only modulate osc 1 or osc 2, not both simultaneously. By connecting a modulation cable from the mod envelope modulation output to the pitch CV input, however, you can get the envelope to modulate the pitch of both oscillators.

Synth Stabs

The word "stab" describes a polyphonic sound that is played staccato and has a loud attack, quick decay, and low sustain level. Imagine quickly stabbing at the keys on the keyboard. The attack is accented with an initial brightness, so there is also a quick filter modulation that decays as fast as the amplitude envelope. Stabs usually have a very subtle pitch modulation, which sounds like the initial attack when a brass instrument finds the pitch after the first burst of wind.

This example demonstrates creating a synth stab patch on the Malström. Mod A is used in one-shot mode to apply pitch modulation that accents the initial attack of both oscillators. The timbre of a stab sound is rich in harmonics, so both oscillators use a sawtooth graintable, with osc B transposed an octave higher. Velocity modulation is applied to the oscillator amp envelopes as well as the filter envelope so that harder stabs will sound louder and brighter.

Polyphony:	8
Osc A octave:	3
Osc B:	On
Octave:	4
Cent:	50
Osc A & B envelope:	A 12, D 43, S 59, R 32
Osc A & B waveform:	Sawtooth*16
Mod A:	
Curve:	10
1-Shot:	On
Rate:	89
Pitch:	19
Osc A to filter B:	On
Osc B to filter B:	On
Filter B:	
Type:	LP12
Env:	On
Kbd:	On
Freq:	66
Res:	16
Filter envelope:	A 12, D 53, S 0, R 49, amount 36
Velocity modulation:	
Level A:	14
Level B:	14
Filter env:	14

Pattern-Controlled Formant Modulation

This patch shows only one of the myriad possibilities for modulating Reason's synth parameters from an external CV source — in this case a Matrix.

- In an empty rack, create a mixer and a Malström Graintable Synthesizer.
- Set the Malström's polyphony to 1 and the portamento to 47.
- On osc A, select the graintable "Voice: Throat."
- Set the osc A motion to −64.
- Enable the osc A routing into the shaper.
- Set the filter A resonance to 42 and cutoff frequency to 42.
- Set the filter envelope amount to 30.

Modulation Section
- Create a Matrix Pattern Sequencer.
- Randomize pattern A1 by selecting Randomize Pattern in the Edit menu.
- Program tied events from step 1 through step 7 and from step 9 through step 15.
- If randomization has created gates on steps 8 and 16, remove them.
- From step 1 through step 8, program C3 notes, and from step 9 through step 16 program G3 notes.
- Bypass auto-routing and create a Spider CV Merger & Splitter.
- Connect the Matrix curve CV output to the Spider splitter A input.
- Connect the Spider splitter A out 1 to the Malström filter modulation input.
- Connect the Spider splitter A out 2 to the Malström index modulation input.
- Set the Malström index modulation trim to 127.
- Set the sequencer tempo to 86 BPM.
- While running the Matrix pattern, edit the curve events to create an interesting rhythm for the voice formants.

Reason MIDI Stack

Reason can be used as a real-time sound generator module. In fact it's a fantastic sound generator, considering the endless possibilities available. A MIDI stack is a combination of several MIDI synthesizers in which they all respond to the same incoming MIDI signals, creating a layered sound. Reason has the facility to route MIDI directly to five different devices simultaneously to create a MIDI stack. Before routing MIDI, the stack of devices in the Reason rack must be created and set up as in a typical Reason song. This example will use a variety of sources to illustrate how a stack containing a thick piano, voice, and synthesizer pad is created.

- Open the Reason Preferences box and select the Advanced MIDI page.
- Assign all four of the external control busses to the same MIDI device or interface driver.
- Switch to the MIDI Preferences page and assign the port to the same MIDI device or interface driver. Set the channel to 1.
- Close the Preferences box.
- In an empty rack, create a mixer.

Synthesizer Section
• Create two Malström Graintable Synthesizers.
• On Malstrom 1, load the patch "Seesaw Breth.xwv" from the Reason Factory Sound Bank\Malstrom Patches\Pads directory.
• On Malstrom 2, load the patch "Lo Texture Pad.xwv" from the Reason Factory Sound Bank\Malstrom Patches\Pads directory.
• Create an NN-XT Advanced Sampler.
• Load the patch "GRANDPIANO.sxt" from the Reason Factory Sound Bank\NN-XT Sampler Patches\Piano directory.
• Create an NN19 Digital Sampler.
• Load the patch "FemaleAhhhFSwp.smp" from the Reason Factory Sound Bank\NN19 Sampler Patches\Voice directory.
• Insert an RV7000 Advanced Reverb between the NN19 and the mixer channel 4 inputs.
• Load the RV7000 patch "ALL Medium Stage.rv7" from the Reason Factory Sound Bank\RV7000 Patches directory.
• Set the RV7000 dry/wet amount to 73.
• Create a SubTractor Synthesizer.
• Load the SubTractor patch "Trad Pad.zyp" from the Reason Factory Sound Bank\SubTractor Patches\Pads directory.
• Insert a UN-16 Unison module between the SubTractor and the mixer channel 5 inputs.

MIDI Routing Section
• On the Reason Hardware Interface, select Bus A, and assign channel 1 to Malström 1 by selecting it from the Device pop-up menu.
• Select Bus B and assign channel 1 to Malström 2.
• Select Bus C and assign channel 1 to NN19 1.
• Select Bus D and assign channel 1 to NN-XT 1.
• On the Reason Sequencer, enable MIDI in to the SubTractor 1 sequencer track.

Performance Section
• Play a note from a MIDI keyboard to hear the Reason MIDI stack.
• Adjust the mixer's faders and panpots to taste.

Chapter 15
Sampling

Since the invention of modern recording technology, there have been many experimental compositions that made use of recorded sound. Many of these were composed long before digital recording technology was available, and used tape machines or phonographs as part of the performance. These experiments in the use of recorded sound, which were called *musique-concrète*, eventually evolved into the sampling technology musicians currently use.

The earliest form of sampling was found in an instrument called the Mellotron, a keyboard instrument that used analog audio recorded on strips of tape. Each strip of tape had an individual note of an instrument, and each key on the keyboard triggered a different tape strip. When a key was pressed, the tape was pulled across the playback head by a spring mechanism. The Mellotron was a multisampler, because every key played a different recording. This multisampling technique is still applied in modern digital samplers, including the NN19 and NN-XT samplers in Reason. A sample zone or keyzone is like a Mellotron tape strip: A unique sound is "mapped" to one or more keys.

Reason's samplers can load individual audio samples or complete sampler patches. Patches contain parameter settings for filters, envelopes, modulation, and so on. They also contain information such as which samples should be loaded from the hard drive, the pitch and loop point for each sample, and a map of how the samples should be arranged on the keyboard. Many of the programming principles outlined in the previous chapter apply to both the NN19 and NN-XT samplers. The main difference between the samples and the synthesizers is the source of sound generation. While the synthesizers use wavetables and graintables, the samplers use audio samples.

Unlike their hardware counterparts, the NN19 and NN-XT can only play back audio samples; they can't record new ones. In order to record a sample, a recording application must be used. Once the audio has been recorded, and the file saved to your hard drive, the sample can then be loaded into Reason. This is not truly a limitation, because most audio interfaces come with basic software that will allow you to record from the audio inputs, and there are shareware audio editors that record and edit audio files suitable for Reason's samplers.

Sample Mapping

Multisampling requires building a key map, in which samples are assigned to different keys. A different sample can be mapped to each of the 128 MIDI notes. Meticulous sample editors will take advantage of file information parameters, which allow root note and tuning information to be stored along with the audio file. For the rest of us, who do not go through the trouble of editing this information, the following examples demonstrate a few shortcuts for creating sample maps using the NN19 and NN-XT.

Quick Sample Key Maps
One of the most tedious aspects of building a multisample patch is mapping samples to different keys of the MIDI keyboard. The NN-XT has many features that far exceed the NN19, but the NN19 is easier to use when it comes to assigning samples to the keyboard. Once an NN19 patch is saved, it can be loaded into an NN-XT for other types of manipulation. Note that if the samples have root keys assigned, this process may not work properly.

• In an empty rack, create an NN19 Digital Sampler.
• Use the sample browser to load the first 15 samples from the Reason Factory Sound Bank\Other Samples\Chords-Phrases-Pads-Stabs directory.
• Disable KBD.TRACK.
• Set the oscillator pitch octave to 3, semi to 8, and fine-tune to 50.
• From the Edit menu, select Automap Samples.
• Save the patch, and play notes from a MIDI keyboard to audition the sample map.

This is easiest way to create a palette of samples that don't require pitch tracking. The NN-XT auto-mapping feature functions differently than the similar feature on the NN19, and will not assign samples to individual keys. The NN19 patch can be saved to disk, then opened using the NN-XT patch browser. Once loaded into the NN-XT, each sample zone can be assigned specific pitch, filtering, and amp envelope parameters.

Pitch Detection & Auto-Mapping
The NN-XT features a fantastic utility for quickly mapping multisamples to create a patch. This is different from making a quick sample palette, such as a collection of kick drums, because each of the samples in the multisample is a recording of the same instrument playing a different note. Two items in the Edit menu will auto-

matically set the root key and map the zones across the keyboard. There is a specific procedure for automatically mapping samples to different key zones.

First, all samples must be loaded in the NN-XT. Once the samples are loaded, select Set Root Notes from Pitch Detection from the Edit menu. Then select Automap Zones from the Edit menu.

The automatic pitch detection is not always perfect, and some editing may be required, but you'll find that many of the samples and key zones are arranged properly. One little issue is that the automatic pitch detection will adjust the tuning of the sample zone. Sometimes the slight tuning adjustment actually helps. If the zone is improperly mapped, then the automatic pitch detection did not successfully analyze the sample, and the zone will require manual adjustment.

Layering NN-XT Samples

The NN-XT can trigger several different samples from a single MIDI note event. This can be used a variety of ways to create layers of different sounds and even different multisample groups. The main limitation to layering samples is the amount of memory available to Reason. This is especially important for people running Reason on Apple MacOS 8 or MacOS 9. Be sure to allocate enough memory to the Reason application.

Ensemble Patch

This example demonstrates how to layer several different samples to create an "ensemble" of samples. When one key is pressed, all of the samples will play back simultaneously. This can be used as a method of sound design, because each sample can have its own envelope, filter, and modulation settings.

• In an empty rack, create a mixer.
• Create an NN-XT Advanced Sampler, and open the Remote Editor.
• Load the sample "170-85_JazzGuitar_mLp_eLab.aif" from the Reason Factory Sound Bank\Music Loops\Fixed Tempo (wave, aiff) directory.
• Set the Group Key Poly to 1.
• Set the sample start to 50%.
• Set the amp envelope release to .54 seconds.
• Select Add Zone from the Edit menu.
• Load the sample "CYM1V10HSH.aif" from the Reason Factory Soundbank\Redrum Drum Kits\xclusive drums-sorted\06_Cymbals directory.
• Set the velocity level amount to 40%.
• Set the pitch keyboard track to 0.
• Set the amp envelope release to 1.54 seconds.

- Select Add Zone from the Edit menu.
- Load the sample "BD1Dub.aif" from the Reason Factory Soundbank\Redrum Drum Kits\xclusive drums-sorted\01_BassDrums directory.
- Set the velocity level amount to 59%.
- Set the pitch keyboard track to 0.
- Set the amp envelope release to 1.05 seconds.
- Select Add Zone from the Edit menu.
- Load the sample "SN2br.aif" from the Reason Factory Soundbank\Redrum Drum Kits\xclusive drums-sorted\02_SnareDrums directory.
- Set the velocity level amount to 47%.
- Set the pitch keyboard track to 0.
- Set the amp envelope release to .40 seconds.
- Set the pan to –22.
- Play notes on a MIDI keyboard to hear the ensemble patch.

Layering Patches

Entire patches can be layered in a single NN-XT. This allows you to stack several multisampled instruments, which will be playable from a single keyboard or sequencer track. This is a fantastic way to create a large brass or string section. This example illustrates a popular technique of layering a female vocal multisample to create an atmospheric choral sound on top of a string orchestra. Building up layered patches involves some work, and you should save the layered patches for later reference.

- In an empty rack, create a mixer and an NN-XT Advanced Sampler.
- Bypass auto-routing and create another NN-XT.
- On NN-XT 1, load the patch "VNS+VCS+BSS.sxt" from the Orkester Sound Bank\Strings\String Combinations directory.
- On NN-XT 2, load the patch "FEMALEAHH.smp" from the Reason Factory Sound Bank\NN19 Sampler Patches\Voice directory.
- Expand the Remote Editor panel on NN-XT 2.
- On NN-XT 2, click on the first group area to select the key zones, and click on Copy Zones in the Edit menu.
- Expand the Remote Editor panel on NN-XT 1.
- Select Paste Zones in the Edit menu. The zones from NN-XT 2 are now combined with the zones on NN-XT 1.
- While the pasted zones are still selected in the NN-XT 1 Remote Editor, set the group amp envelope gain level to –11dB, and set the velocity-to-amp envelope attack modulation to –22%.
- Delete NN-XT 2.
- Enable MIDI on the NN-XT 1 sequencer track and play notes from a MIDI controller to audition the layered patch.

Audio Manipulation

Manipulation of recorded audio is one of the most interesting aspects of using samplers. The audio data can be tweaked and played as if it were a synthesizer. The pitch can be modulated with an LFO, short segments of sample can be used as a waveform, and sample playback can be reversed. A wide variety of effects can be applied to samples to create unique timbres. The following examples illustrate a few ideas that you may find inspiring and that may lead you to further experimentation.

Envelope-Modulated LFO Rate

The NN-XT is the only device in Reason that allows CV control over the LFO rate. This can be used to create unique pitch modulation patterns. In the example below, the Matrix pattern sequencer CV/gate signals are split to trigger both the SubTractor and the NN-XT. The SubTractor's filter envelope signal modulates the LFO rate on the NN-XT.

- Start with an empty rack, and create a mixer.
- Create a Matrix Pattern Sequencer and a Spider CV Splitter & Merger.
- Connect the Matrix note CV output to the Spider CV split A input.
- Connect the Matrix gate CV output to the Spider CV split B input.
- Pencil in tied gate events from step 1 through step 8 on the Matrix.
- Bypass auto-routing and create a SubTractor Synthesizer.
- Connect Spider CV split B output 1 to the SubTractor sequencer control gate input.
- Set the SubTractor polyphony to 1, enable low BW, and set the filter envelope decay to 75 and filter envelope release to 45.
- Create an NN-XT Advanced Sampler and open the NN-XT Remote Editor.
- Load the Sample "CYM1 1OHSH.aif" from the Reason Factory Soundbank\Redrum Drum Kits\xclusive drums-sorted\06_Cymbals directory.
- Set the NN-XT amp envelope release to 7.06 seconds, and the LFO1 pitch modulation amount to 1350 cents.

Figure 15-1.
A Matrix triggers both the NN-XT and SubTractor. SubTractor envelope controls NN-XT LFO rate.

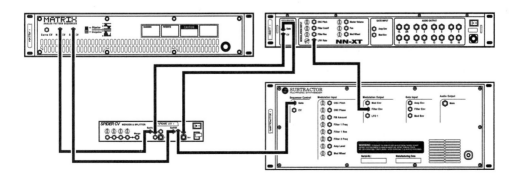

- Connect the SubTractor filter env modulation output to the NN-XT LFO1 rate CV input.
- Connect Spider CV split A output 1 to the NN-XT sequencer control CV input, and Spider CV split B output 2 to the NN-XT sequencer control gate input.
- Set the NN-XT LFO1 rate CV trim to 93.
- Run the sequence.

Turntablist

A turntablist is a DJ who uses the turntable as an instrument. The effect described below is quite extensive and requires a lot of fine-tuning, but the results are astonishing. This effect emulates the sound of a vinyl record being scratched on a turntable by triggering samples that play forward and backward. The modulation envelope controls pitch and filter settings that create the sound of the sample accelerating and decelerating.

- Start with an empty rack, set the tempo to 84 BPM, and set the pattern shuffle amount to 29.
- Create a mixer.
- Create an NN-XT Advanced Sampler, and open the NN-XT Remote Editor.
- Using the sample browser, load the sample "Peff_BrassAction.aif" from the *Power Tools for Reason* CD Audio Samples directory.
- Duplicate the sample zone "Peff_BrassAction.aif" five times.
- Set the NN-XT group parameters as follows:

NN-XT Group Parameters

Key polyphony	1
Mode	Legato
Portamento	36

The NN-XT sample zones all have the same name, so they are referenced from their order from top to bottom. Only adjust the parameters indicated in the charts. Only parameters of the selected zone selected will be modified, so click on the sample name before editing the parameters. Start with the NN-XT sample parameters found along the bottom of the Remote Editor display:

NN-XT Sample Parameters

Zone	Root	Start	End	Play Mode	Lo Key	Hi Key
1	C3	0.0%	100.0%	FW	C 3	C 3
2	D3	35.6%	100.0%	FW	C♯ 3	D 3
3	E3	0.0%	74.4%	BW	D♯ 3	E 3
4	F3	0.0%	40.4%	BW	F 3	F♯ 3
5	G3	0.0%	14.9%	BW	G 3	G♯ 3

Two zones are used for forward playback and three are set for reverse playback. The start positions are offset to recreate the effect of scratching at varying points of the record. The sample end parameter is actually the sample start position for zones set in BW play mode.

The NN-XT synth parameters can be set for a single zone or for a group of zones. Each sample zone in this patch has specific parameters, so be careful not to select the group or more than one sample zone. Start with the velocity modulation parameters:

NN-XT Synth Velocity Parameters

Zone	Mod Dec	Sample Start
1	−9%	56%
2	−22%	44%
3	11%	0%
4	31%	0%
5	25%	0%

Samples in BW play mode play from the end position sample parameter, and because the playback duration will be fairly short, modulation of the sample start parameter will be insignificant.

The modulation envelope is assigned to the sample playback pitch. The envelope is set with very short ramps to create the sound of the record speeding up and slowing down.

NN-XT Synth Mod Envelope Parameters

Zone	Attack	Hold	Decay	Sustain	Release	Pitch	Filter
1	48.5ms	Off	1.13 s	0%	44.8ms	2269 cents	44%
2	0.10 s	Off	36.4ms	0%	20.6ms	1875 cents	44%
3	7.2ms	Off	0.30 s	0%	0.14 s	379 cents	44%
4	22.7ms	Off	0.20 s	0%	0.36 s	1517 cents	44%
5	48.6ms	Off	0.36 s	28%	20.6ms	2269 cents	44%

The filters are given a dynamic character from the envelope modulation source. Verify that all zones have the filter section switched on, or turn the filter on for the entire group. Set the following filter parameters:

NN-XT Filter Parameters

Zone	Freq	Res	Mode
1	547Hz	0%	LP 6
2	1.3kHz	50%	LP 6
3	3.2kHz	41%	LP 12
4	707Hz	25%	LP 12
5	28.2kHz	0%	LP 6

The amp envelope parameters are the same for all of the sample zones, and can be applied to the entire group of zones. First select the group of zones by clicking on the group region on the Remote Editor display. (This is the column to the left of the sample names under the letter "G".) Program the following amp envelope parameters:

NN-XT Synth Amp Envelope Parameters (Group)					
Zone	Attack	Hold	Decay	Sustain	Release
Group	0.5ms	Off	60ms	0.0dB	19.1ms

For those who are new to programming NN-XT patches, this patch is probably a long task. It's recommended that you now save the NN-XT patch to a convenient location on your hard drive.

The playback of the sample patch can be rather unpredictable, so it's necessary to add some compression and equalization to the NN-XT outputs:

• Insert a Scream 4 distortion unit between the NN-XT audio outputs and the mixer channel 1 inputs.
• Connect the Scream 4 auto CV output to the P1 CV input.
• Set the P1 CV trim to 34.
• Program the following settings on the Scream 4:

Scream 1 Settings		
Damage: *on*	Damage control	30
	Algorithm	Tape
	P1	24
	P2	99
Cut: *on*	Lo	−26
	Mid	42
	Hi	5
Body: *off*	Reso	
	Scale	
	Auto	
	Type	
	Master	

Pattern Control Section

While this effect can be controlled via MIDI, a Matrix pattern sequencer is the most convenient way to trigger the scratch events on the NN-XT. Scratching is a very rhythmic process, and the configuration is designed to take advantage of all three Matrix control voltage outputs:

• Create a Matrix Pattern Sequencer, and switch it to bipolar mode.
• Connect the Matrix note and gate CV outputs to the NN-XT sequencer control CV and gate inputs.
• Connect the curve CV output to the NN-XT osc pitch modulation input.
• Adjust the NN-XT osc pitch CV trim to 14.

Scratch Pattern Programming

This is probably the most difficult part of the Turntablist effect. While the example provided below creates a basic pattern, more complicated scratching can be created with careful programming. Keep in mind that the samples on C3 and D3 play forward while the samples on E3, F3, and G3 play backward. Alternating between forward and backward requires separate gate and note events.

The Matrix curve CV controls the oscillator pitch, and this should be varied for each gate event. Scratching does not have a consistent pitch, so varying this control value adds more realism.

The velocity modulation on the NN-XT is set to mimic the push and pull speed. With the forward playback sample zones, velocity will also shift the start position. Gate events with high velocity settings will start these samples at a point further from the original start position. Velocity will also change the rate of the modulation decay. This creates the variation in acceleration/deceleration speeds. Mixing up the gate velocities is another way to add realism to the effect.

• Select Matrix pattern A1, set the pattern resolution to 1/32, and enable shuffle.
• Program the following on Matrix pattern A1:

Matrix Pattern

Step	1	2	3	4	5	6	7	8	9	10	11	12	13	14	15	16
Curve	0	0	20	20	−32	−32	63	−64	32	0	0	0	15	20	36	50
Note	C3	C3	F3	F3	D3	D3	G3	C3	F3	C3	G3	D3	E3	E3	E3	E3
Gate	L		L		L		H	M	M	H	L	H	TM	TM	TM	

• Run the Matrix pattern.

Chapter 16
MIDI Sequencing

MIDI is an acronym that stands for Musical Instrument Digital Interface. Developed in the early 1980s as a standardized method of communication between electronic music instruments, MIDI can be used to establish a digital network that connects synthesizers, other sound generators, and computer sequencers. Data transmitted along the network of MIDI cables can trigger synthesizers and samplers to play notes, change patches, and respond to controller movements. MIDI can also be used to synchronize timing between sequencers and drum machines. MIDI is still the basis of all current sequencing applications, including Reason.

The MIDI sequencer revolutionized the way music is created. Even before MIDI sequencing, artists could use multitrack audio tape, which allowed a single person to record every part of a complex arrangement. The musician would have to play all of the parts without mistakes, however. Using synthesizers and a sequencer, composer/performers can freely edit their tracks after recording — fixing the timing, transposing the part to a new key, or using an entirely different timbre, for example. Changes to a sequenced track are instantaneous, offering amazing flexibility.

At the heart of each Reason song is a MIDI sequence, in which note events and controller data are recorded, arranged, and routed to the devices in the rack. The sequencer's edit mode features the tools necessary for making microscopic adjustments to MIDI events, and the arrange mode is used to structure the entire song. This chapter will focus on methods that make arrangements easier to handle, and hopefully will improve your productivity when developing tracks in Reason.

Sequencer Tracks

Each time a sound generator module is created in the Reason rack, a corresponding sequencer track is added. This is convenient feature, but it can also lead you to work in a manner that is somewhat narrow-minded. Just because Reason adds one sequencer track per device does not mean you have to work with only one track per device. In fact, using multiple tracks per device can be more efficient. This has already been demonstrated in previous chapters, where multiple tracks are used to rearrange REX slices. The next few sections discuss more ways of using multiple sequencer tracks.

Automation Tracks

Rather than recording automation data to the same track as the MIDI note events, create a separate track in which only the parameter automation for the instrument is recorded. Having the automation controls on a separate track allows you to disable parameter automation quickly by muting the track. By Option/Alt-clicking or using the contextual menu item, you can go directly to the sequencer track display containing the automation data.

Parameter change information can be used like a Matrix curve CV pattern that modulates several different parameters simultaneously. A measure or group of measures can be duplicated to repeat through the course of the sequence from the arrange view. This can also be achieved by selecting and duplicating individual blocks of controller lane data, but it's much faster to use the arrange window.

Certain parameters, such as the mod wheel, pitchbend, filter cutoff frequency, and volume, function in the same manner on various devices. Controller automation of these parameters can be assigned to other devices by duplicating the automation track and changing the destination device. For example, if the master volume level of a Malström is used to create a swell in dynamics for a pad sound, the level automation track can be duplicated and applied to any of the sound modules in Reason. ECF-42 filter cutoff and resonance parameter automation can be duplicated and will control the Dr.REX and NN-19 filters, filter B of the Malström,

Figure 16-1.

Filter events recorded on an ECF-42 automation track duplicated and routed to a SubTractor.

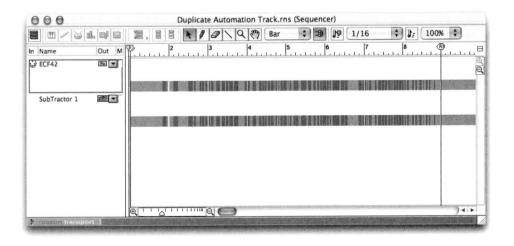

filter 1 of the SubTractor, and the NN-XT global filter control. However, it's not possible to cut and paste controller data from one controller lane to another (for example, to get the same movement on both filter cutoff and filter resonance).

Splitting Note Events

In an effort to get a track started as quickly as possible, one may record polyphonic events consisting of bass octaves played on the left hand and triads (or more) played on the right hand. This is a useful method for developing chord progressions, but the resulting track can sometimes overwhelm a mix. Naturally, this sequence is recorded live, but with a little editing, it can be distributed over several tracks.

• Duplicate the original track twice, and mute the original track.
• Enter edit mode to view the key lanes of the first duplicate track.
• Zoom out the sequencer view to see all of the note events.
• Select and delete all of the bass octave note events.
• Switch to the second duplicate track.
• Select and delete all of the right-hand chords.

Having the chord progression split to two different tracks allows more flexibility in changing the voices of the sequence. The bass octaves might be assigned to a synth pad played on a Malström, while the chords might be assigned to a choir multisample on the NN-XT. Or you might elect to delete the bass part entirely in favor of a more active, syncopated line. The separation of tracks also makes arrangement easier since the chord events and bass octave events can be deleted or duplicated as separate groups in the arrangement window.

Left-Hand Controller Overdubs

Overdubbing pitch-bends and mod wheel moves into a track that already contains some of the same type of data is a bit tricky in Reason, because the program treats these controllers like other types of automation. While in record mode, once you touch the left-hand wheel you're overdubbing, Reason will erase any other data of this type in the track as the play cursor moves over it.

The solution is to overdub new controller moves on a separate track assigned to the same synth. Once you have the modulation moves the way you want them, you can cut them from the overdub track and insert them at a corresponding point in the main synth track.

Redrum Tracks

Pattern-based Redrum programming has its advantages because it supplies a certain amount of instant gratification when a drum groove is programmed very quickly. Using multiple Redrum patterns and the pattern lane to develop an arrangement is fairly simple. One problem with this method is that it's not easy to make specific pattern changes. The occasional crash cymbal can be added to the drum lane of a Redrum sequence track, but a snare can't be removed without going through a number of steps to record a mute event or duplicate and reprogram the pattern and then edit the pattern automation.

Once a programmed drum arrangement has been established for the structure of a song, it can be converted to MIDI sequence events that trigger the Redrum channels. Pattern changes can be easily recognized, as pattern groups will be assigned different colors. Simply set the left and right loop locators to the boundaries of the track region where pattern A1 is playing, copy the pattern, move the locators to the next pattern region, and so on. Do this once for each pattern. Once all of the patterns have been copied to the track, switch off "Enable Pattern Section" on the Redrum. Then use group duplication in the track view so each pattern will play in the sections where it's needed.

Sometimes starting with a single Redrum pattern used as a metronome track is useful. The base pattern can be modified in edit mode, while percussive embellishments like snare rolls or crash cymbals can be programmed on separate sequencer tracks so that they can be quickly identified in the arrangement window. This provides a better overview of the entire drum arrangement.

Redrum patterns converted to MIDI sequence events can be split in the same manner as tracks with note events. For example, a converted Redrum pattern may use six different channels: bass drum, snare drum, rim shot, open hi-hat, closed hi-hat, and crash cymbal. Each of these elements can be split into its own track. One drum arrangement technique, especially with programmed drums, is to mute out different elements for a certain period of measures. Having each of the drum events on its own sequencer track makes this process simple, because the data can be deleted from the arrangement wherever the drum sound should be silent.

Once the Redrum notes are being played from the MIDI track rather than from the Redrum patterns, you can freely add snare "ghost notes" to individual measures, humanizing the track. This can be difficult in a Redrum pattern because the clock resolution of the pattern is fixed (to sixteenth-notes, for instance). Another advantage of copying Redrum patterns to tracks is that the drum sounds are no longer limited to three velocity levels. Each note can be given its own velocity with the pencil tool, and you can draw smooth crescendos and diminuendos with the line tool.

Groups

Most music is repetitive by nature, and elements of a music arrangement often recur throughout a track. Repetitive elements of a sequence can be recorded once and then duplicated for each instance where they occur. The key to arranging and duplicating musical phrases in a sequence is to use the group features. Regions of the song can easily be grouped using the pencil tool in the arrange view, or by selecting a range of measures with the arrow tool and selecting the Group command in the sequencer edit menu. A single group can be moved by selecting it and dragging it to a different position on the sequencer track, and the same can be done with several selected groups.

Arrangement groups add a visual element to the structure of a sequence. Not only does this provide a method of quickly moving to different parts of the sequence by dragging the position marker, the loop locators can quickly be set at the boundaries of a long group so you can work on a section of the music while listening to it.

Inserting Measures

The name of the Insert Bars Between Locators command in the sequencer edit menu is somewhat misleading, because it is not restricted to full measures. The loop locators can define a space of any length, and the insert command will shift events to the right by exactly the distance between the locator markers. Using the snap-to-grid feature with the resolution set to Bar will ensure that the space inserted is exactly on a measure, otherwise it may end up being less than a full measure.

Sometimes inserting a half- or quarter-measure space between passages can add a dramatic pause to a track. The are several pitfalls to be aware of when using this technique, however: Groove, shuffle, and user quantization will be useless, in the section after the break, and if Matrix or Redrum patterns are used, special 4-step or 8-step patterns may need to be programmed to occur during the break. It's a lot of work to add this timing shift to a track, but the effort is sometimes worth it. It may be easier to simply insert a one-measure gap, then shorten the gap using an audio editor after the song is finished and mixed.

Splitting All Groups

When you start moving individual groups around in the arrangements, the group regions will usually start and end at different measures. The Insert Bars Between Locators command can be used to insert a split point across all groups at a specific point in the sequence. Set the right and left locators to the same position, and then use this command. A space of zero measures is created, which splits all of the groups. This can be performed at another position to mark the start or end of the region, and the various groups in between can be selected and grouped as a single phrase.

Chapter 17
Reason Accessories

Reason alone is a fantastic application. You may not need anything else to turn your creative ideas into complete compositions. Other software applications can be used in conjunction with Reason to expand production possibilities. Discussed in some detail in earlier chapters is ReCycle, the application used to create REX loops. Registered Reason users can also download Reload and ReFill packer from the Propellerhead website. Using the ReWire protocol, Reason can be interfaced with many other software applications, and ReBirth RB-338 users can integrate the 303 synth bass and drum machine patterns from ReBirth into a Reason production.

Reload

Reload is a utility that converts Akai S1000 and S3000 sampler libraries into samples and patches that are usable in Reason. Reload will convert data from sample CD-ROMs and removable storage media. The application extracts and converts the audio data into AIFF format, and converts the Akai sampler patch information into SXT patches that are usable in the NN-XT sampler. Hundreds of commercial sample libraries are available for Akai samplers, and Reason users have convenient access to this vast collection. It's important to note that Reload will only run on Apple Mac OS X or Microsoft Windows XP operating systems. If you need an operating system upgrade in order to use Reload, please research all of the implications of the upgrade before performing it. Older software, including audio and MIDI device drivers, may become unusable under the new OS.

Using Reload is quite simple. When the application is launched, it waits until an Akai format CD-ROM or other removable storage media is inserted. Once the media is verified, Reload gives you the option of either extracting the data into a folder or packing the data into a ReFill file. If the CD-ROM has many small individual samples, the extraction process takes longer than if there are a few large samples. It can take as long as 45 minutes to convert a standard CD-ROM on a slow computer. The process can take still longer if you opt to pack the folder into a ReFill. After the extraction process, Reload will launch the ReFill Packer utility to create the ReFill.

Extracting the Akai format media to a folder is useful if you want to have direct access to the individual sample files. Perhaps only one of the partitions from the library is needed, and the rest will most likely never be used. If you want to modify some of the files in a sample editor, then having access to the AIFF files is necessary. Packing an Akai CD-ROM into a ReFill is useful if you want to take advantage of the ReFill file compression feature. ReFill can compress sample data with around a 2:1 ratio, and this will definitely economize hard drive space. The latest version of ReFill Packer must also be installed if you intend to create ReFills from sample libraries imported using Reload.

Custom Patch Directory

The NN-XT patches converted from Akai patches are located in the same directory as the sample files. Navigating through the folders can be a little confusing, mainly because the names given them will be "Partition A," "Partition B," etc. Patches of certain sample banks that you find useful should be saved in a separate directory so that they are easily found. If you have extracted the Akai media to a folder, then create an NN-XT Patches directory in this folder, or in some other convenient location on your system. Load the patch into the NN-XT, then save the patch into the NN-XT Patches folder. You can't copy the NN-XT patch file from the partition directory into the NN-XT Patches folder, because if you do, the file pointers to the samples will point to the wrong folder.

ReFill Packer

ReFills are add-on files that contain samples, ReCycle loops, patches, and songs usable by the different devices in Reason. The Reason Factory Sound Bank and Orkester files are the ReFill libraries installed with the Reason application, and dozens of commercial ReFill libraries are available. In the Reason user community, there exists a subculture surrounding the ReFill Packer utility. Several users produce ReFills that can be downloaded from the Internet and used freely.

Before creating a ReFill, you should organize the directory layout in a manner similar to creating a project folder for song projects. All the content of the ReFill must go into this folder before it can be packed. Included on the *Power Tools for Reason* CD is a directory named "ReFill Production Template," which provides an example of how to structure the directory hierarchy. You can duplicate this folder to your hard drive, rename it, and move the content into the appropriate directories within it.

Besides the Reason content, two other files must be included in the ReFill project folder — the info.txt and splash.jpg files. The splash.jpg is a small image that can be used to brand the ReFill. The file must be in jpeg format, and must have the exact dimensions of 64x64 pixels. If the image does not meet these requirements, ReFill Packer will reject the file and abort the packing process. The info.txt file is a text file that contains information about the ReFill: its name, copyright, and any comments. The name indicated in the info.txt file is extremely important, because Reason is sensitive to ReFill names. If two different ReFills have the same name indicated in the info.txt, one or both may be rejected when Reason looks for them.

The ReFill Packer utility should be moved into the same directory where the Reason Factory Sound Bank is located. When preparing to compress the project folder, ReFill Packer requires access to the Reason Factory Sound Bank.rfl file. If it can't find the Reason Factory Sound Bank, a prompt will appear asking for the Factory Sound Bank CD.

Samples and File Paths

Samples and patches that are associated with the samples can be copied into the ReFill project folder, but patch and audio sample files must reside in the same directory. The NN-XT, NN-19, and Redrum patches contain information about file paths that tell Reason to look for the sample in a specific location on a hard drive. ReFill Packer checks this information to verify that the audio file locations properly link with the patches.

Once the sample and patch data is copied into the ReFill project folder, you can open the patches, then resave them into the patch folders. When the patch is resaved, the file path to the audio samples is updated to reflect the new location of the audio samples. Simply moving the patch files will not work, because the file path is not updated, and ReFill Packer will abort when it discovers the problem.

Production Strategy

In order to build a ReFill, you must have a Reason song file open in which you can open and resave patches to update the file path data. This song file should be saved in the ReFill project folder so that it can be easily accessed. Reason song files are also affected by the file path information, and if the samples load properly into the song file, then they will function properly as part of the ReFill package.

As the previous chapters in this book have illustrated, cabling schemes are very useful, and custom effects chains and effects templates can be saved into the Reason song file folder. If the ReFill is going to be distributed as a commercial product or a free download, prepare a demo song that shows users the potential use of the content. Developing content around a song is a very effective technique for creating a palette of samples, synth, loop, and effect patches that work together. When the different elements of the content work in harmony, using the content is much easier for the end user.

ReWire

Reason can be connected to other software applications using ReWire. This is a protocol that shuttles audio, MIDI, and synchronization data back and forth between ReWire-compatible programs. The current versions of applications such as Pro Tools, Logic Audio, Ableton Live, Nuendo, Digital Performer, Max/MSP, and others support ReWire. Using ReWire, Reason can be incorporated into larger productions that require audio recording and hardware synthesizer sequencing.

The ReWire system is hierarchical: One application acts as a ReWire host while another functions as a ReWire slave (some people prefer the word "client" to "slave"). Before enabling ReWire between Reason and a ReWire host, quit both applications. The ReWire host application must be launched first, and ReWire channels to Reason must be enabled. Once the ReWire channels are enabled, launch Reason. If the connection is properly established, the ReWire lamp will illuminate on the Reason Hardware Interface. After the session, Reason must be shut down before the ReWire host application can quit. Some applications, such as Pro Tools 6.1, are scripted to automatically launch and quit Reason in the proper order.

Once the connection is established, MIDI data can be sent from the host application to the devices in the Reason rack, and the audio from the Reason devices can be routed through the mixing suite and plug-in effects of the host application. The transport, tempo, and loop controls are also perfectly synchronized between Reason and the host application, and sample rates are locked.

Preparing for ReWire

Using Reason with a ReWire host application does present more flexibility, but the added features can be a bit cumbersome. A large part of a piece of music can be created using Reason alone, after which the host application will only be necessary before mixdown. Using the audio inputs on the Reason Hardware Interface, 64 individual audio signals can be connected from Reason to the host application.

One way to prepare for the ReWire connection is to use Spider Audio splitters to split the mixer input signals. Devices from the rack can be split so the signal is connected to the mixer and also to the Reason Hardware Interface. The outputs of the individual devices can then be accessed directly from the host application. The mixer master outputs should stay connected to input 1 and input 2 on the hardware interface as a way to listen to the music while you're developing the basic tracks in Reason. Once you get to the mixing stage and start adding plug-in effects in the host application, the Mixer 14:2 can be muted or disconnected. Note that if you use this method, you'll need to automate the output levels of the devices in the rack using their own master volume faders rather than using the mixer faders.

Another useful technique is to bus signals from the Mixer 14:2 into the host application through aux send outputs. The aux send outputs can be connected into pairs of channels on the Reason Hardware Interface, and different groups of input signals can then be directed to the busses using the aux send attenuation controls.

Reason Adapted

Reason Adapted is a limited version of the full Reason application. It's customized specifically for third-party distribution, and is based on features in Reason 2.5. There are several different versions of Reason Adapted and the features may differ, but typically the program contains a fixed set of devices, such as a mixer, a few effects devices, a synthesizer module, a sampler, a Dr.REX, a Matrix, and a Redrum. The devices themselves function in the same manner as in the full version.

When a new Reason Adapted song is created, the rack components are already created and can't be changed. Fortunately, cabling can still be modified, so Reason Adapted users can manipulate the signal paths. The sequencer tracks are also fixed, but one is assigned to each of the devices so automation is still available, and all of the devices will respond to MIDI.

Reason Adapted usually comes with a limited sample set packed in a special ReFill sound bank. The sampler and Redrum can load audio samples from a hard drive, but Reason Adapted can't access ReFills created for the normal version. The same applies to sampler, Redrum, synthesizer, and effect patches, and patch saving is not available.

Reason Adapted users should still develop the habit of creating project folders to keep samples and backup song files organized. Song files created with Reason Adapted will open in the full version of Reason. Users who upgrade to the full version of Reason will be able to open their old song files, which can then be further modified.

On the CD

Reason provides a great many useful tools for creating music, and it's very easy to use Reason alone to create complete productions. The real power of Reason lies in using the application as a creative conduit to shape a composition by transforming the palette of timbres as needed. In addition to demo versions of Propellerhead Reason, ReBirth, and ReCycle,* the CD-ROM contains a variety of samples, demo songs, and examples for using Reason with outside resources. Several examples in this book refer to audio sample files found on the *Power Tools for Reason* CD-ROM. Use of these particular samples is important to achieve the correct results. These samples are AIFF and ReCycle RX2 files, and work with the demo version of Reason 2.5.

The demo songs are presented in Reason Song File format, which requires the full version of Reason 2.5. MP3 files of the demo songs are also included. The diversity of styles demonstrates the flexibility of the application. The CD-ROM also showcases the talents of many people who contributed audio samples, engineering, and graphics design. Please refer to the "CD_Rom _Info.html" file for photos and biographies of the artists, musicians, and engineers who participated in this project. The info file also includes internet links to other resources for Reason users.

Readers currently using Reason 2.5 can expand their sample libraries with the ReFills included on the CD-ROM. The ReFills include a variety of samples, ranging from bizarre electronic effects and sampled acoustic instruments to palettes of musical riffs and bass loops produced specifically for this project. Those interested in developing their own Reason sample libraries should refer to the ReFill Production Template. This folder can be copied to a local hard drive, where custom samples, loops, and patches should be saved into the appropriate subdirectories.

Several song production examples are included on the CD-ROM. The Song Project Template folder shows how to organize the various files associated with a Reason track, and the custom set of Reason folder icons can be copied to a local drive to identify the various types of patch, sample, and song files. Several ReWire setups are included for those who may use Reason with Pro Tools, Logic Audio, or Max/MSP.

*©2003 Propellerhead Software. All rights reserved. All specifications subject to change without notice. Reason, ReBirth, and ReCycle are trademarks of Propellerhead Software AB, Stockholm, Sweden.

Index